The **Philly Fan's** Code

The
Philly Fan's
Code

The **50** *Toughest, Craziest,*
Most Legendary Philadelphia Athletes
of the Last **50** *Years,*

MIKE TANIER

Temple University Press · Philadelphia

TEMPLE UNIVERSITY PRESS
Philadelphia, Pennsylvania 19122
www.temple.edu/tempress

Library of Congress Cataloging-in-Publication Data
Tanier, Mike, 1970–
    The Philly fan's code : the 50 toughest, craziest, most legendary
Philadelphia athletes of the last 50 years / Mike Tanier.
        p. cm.
    ISBN 978-1-4399-0599-9 (pbk. : alk. paper) — ISBN 978-1-4399-0600-2 (e-book)
    1. Sports—Pennsylvania—Philadelphia—History. 2. Athletes—Pennsylvania—
Philadelphia—History. I. Title.
    GV584.5.P46T36 2011
    796.09748'11—dc23

                                                                        2011017778

Printed in the United States of America

2 4 6 8 9 7 5 3 1

Contents

The **Philly Fan's** Code

Introduction

A S PHILLY SPORTS fans, we have to stop lying to ourselves. We aren't bad fans. We're not the "uncontrollable mob scene" Mike Schmidt described or the Santa-hating thugs national sportswriters describe when blending 40 years of unrelated incidents into one stereotype. At the same time, we're not "the best fans in the world," as Eric Lindros once called us and as we often call ourselves. We're not the "most passionate, most knowledgeable" fans (a default compliment bestowed on us by dozens of players and announcers), nor are we boozers who throw up on children and beat up tourists wearing the wrong colors. We're not front-runners, as Jimmy Rollins once called us, but we're not as loyal as we claim to be, and while Ryan Howard compared the fan-player relationship in Philly to "brotherly love," he hasn't yet seen how rough his older sibling can be.

As a fan base, we are quick to anger and hold long grudges. We are pessimistic, suspicious, and judgmental. We assume the worst about players' motives, take innocent mistakes personally, interpret weaknesses as character flaws, then dwell on them until they outweigh the strengths. We never let facts get in the way of our opinions, and we rush to form-fit players into our mythology of failure: instead of wondering how a player can help win a championship, we brace ourselves for the moment he will lose one. We also can be quick to forgive, protective, and gracious, but we have a bad habit of hiding those virtues from players until they have been retired for 20 years.

Worst of all, we back the wrong horses. We hate players we really should love, and we sometimes embrace players we would be better off holding at arm's length. Winning a championship is an easy way for a player to get on our good side, but it isn't foolproof, as Mike Schmidt will tell you. Players who fall short of a championship get it far worse. It's one thing to forever curse the name Terrell Owens or Shawn Bradley, but we bared our teeth to inoffensive guys like Scott Rolen, and we've had more sympathy for scandal-ridden politicians on their way out the door than for the typical Eagles quarterback. Meanwhile, we make a hero of Len Dykstra, a marginal star and disagreeable person, and we celebrate hard hitters like the Buddy Ryan-era Eagles, even though they were a danger to both themselves and others.

Our most fascinating sports heroes occupy a buzzing bipolar region of our collective psyche. We try to simultaneously love and hate them, cheer them and vilify them. These are the players who truly shape Philly sports history: Dick Allen and Donovan McNabb, Eric Lindros and Allen Iverson. They weren't the greatest players, but they dwell in our pantheon beside immortals like Julius Erving and Bobby Clarke because they were so remarkable, so relevant, so likely to come up in conversation 10 years after their retirement and provoke an argument.

If we can unlock the secrets of our fan neurosis, understand why we love so madly and hate so badly, and accept as fans that our relationship with these players is not healthy, then we can move forward. This book is many things: a history, a countdown, a moody Valentine to the players who shaped our lives. But it's also an *intervention*. We make ourselves miserable. It's not the teams or the players, at least not totally. It's us.

I can say this because I am one of you. I cried during Super Bowl XV, nearly threw up after Game 6 the 1993 World Series, tossed and turned in my sleep after NFC Championship losses that spanned nearly a decade. I endured the quarter century of misery from 1983 to 2008, growing from a preteen in a Ron Jaworski jersey to a writer watching Ryan Howard strike out from the press box. It was 25 years of disappointment, worse than anything our parents endured. At least the old-timers who dwell on the Phold of 1964 could enjoy the 1960

Eagles and 1966–1967 76ers. Children grew to be parents wondering what a championship parade down Broad Street would look like. It was brutal.

But it wasn't all misery. There were pennants and Stanley Cup Finals and Bounty Bowls. There were cheers, celebrations, and playoff parties. Yet we reflexively forget the good times, because we're conditioned to perceive anything short of a championship as a catastrophe. So we have dwelled on the failures and turned against our best players. We've all done it. But it isn't good: not for the players, the teams, ourselves, or one another.

But our best players let us down, you say. Many of them did. But championships are rare, everywhere but in New York. A player can be great even if he falls short of a championship. A player can be laudable and praiseworthy even if he doesn't come across as the toughest, meanest, craziest guy on the field (ice, court). The sooner we accept these things, the less miserable we can all be about the fan experience. Every sports hero in the world doesn't have to live up to the Chuck Bednarik standard.

· · ·

I COME BOTH to praise Chuck Bednarik and to bury him.

Five decades ago, Bednarik, aka Concrete Charlie, aka the NFL's last 60-Minute Man, led the Eagles to their last championship. Bednarik played 58 minutes in the championship game, playing center on offense, linebacker on defense, and snapping for field goals and punts. He made the game's final tackle, stopping Hall of Fame running back Jim Taylor at the 9-yard line, helping the Eagles defeat the Packers 17–13, handing Vince Lombardi his only career postseason defeat.

Bednarik didn't just win a championship. He captured the imagination of Philly sports fans so thoroughly that his impact spanned generations. He was great, of course. He was also tough, a World War II veteran who knocked Giants pretty-boy Frank Gifford out of football for a year and a half and played until his fingers were gnarled and twisted. He also was eccentric, or at least he came to be perceived as eccentric as eras passed and 60-Minute Men who poured concrete in the off-season became as relevant to sports fans as medieval jousters. He was everything a city like Philadelphia could ask for in a champion:

Chuck Bednarik
(Courtesy of Temple University Libraries, Urban Archives, Philadelphia, PA)

a local guy, a blue-collar hero, a growling, scrapping overachiever who stuck it to both the Giants and the unbeatable Packers.

Bednarik set a high standard for sports heroism. Too high. The more mythic his accomplishments became, the more unattainable that standard became. As decades passed and memories faded, a hagiography grew around Bednarik, one that he fueled with regular interviews and media appearances. His tall tales grew taller, his condemnations of modern players a little more self-serving. His nostalgia dissolved into fogyism, with frequent remarks about how modern players "couldn't tackle my wife, Emma." He became our curmudgeon emeritus. By the 2005 Super Bowl, Bednarik was openly rooting against the Eagles, his feelings hurt by some disagreement with the team's front office.

Despite the negativity, or maybe because of it, Bednarik inspired an ever-increasing reverence, even among fans who never saw him play.

Tom McAllister cited Bednarik as his favorite player in his book *Bury Me in My Jersey*, even though McAllister admits he's too young to remember watching Jaworski, let alone a player he knew only from faded photographs and old stories. Bednarik retired in 1962. He's as real to the last two generations of fans as Superman, a Superman who has gotten old and has nothing nice to say about today's "pussyfoot" heroes. The last five decades have been a ceaseless application of a Bednarik litmus test. We take each player, compare him to the Concrete Charlie we've constructed from Grandpa's stories, NFL Films, and documentaries, and assign a pass-fail grade. Bobby Clarke: pass. Mike Schmidt: too aloof, so fail. Moses Malone: a mean and nasty champion, so pass. Donovan McNabb: epic fail. Ryan Howard: to be determined.

As great as Bednarik was, he has become a symbol to us, not a player. That's why he's consigned to this introduction. The chapters of this book are about real players, guys we still remember clearly enough to say bad things about them. Modern fans love Bednarik and Richie Ashburn, and we'll say nice things about Steve Van Buren and Grover Cleveland Alexander because we've been told to. This book is about the standard Bednarik helped set, and why we've found it so hard to feel satisfied in the half-century since his retirement.

●   ●   ●

TO CLARIFY FROM the outset, the Philly Fan's Code described in this book isn't a ranking of the greatest players in Philadelphia sports history. Obviously, Pat Burrell wouldn't make that list, even though he made this one. A listing of all-time greats, even one with a five-decade time limit, might include such players as Pete Retzlaff and Bob Brown, Johnny Callison and Garry Maddox, Paul Arizin and George McGinnis, and a bunch of other guys who won't come up once in a thousand barstool conversations or a hundred hours of sports-talk radio. Those players were great, and some were interesting, but they aren't very relevant.

The Philly Fan's Code isn't a ranking of the most beloved players in Philadelphia sports history. That list would be dominated by Broad Street Bullies, along with Erving, some current Phillies, some Buddy Ryan Eagles, and lovable curiosities like Vince Papale. A book about "beloved" stars would have to pussyfoot around our awkward relationships with Mike Schmidt, Charles Barkley, Donovan McNabb, and others, and Bednarik taught us to hate pussyfooting. It would be dishonest to write a book about how we really loved Schmidt or McNabb all along. Any book that reflects the true Philly sports experience must address the love-hate. It must admit that some of our most respected players were booed mercilessly and some of our most disappointing stars were once hailed as heroes.

The Philly Fan's Code is about *relevance*: the ability of a player to occupy our gray matter, to make us laugh or curse 10 or 20 years later. It's about our need to boo Pat Burrell even though no one can put a finger on what he did wrong. It's about our inability to notice Chase Utley's slumps and our inability to ignore Ryan Howard's. It's about why we remember the 1993 Phillies more than the 1987 Flyers, why we loved Buddy Ryan's Eagles but thought the worst of Andy Reid's team. It's about rattling off the 10 players who have meant the most to us as fans and realizing that we've named guys like John Kruk and Ron Hextall: quirky, frustrating, flawed stars, not champions or even the best players we've ever seen.

This book started as a *New York Times* article. When the Phillies faced the Yankees in the 2009 World Series, the *Times* asked me, as the sports section's resident comedian and Philly guy (the two jobs are closely related), to write about why Philly's pantheon of sports heroes is such a rogue's gallery. After some soul searching, I realized that we value toughness and craziness over excellence. Fans in every city like to root for "dirty uniform" types, but we make a fetish of it, and it throws our judgment way off when evaluating our best players. The article earned a lot of attention—good and bad—so I began to expand on the concept of a code, or a rubric, that could be used to rank Philly stars on their Philly-ness.

Along the way, I discovered an untold history of Philadelphia sports. I didn't set out to write a revisionist history, but much of this book contains stories that diverge from our civic folktale, the one that bounces from Bednarik to Broad Street Bullies to the present day with a few pit stops of glory scattered along vast wastelands of disappointment. I excavated standing ovations for Scott Rolen and boos for Harold Carmichael, rediscovered the fascinating 1961 Eagles, even found a Julius Erving who would be torn to shreds by the modern media culture. You may not recognize the 1964 or 1993 Phillies as they appear in this book, and you may not recognize yourself, the fan who booed Ron Jaworski in favor of Randall Cunningham, the one who threw batteries at Dick Allen, the one who called Eric Lindros a wimp after his fifth concussion.

You can try to deny it. That wasn't you. "Real" Philly fans don't do those things. Those are the actions of an unruly handful of malcontents. It's odd that those malcontents are always there, always shouting down the cooler heads. They were there in 1964, booing even when the Phillies were in first place. They were there in 2010, turning on Ryan Howard for slumping through the NLCS (he batted .318 with four doubles, but never mind).

They are always there, because they are us. We may not all be morons who boo Santa or run onto the field to get tased by security, but we are all guilty of giving up too quickly, expecting too much, turning uglier than we have to after a strikeout or a loss. We are a lot like the players we root for: we can be a little tough and a little crazy, have great moments and awful moments, come up big and come up short. And we could do a little better.

The Philly Fan's Code is about 50 remarkable players, but it's also about millions of remarkable fans: why we love, why we hate, and what five decades of frustration, bitterness, and longing mixed with brief episodes of euphoria and a lot of irrepressible hope tells us about ourselves.

THE RUBRICS

The Philly Fan's Code is just that: a code, an analytical tool for quantifying our emotional responses to athletes. In this book I've used the code to calculate the precise impact that 50 of our most remarkable athletes had on our regional psyche, how much they contributed to the mind-set and psychological stability of the contemporary fan.

This is all very scientific. I swear.

Each player is evaluated along four axes: Greatness, Toughness, Eccentricity, and Legacy. Once a player gets a one-star to five-star score in each of those categories, the scores are weighted, then totaled. The higher the score, the more remarkable the player is, and the more worthy of the title Philly Sports Legend.

Amazing, right? And it works. Just thumb through the book. Bobby Clarke is near the front, Mo Cheeks is toward the middle, Pat Burrell is at the end, and Charles Shackleford is nowhere to be found. Science works!

A few notes before I explain the rubrics. First, players are rated on their post-1960 accomplishments. That affects Tommy McDonald, Hal Greer, and a few others. Second, players are generally rated and assessed for their contributions to the Philadelphia sports scene, not for contributions over their entire careers. Pete Rose is rated for his five years with the Phillies, not for anything he did with the Big Red Machine or was accused of in the Dowd Report.

Sometimes, though, it's impossible to rank a player on just his Philadelphia accomplishments: Wilt Chamberlain is just too big and important to talk about him simply as a center for the Warriors and Sixers, and we lose a lot of Cheeks and Curt Schilling if we don't mention things they did for other teams. But even when we veer away from Philly, in thinking or talking about a player, we are concentrating on the player's impact on us. When we examine Cheeks's National Anthem duet or Schilling's embarrassing blogging career, we do it through a Philly-focused lens: the Philly fan perceives these events a certain way, and some of them reflect back upon our region, even when the player is gone. For the most part, though, you'll see that each player's story ends when he leaves Philadelphia.

Now that we've settled that, here are the four categories and an explanation of the scoring. Each category is accompanied by a rubric that explains the scoring criteria. There are also benchmarks to guide rankings: it's one thing to rate toughness arbitrarily on a one-to-five scale, but once you start saying that a player is between Darren Daulton and Brian Dawkins on the toughness scale, you are really taking the guesswork out. Well, some of the guesswork.

GREATNESS

A player doesn't have to be great to be loved in Philly, and being great doesn't always help. Philadelphia fans have been notoriously unappreciative of some of Philly's best players and have been downright cruel to many talented players whose only crime was falling short of expectations. And it's not like those expectations are too high: all a player has to do is single-handedly erase decades of painful sports memories by winning multiple championships . . . while playing through injuries . . . for a league-minimum salary.

Still, if a player plans to linger in the minds and hearts of sports fans for decades, if he hopes to inspire debates, tears, or sighs of resignation long after he's retired, and his name isn't Jeff Ruland, he at least has to be a very good player for a few years. The greatness rubric rewards old-fashioned, individual excellence: Hall of Fame recognition, All-Star appearances, touchdowns, home runs, and so on.

In some regions, fan appreciation begins and ends with greatness. New Yorkers, of course, can fill their household shrines with unassailable superstars; there's little need to dredge up Bobby Murcer when Babe Ruth's bust is over the mantle and Derek Jeter is on deck. Heck, even New York's plucky auxiliary stars, their Phil Rizzutos and Harry Carsons, make it into the Hall of Fame. Smaller cities, like San Diego, have few champions but fewer disappointments, so they cherish what they have: Tony Gwynn's hits and Dan Fouts's touchdowns.

Philadelphia lacks New York's trophy case and San Diego's fabulous weather. With so few five-star, transcendent legends to reminisce about, we look elsewhere for sports validation. That's what the Philly Fan's Code is all about, and it's why greatness is just one of four axes on which players are ranked, and not even the prominent one. Rest assured that if Dan Fouts played here, we'd still be obsessing about his 16 career playoff interceptions (one fewer than made by Donovan McNabb, but in nine fewer games) and wishing we had a tougher, grittier quarterback in the late 1970s, like Archie Manning or someone.

Rubric

One Star: The player was ordinary, a run-of-the-mill starter for a few seasons or a backup for a long time. To even register on the Philly Fan's Code with one star, you have to be a legendary bust (Jeff Ruland, Mike Mamula) or famously spunky. Benchmarks: Vince Papale, Jim Eisenreich.

Two Stars: The player was a productive starter who made a few All-Star games in his best seasons and is known for a handful of specific personal accomplishments, like being the best defensive player in the game or leading the league in penalty minutes. Benchmarks: Dave Schultz, Bob Boone, Andre Waters.

Three Stars: The player was an All Star in his best seasons and was a productive player for many years. Or, the player had one or two seasons of tantalizing excellence mixed among several mediocre, disappointing seasons. Or, the player had one amazing ability that separated him from the typical two-star player—like tape-measure home runs, tip-in goals from the crease, or backboard-breaking—but never achieved on a par with a four-star player. Benchmarks: Tim Kerr, Greg Luzinski, Darryl Dawkins.

Four Stars: The player was a second-tier Hall of Famer, a near Hall of Famer, or someone who looked unmistakably like a Hall of Famer for a few seasons. Such a player should have an MVP award and several All-Star appearances on his résumé, plus other awards (Rookie of the Year, Conn Smythe) and statistical accomplishments like batting titles. Four-star players may also be first-ballot Hall of Famers who achieved a large amount of their success outside of Philly, like Moses Malone. Benchmarks: Bill Barber, Reggie White, Steve Carlton.

Five Stars: An unquestioned first-ballot Hall of Famer, the kind whose name is brought up among the legends of the sport, and one who accomplished nearly all of his feats for a Philadelphia team. Benchmarks: Bobby Clarke, Mike Schmidt.

TOUGHNESS

There are three kinds of toughness to explore here: physical toughness, mental toughness, and perceived toughness.

Physical toughness includes the ability to play through pain and the willingness to inflict it. Every sports fan likes a hard-hitting free safety or an enforcer on the ice. Only Philly fans expect hard-hitting goalies and enforcers in the bullpen. For players who aren't supposed to beat the daylights out of their opponents, we can judge toughness by determining how often they overcame major injuries and how frequently they played a full schedule.

Mental toughness is the ability of a player to break out of slumps, endure criticism, escape controversy, drive the lane, stay in the pocket when Lawrence Taylor is blitzing, or listen to three years of Larry Bowa screaming in his ear without strangling him. There's an ironic element to mental toughness: if a player can keep performing at a high level even when half the fans in the city are sure he lacks mental toughness, chances are he doesn't lack mental toughness.

The perception of toughness is all of that dirty-uniform stuff: players ranting and raving after losses, crashing into the center field wall, not combing their hair, and so on. While many players who were physically and mentally tough also radiated this "perceived" toughness, like Brian Dawkins, there are plenty of otherwise tough players who took a lot of criticism because they didn't put on a fire-breathing façade (Schmidt), and there are plenty of blustery loudmouths in our sports history who were better at looking and acting tough than at being tough (half of Buddy Ryan's roster).

Finding a balance between the three kinds of toughness is tricky, as is assigning one "toughness" score for a whole career. Often, we call a player tough when we love him and soft when we hate him, tough when he's on the rise and soft when he's on the decline. If you don't believe that, I can pull a dozen newspaper articles from the 1997–1998 archives about Scott Rolen's toughness for you. These benchmarks help separate the truly gritty from the mushy.

Rubric

One Star: The player was soft, and it showed. He avoided contact, didn't hustle, and couldn't handle criticism. He may even come across as a wimp. It's difficult to have a long career with one-star toughness in any sport; it's probably impossible in hockey and boxing. Even some of Philly's most well-known china dolls get a star-and-a-half, because bouncing back from 71 sacks requires a degree of resilience. There's one player in this book who earned less than one star, and I don't even have to name him, because you've already thought of him. Benchmarks: Von Hayes, Bobby Hoying.

Two Stars: This is the realm of the "paycheck" guy: he wasn't a wimp, but he didn't show much interest in fighting for the extra yard or diving for the loose ball. It's also the rating for players who were too flighty to approach the game properly, or who had an off-putting pretty-boy persona. Benchmarks: Derrick Coleman, Bobby Abreu, Mitch Williams, Peter Zezel.

Three Stars: This is the baseline for many of the rank-and-file players in this book. Three-star toughness means showing up every night and putting out an honest effort without making a big show of it. It means battling through injuries multiple times. Some of our three-star players wore the aloof-sensitive-momma's boy tag for part of their careers but showed plenty of competitive fire and resilience other times. Some made excellence look too easy; at least one made it look harder on purpose but was still a formidable foe once you cut through the theatrics. Benchmarks: Hal Greer, Eric Lindros, Donovan McNabb, Tug McGraw.

Four Stars: These are the big hitters, fighters, and scrappers. The four-star player has a chip on his shoulder, plays through pain, overcomes obstacles, bristles with competitive fire, and inspires other tough-guy clichés. Many of our most beloved players have four-star toughness. Benchmarks: Bobby Clarke, Charles Barkley.

Five Stars: This is the Bednarik standard. To get to five stars, a player has to flaunt the toughness until it is almost mythical. The five-star player not only does anything possible to win, but scares the hell out of you if he loses. Benchmarks: Chuck Bednarik, Moses Malone.

ECCENTRICITY

Most American sports stars aren't particularly crazy. They play the game, deliver some noncommittal sound bites from the locker room, then go home. After retirement, they become announcers or coaches, or they just fade away. Even their "odd" behavior falls into predictable patterns: end-zone dances, blue-line scuffles, self-promoting press conferences, sad lapses into drug abuse or antisocial behavior, post-retirement lunges into reality television.

Philly sports stars do sit-ups in suburban driveways, deliver locker room soliloquies about other planets, and beat up visiting Russian teams. After retirement, they retreat into bunkers, manipulate the stock market, write New Age manifestos, and deliver racist rants to state legislatures. Many of our greatest players acted a little neurotic during their playing days. A few acted downright delusional. One or two were just terrifying. Their eccentricities made them fascinating during the long droughts between championships. We couldn't always have the best players, but Philly always had a player around who could make the rest of the nation (in Bobby Clarke's case, the world) laugh, gasp, cringe, or cower.

It may be going too far to call most of our sports heroes "crazy." It's better to say that they were eccentric, in about a dozen different ways. In a few extreme cases, we might have made them that way. At any rate, to score highly on this axis of the Philly Fan's Code, a player had to do more than show up and win a few games. He had to kick up a lot of loony dust in the process.

Rubric

One Star: The player came across as normal, well-adjusted, and pleasant, on and off the field, during and after his career. We're rarely interested in these guys, even when they are quite good. Benchmarks: Hersey Hawkins, Brian Propp.

Two Stars: The player has one or two odd, endearing quirks, or the player has an inflated sense of self-worth, though not Randall Cunningham-level inflated. Benchmarks: Brad Lidge (quirks), Scott Rolen (inflated).

Three Stars: The player is rather unpredictable on and off the field. He's capable of saying something wacky at a press conference or doing something unusual-dangerous-dumb on the field, though for the most part his behavior falls within reasonable parameters. Or, the player is perceived as exceptionally moody, sullen, or introverted. Benchmarks: Wilt Chamberlain, Dave Schultz, Jimmy Rollins.

Four Stars: The player made a career out of off-kilter behavior and was known as an eccentric during his career. Or, the player's behavior became inexplicable after his career. The difference between a four-star and five-star player typically comes down to the player's belief in other planets or conspiracy theories, or his number of police-related incidents. Benchmarks: Randall Cunningham, Charles Barkley, Terrell Owens.

Five Stars: Houston, we have a problem. Benchmarks: Steve Carlton, Darren Daulton.

LEGACY

You may not have noticed, but we don't throw many championship parades in Philadelphia. The handful of champions we have crowned linger for a long time in our consciousness. There are plenty of 17-year-olds in Philadelphia who can tell you more about Bernie Parent than about whatever they learned in history class last week. Parent and the 1973–1975 Flyers left a legacy, easily the richest and most enduring of the last 50 years.

Some nonchampionship teams left long legacies as well, most notably the Buddy Ryan Eagles and 1993 Phillies. Second-rate players on these beloved teams are better remembered than the stars of weaker teams. Other near-championship teams didn't have the same impact. The 1983 Phillies were a lot of fun, but John Denny and Joe Lefebvre didn't make it into this book.

There's another kind of legacy in Philly, however: the legacy of controversy, scandal, shame, doubt, and disappointment. Once a player has spent a few seasons in the crosshairs, he is with us forever. If you can't win a championship, the best way to get talked about in this town is to be the most recognizable player who *didn't* win, and to hold that title for a few years. A lot of our most remarkable heroes, particularly from the last 25 years, were the mosquitoes who got trapped in the amber. They got stuck, weren't good enough to escape, and the inevitable flow of our obsessive criticism engulfed them, preserving them forever.

A player's "legacy," of course, seeps into the other Philly Fan's Code categories: being great, tough, and/or crazy leaves a lasting impression. The legacy rubric accounts for achievements that weren't rewarded elsewhere. A one-star legacy may sound low, but it's low only by the standards of our top 50 players. Typical players, even good ones who hang around for five or six years, have a zero-star legacy. Johnny Dawkins has a zero-star legacy. So do Kevin Gross and Danny Briere, Andy Harmon and Larry Christenson. A zero-star player is remembered by diehards. A one-star player is remembered by casual fans. A five-star player is a civic treasure.

Rubric

One Star: The player was a well-known starter and sometime star for one of our less-renowned teams. Or, the player was noteworthy only for some dubious accomplishment, like being an all-time bust. The one-star player's accomplishments fade with time, which is why George McGinnis and Bill Bergey aren't in this book, though a handful of one-star types make the cut. Benchmarks: Mark Howe, Harold Carmichael.

Two Stars: The player was a low-key starter on a championship team; this includes mercenaries who played only a few seasons in Philly. Or, the player was one of the ensemble stars for a beloved near-miss team. Or, the player was otherwise ordinary, or downright bad, but generated a lot of scandal. There are many two-star legacy players who aren't in this book (Reggie Leach, Garry Maddox, Jamie Moyer). Benchmarks: Mo Cheeks, Brian Westbrook, Ricky Watters.

Three Stars: The player was one of the secondary stars on a championship team but was always a supporting character. Or, the player was a star for a near-miss team, enduring the typical amount of controversy such a player receives (for "not winning the big game," and so forth). Or, the player spent several seasons as our sports whipping boy. Benchmarks: Bernie Parent, Eric Lindros, Charles Barkley.

Four Stars: The player was the superstar on a championship team. Or, the player was a superstar of a near-miss team but was so controversial, in Philadelphia and nationally, that his career shaped the Philly sports experience for several seasons. Benchmarks: Chase Utley, Allen Iverson.

Five Stars: The player was the superstar on a championship team and became a nationally recognizable symbol for the Philadelphia sports experience. If you could put a picture of only one player in a time capsule so your great-great-grandchildren could understand the Philly sports experience, this is the player you would select. Benchmark: Julius Erving.

· · ·

ONCE EACH PLAYER is rated along all four axes, his scores are weighted, with toughness and eccentricity worth a little more than plain-old greatness. Legacy gets its own small bonus. The result is a list that accurately maps the geography of the typical Philly fan's brain: who commands the most synapses, who inspires the most heated lunch-table arguments. Some selections and rankings may appear to be controversial, but before you send me an angry e-mail, explore your own fan experience. Who did you really spend most of your time cheering for, booing, worrying about, complaining about, pretending to be in the schoolyard, hoping to see when you bought a game ticket? Unless you are 70 years old, it wasn't Chuck Bednarik. It was one of the guys on this list.

ALLEN IVERSON

The Answer in Theory, but Not in Practice

Greatness: ★★★★
Toughness: ★★★★½
Eccentricity: ★★★★
Legacy: ★★★★

THE SIXERS HAD just lost to the Lakers, but Allen Iverson still clapped and cheered. It was Game 2 of the 2001 Finals, and the Sixers' fourth-quarter rally had just come up short. They were headed back to Philadelphia with the series tied. Winning Game 1 was an impressive accomplishment for the overmatched Sixers, and they didn't go down without a fight in the second game. So Iverson was charged up. The Sixers hadn't won, but they had proven their point. "Nobody's going to walk over the top of us," Iverson said after the game. "Won't happen."

Watching the game, we knew that moment was the high-water mark, not just of the Sixers' season, but of the Iverson era. Sure, we talked about taking two of three in Philly and returning to the Staples Center with a lead, but it was talk. We watched Iverson shoot 10-for-29, saw him get butchered all game and go to the line just four times (missing all four free throws), saw Shaquille O'Neal pull down 20 rebounds and dime out nine assists as the Tyrone Hills and Aaron McKies of the world collapsed in vain trying to double him. We knew that was the best we would get. It was the Rocky moment. The clenched jaw in the face of defeat.

In Bury Me in My Jersey, Tom McAllister explains the dilemma at the heart of Philly fandom. "True success is so foreign to you that you learn the only real measure of your character is how close you can get, and how you cope with your loss afterward. Loss is inevitable; it's up to you to handle it stoically, like a man." Iverson was more than stoic. He was defiant. He promised to "spread the war" in the Lakers series, and that's what he did, careening through the lane on drive after futile drive, night after night, making sure that the Sixers died a warrior's death. In 2001, almost 20 years after the city's last championship, we had forgotten that there was anything more we could have asked for.

• • •

WHEN THE EAGLES stink, they stink in the limelight, in front-page headlines and endless sports-talk arguments. When the Phillies stink, they languish across the summer, lingering in our minds because there's nothing else to watch or think about. When the Flyers stink, the hockey diehards preserve the flame, but the Flyers rarely stink: they dip out of the playoffs for a year or two, then climb back to respectability quickly.

When the Sixers stink, they vanish. Basketball purists head to the Palestra. The national spotlight turns to the Celtics. The sports-talk guys wait for spring training.

The Sixers existed in the mid-1990s, though there is scant evidence of it: statistics on BasketballReference.com, deposits in Shawn Bradley's bank account, the rare Dana Barros jersey excavated from the back of the closet. There are certainly no memories. Even Iverson's first seasons are fuzzy. How clear are your recollections of Tim Thomas? Jim Jackson? Did you know that Clarence Weatherspoon was still on the team in 1998? Have you repressed all memories of Clarence Weatherspoon?

Unless you are a hoops addict or a masochist, you ignored the Sixers completely until 1996, when Iverson and Jerry Stackhouse shared the backcourt and little else. Their Sixers were a fascinating disaster, two great talents with the same skill set trying to saw a basketball on half so they could both penetrate. Then Stackhouse left, Larry Brown built around Iverson, and the Sixers suddenly became relevant again.

Iverson quickly grew from exciting youngster to true NBA superstar. In January 1998, he scored 31 points and dealt six assists as the Sixers beat the Bulls—who were still The Bulls, reigning champs led by Michael Jordan—for the first time since 1993. The Sixers lost to the Heat a few days later, but Alonzo Mourning, who knew Iverson through his Georgetown connections, was shocked at how quickly the ball-hogging layup machine had grown into something more. "He's really turned himself into not just a scoring guard, but a guard that's controlling his team, making great decisions, distributing the ball. And he's still scoring."

Already, though, there were the extracurricular activities: arrests, rumors, distractions. Iverson was arrested while riding in a car full of guns and marijuana in 1997. His bodyguard was charged with rape in Hampton, Virginia. Sean Combs, aka Puff Daddy, expressed interest in becoming Iverson's agent. The NBA left Iverson off the 1998 All-Star team, wary of his tattoos and ghetto bona fides. The league had spent years cultivating a whistle-clean image, represented by Jordan and O'Neal. Iverson was a little too real. The NBA liked Will Smith; Iverson was Snoop Dogg.

Iverson's straight-from-the-hood sensibility made him tough, able to intimidate players a foot taller than he was and drive through half a dozen forearms and elbows to reach the basket. As the years passed, though, the hood slowly swallowed him whole.

. . .

IT WAS SOMETHING out of a television show like *The Wire* or *The Shield*, something from an Elmore Leonard crime novel. But it happened in Philadelphia. Hell, it happened on the Main Line. It happened a little more than a year after that high-water mark, just 13 months after Iverson gave his all against the Lakers, then married his longtime sweetheart in a ceremony that took him from the sports page to the society page.

According to police reports, that sweetheart was hiding in a West Philadelphia apartment, hiding from the rampaging husband who threw her out of their suburban mansion and then pursued her through the city for two days with a gun. The story unfolded in July 2002, a surreal saga of jealousy and rage that was impossible to digest. It dominated the news for weeks, then suddenly disappeared as witnesses, starting with Iverson's wife, refused to testify against him. The sudden silence—the case was out of the judicial system by September—was scarier than the allegations themselves. Maybe it was all a domestic misunderstanding. Maybe this was really Godfather territory.

Even more surreal: Iverson's "practice" rant, which occurred just two months earlier, is better remembered than his domestic violence arrest. In a way, it's understandable. We can joke about missing practice. We can comprehend missing practice. We can cite missed practices as a reason to trade a player without having to contemplate the horrible. Iverson said it himself. "We're talking about practice, man. We're talking about practice. We're talking about practice."

But what's most surreal of all was that Iverson spent four more full seasons in Philadelphia after those incidents. We endured four years of arguments with coaches, late arrivals for fan appreciation nights, and diminishing returns. There were casino scuffles and more incidents involving his bodyguards. Coaches got fired and lineups got shuffled to accommodate Iverson.

Why? Didn't the Sixers know the high-water mark when they saw it? Philly turned on superstar athletes for crimes far less serious than allegedly kicking down doors with a loaded firearm in their hands (which is a pretty serious crime compared to, say, disagreeing with Larry Bowa). Instead of trading Iverson or releasing him, the Sixers kept trying to build around him. Iverson kept averaging over 30 points per night, but the Sixers got a little worse every season. Perhaps Billy King and the Sixers knew that, for all of his problems, Iverson was keeping the Sixers from disappearing. No one was going to go to Broad and Pattison to see Chris Webber and Samuel Dalembert.

In December 2006, the Sixers finally traded Iverson for Joe Smith, Andre Miller, and some pocket lint. Poof! The team disappeared.

●   ●   ●

IT WAS YEAR 3 of the Andre Iguodala–Dalembert era in Sixers history, and no one cared. The Phillies had just made their second straight World Series appearance. The Eagles were in the midst of a typically dramatic autumn. The Villanova Wildcats were ranked. Iguodala was the face of the franchise, but in terms of fan recognition he ranked somewhere between Raul Ibanez and Quintin Mikell. The proud Sixers franchise was an afterthought locally and a nonentity nationally.

Then, Iverson returned. He wore out his welcome with various NBA teams, but after contemplating retirement, Iverson was back in a Sixers uniform. With that, the sports-talk phones lit up. The water-cooler discussions began. And when Iverson stepped back onto the court, he received the same prodigal son welcome we gave Dick Allen, Ron Hextall, and others. We cheered harder than we had in years.

A few months later, I sat in the WIP studios with overnight host Big Daddy Graham while working on an article. The Sixers were going nowhere, and the novelty of Iverson's return had worn off, but Iverson still sparked conversation. "No one gets people talking like Iverson, except maybe Lindros a few years ago," Graham told me. Long into the night, Graham talked basketball, even though the Sixers were losing and Iverson was coming off the bench.

Iverson's comeback was short lived. In February 2010, Iverson left the Sixers to deal with family problems. Soon, the team released him, and his wife—the same woman he allegedly threw out of the house naked in 2002—filed for divorce. Stephen A. Smith published tales of out-of-control drinking and gambling, rumors that fit our tragic image of Iverson. In October 2010, Iverson signed with a Turkish basketball team, and every blogger on the Internet frantically searched for the Turkish translation of "practice." Chances are, we'll hear from Iverson again soon, before the first Hall of Fame ballots are cast in 2015. Chances are, sadly, that the news won't be good.

We are still fascinated and polarized by the former superstar. We debate his legacy. We wonder about the truth: how often he really practiced, how violent his personal life really was, what really happened in July 2002. We speculate whether there was a better, more disciplined player in Iverson, or if what we saw was the best we could hope for: a penetrating scorer in a tiny point guard's body, a warrior for 48 minutes who found it impossible to turn on the intensity in an empty gym, a young man who could get only one foot out of the old neighborhood no matter how hard he tried.

But there's one thing we never do. We never look back on 2001 as a missed opportunity. Those 2000–2001 Sixers weren't the 1980 or 2004 Eagles or the Lindros Flyers. They weren't going to beat the Lakers. We wanted them to, but we knew they couldn't, and we wouldn't know what to do if they did. But Iverson gave the Lakers all they could handle in that series, and he gave us all we could handle at that point in history: pride in the face of defeat, joy and self-respect in the act of spreading war to an invincible foe. Iverson—tiny, terrifying, wide-eyed, intense, gifted, flawed, loved, reviled, dangerous, and misunderstood—gave us a loss we could admire, a rare example of finishing second without coming up short. In the long drought between championships, he defined the character of Philadelphia sports.

BOBBY CLARKE

The Bully Who Made Us Believe

Greatness: ★★★★★
Toughness: ★★★★
Eccentricity: ★★ ½
Legacy: ★★★★★

IMAGINE PHILADELPHIA SPORTS history without Bobby Clarke. Without Clarke, there are no Broad Street Bullies, no Stanley Cups, none of the parades that seeped into our regional memory and made lifelong sports fans out of thousands. Without Clarke, Bill Barber and Reggie Leach lead the 1970s Flyers to a few playoff berths, and Dave Schultz gets into a lot of fights. But without the glory of a championship, Flyers hockey starts to resemble pro wrestling, and Philly never becomes a great hockey town.

Who knows what other Butterfly Effect-type changes Clarke's absence would cause? It's not a stretch to imagine the following: without the Flyers to cheer for, frustrated fans turn against Julius Erving when he cannot produce a championship. Erving demands a trade and ends up on the Knicks. Pete Rose sees the way Erving is treated and refuses to sign with the Phillies. Movie producers convince Sylvester Stallone to shoot *Rocky* in Chicago. The Eagles move to Phoenix. Flash forward to September 2010, and a few thousand loyalists stagger into crumbling Veterans Stadium to watch Chase Utley one last time, knowing the cash-strapped, unloved Phillies will trade him for prospects and money during the winter meetings. You never even meet your wife, who becomes the spinster who rewinds microfilm in the basement of the Free Library.

Okay, that may be taking things too far. But a lot of civic self-esteem is wrapped up in those Stanley Cup teams, and Clarke was the heart and soul of those teams. Even after they won, many fans still thought of Philly as "Loserville." Who knows how we would have felt if they hadn't won.

. . .

CLARKE WAS AN archetypal hockey player and an archetypal Philly sports hero. He was a Platonic ideal on skates. His story has been told so often that it has lost its impact. He came from Flin Flon, Manitoba (in our imaginations, the town is Tatooine on ice), where the team's long underwear froze solid in the storage compartment of the bus, and players skated extra fast just to warm up. He was diabetic and needed a special diet of Coca Cola and sugar to get through games. He slipped into the second round of the 1969 draft, where Ed Snider (who wanted Clarke in the first round) ordered his general manager to draft him. Snider and his staff then drafted Dave Schultz, Don Saleski, Bill Clement, and Bob Kelly to join Bill Barber, Bernie Parent, and other incumbents.

In a few years, the Flyers had two Stanley Cups, a nickname, and an identity. They were the people's champions. They couldn't skate a victory lap with the Cup without getting mobbed. Their championship parades devolved into South Philadelphia block parties. Bobby Clarke was loved like no sports figure before him in the Delaware Valley.

He was hated everywhere else. But that's part of his appeal. Philly fans love to root for underdogs and villains. Clarke was both, as were Allen Iverson and a few others throughout our history. If America hates you, good. If other countries hate you, even better. We loved the 1993 Phillies because we feared they would cause an international incident when they played World Series games in Toronto. They had nothing on Clarke, who caused several international incidents . . . with Russia . . . during the cold war.

"The Slash" occurred when Clarke was playing for Team Canada, though he was also a member of the Flyers when Canada faced Russia in the 1972 Summer Series. Clarke took Russian star Valeri Kharlamov out of the series with a two-handed slash across an already sore ankle. "If I hadn't learned to lay on a two-hander once in a while, I'd never have left Flin Flon," Clarke famously told the Canadian press. A CBSSports.com feature named it the fourth-worst incident of hockey violence ever. Amazingly, it's the only incident on the list to involve the Flyers in any way.

Clarke was just warming up. Four years later, the Russian Central Red Army team arrived in Philadelphia on a Goodwill Tour, a national All-Star team ordered to prove the righteousness of communism by beating ordinary Rangers and Bruins teams. The Flyers gave them a Philly welcome. Clarke wasn't an instigator—Barber, Moose Dupont, and finally Ed Van Impe delivered the blows that convinced Russian coaches to order their team off the ice for 17 minutes—but he was the ringleader. "We made every place they went on the ice miserable for them, and they quit," Clarke said of the Flyers' (and America's) victory.

Hacking and slashing Russians was acceptable, even laudable, to North American hockey fans. Ruthlessly brutalizing fellow NHL players was another matter. Clarke's reputation is as checkered around the continent as it is spotless in Philadelphia. "Bobby Clarke could have become a national hero," according to the NHL Hall of Fame Web site. "But Clarke's behavior on ice was far from heroic. Under the captaincy of Clarke, Philadelphia played a very aggressive game of hockey."

Aggressive? How polite. How . . . Canadian. We wouldn't want our hockey legends to be too aggressive, would we?

Hockey columnist (later historian) Stan Fischler called Clarke out for his style of play back in 1974. "For years, we've been spoon-fed stories about Bobby Clarke earth-angel, super Boy Scout and, of course, arch-savior of the Philadelphia Flyers," he wrote. "But that's all in the past. A guy can cut up the opposition just so much before the enemy starts yelling and screaming." Opposing coaches were complaining about Clarke's slashes, about the "Ferocious Flyers" (Broad Street Bullies hadn't caught on yet) and their bloody tactics. Of course, the Flyers were branded as the instigators, hooligans in the otherwise pristine world of professional ice hockey, but that's only because they usually were.

In the same season that Fischler wrote that column, California Golden Seals forward Barry Cummins slammed his stick into Clarke's skull while trailing a play, knocking the Flyers' captain to the ice. Clarke later required 20 stitches. You can imagine the reaction of Clarke's teammates: Cowboy Bill Flett pounced on Cummins, followed by Bob Kelly, who shot from the bench like a rocket. Photos of the fight show an enormous pile of Flyers, presumably with Cummins on the bottom.

Four minutes of game time later, another fight broke out. By the time Dave Schultz started chasing Hilliard Graves around the ice, the referees decided to send both teams to the dressing rooms so they could dole out 115 minutes of penalties and clean up the blood. The Flyers won the game 5–1, though it's not clear how, because all newspaper accounts of the game devote 90 percent of their words to the brawls. "It was ugly," Paul Giordano wrote at the time, though today it sounds strangely beautiful.

Cummins lived, but he earned a fine, which sounds appropriate until you hear Fred Shero's take on how the play started. "Bobby was pulling away from him, but his stick was caught around Cummins's neck. When he tried to pull his stick away, it hit Cummins in the face." Ah, it was an accident: Clarke's stick just happened to be hooked around Cummins's neck. That explains everything.

Aggressive? Absolutely. Cheap? Maybe a little. Philly? One hundred percent.

Play like that apparently kept Clarke from becoming a national hero. America has enough heroes. Canada has enough heroes. Philly needed a hero. Clarke fit the job description.

· · ·

CLARKE'S STORY JACKS straight into our cerebral cortex. Working class underdog, high-effort overachiever, toothless brawler, competitor willing to make the Doomsday Clock tick if it meant winning a game, champion who walked and worked and drank among us. He played for 15 years, usually as the captain, sometimes as an assistant coach. He played 136 playoff games, the equivalent of almost two full extra seasons, scoring 152 points against the best competition in the NHL. He skated at full-speed and played with full force until 1984. If only he were assumed body and soul into heaven (or somewhere) at the end of his playing career. Instead, he was assumed into the front office. But that's a story for another chapter. Several other chapters.

There have been better players in Philly sports history than Clarke. There have been more exciting players, arguably even tougher players. In time, we may crown even bigger winners than Clarke, as the Phillies shows no signs of letting up.

But no player is more irreplaceable than Clarke. Erase Erving, Schmidt, or Utley, and you erase a title, which would be sad. Erase Wilt

Chamberlain, and you erase a legend, which would be tragic. Erase Clarke, and you erase the Flyers. You erase hockey. For a generation of fans who identified with the Broad Street Bullies, you erase hope.

Yes, the butterfly effect can be taken too far: Philadelphia itself wouldn't have crumbled without Clarke, our lives wouldn't be in ruins and we wouldn't all be drinking vodka and calling each other "comrade." Probably. We would just be fans without a touchstone, without a golden age to point to in our past and strive for in our future. We would be unrecognizable to ourselves. Clarke made the Philly sports experience what it is. He made us who we are. That's how important he is.

MIKE SCHMIDT

The Slugger Who Won Our Hearts, Eventually

Greatness: ★★★★★
Toughness: ★★★
Eccentricity: ★★★ ½
Legacy: ★★★★

IT MAY HAVE been the greatest upset in Philadelphia sports history, greater than the 1960 NFL Championship.

The *Philadelphia Daily News*, in conjunction with the Temple University Sport Industry Research Center, conducted a poll in the spring of 2010 to determine the greatest athlete in Philadelphia sports history. Voters could choose from among 18 athletes, all of whom are featured in this book. Wilt Chamberlain was there, as were Julius Erving and Bobby Clarke, among others. Mike Schmidt won the vote in a landslide, appearing on 60 percent of ballots.

Mike Schmidt, Philadelphia's People's Choice. It was a triumph of selective memory, if not revisionist history. *Daily News* writer Mark Kram acknowledged the irony when presenting the list. "Could this be the same Mike Schmidt who the fans just could never cozy up to? Who was so haughty, so aloof and so sensitive when it came to fielding criticism?"

Saying fans "never cozied up to" Schmidt is like saying we never warmed to the Cowboys or Mets. When Schmidt gave his Hall of Fame induction speech in 1995, many observers expected boos. And not just the Philadelphia bashers: Richie Ashburn, inducted at the same time as Schmidt, expected Schmidt to get booed, too. And no wonder: Schmidt committed a cardinal sin just weeks before his induction, a mistake he made again and again throughout his career: he admitted that he cared about the criticism. "It's hard for me to have good things to say about a town that never did anything for me and made life miserable for me," he said in an article in *Philadelphia Magazine.*

It may have been the most complex relationship an all-time great has ever had with his hometown fans. Schmidt excelled but was reviled. His strikeouts were seen as lapses of effort, his complaints as evidence of weakness. He was written off as "aloof" so many times that it became a watchword, like "passionate" (our catch-all excuse for treating great players terribly). Other Philly sports legends would suffer the same torment—Donovan McNabb's relationship with the fans was amazingly similar—but Schmidt remained at war with the fans even after winning a World Series, winning three MVP awards, achieving Hall of Fame status, and stepping onto the risers at Cooperstown.

Columnist David Ramsey called Schmidt a "tormented victim of fandom gone bad" at his Hall of Fame induction. He noted that Schmidt looked "grim" as he approached the podium. Writing for the *Syracuse Herald-Journal*, Ramsey found the spectacle of Phillies fans suddenly supporting Schmidt most unusual. "For 18 years these fans booed Schmidt without mercy and without good reason. Now, they treat him like teen-age girls treated the Beatles in 1965."

At the podium, Schmidt addressed his unfortunate relationship with us. "Can we put that to rest here today?" he asked. "Sure, there were tough nights and tough games at Veterans Stadium. . . . But I remember most your cheers of anticipation as I would come to the plate for a big at-bat. The curtain calls after big home runs. And that number 20 being hung on the outfield wall of Vet Stadium forever." Ramsey felt Schmidt's words didn't "ring true," but biographer William C. Kashatus called the speech "a valiant effort to forgive and forget."

* * *

FIFTEEN YEARS AFTER his Hall of Fame speech, the man voted the Greatest Athlete in Philadelphia History sounded more at ease. "I sense a warmth from fans in Philly when I visit and it feels good," Schmidt said in response to the *Daily News* vote. Oddly, many fans felt that Schmidt had changed, not the circumstances. "His personality has changed," said one fan in the *Daily News*. "During his playing days, he seemed aloof."

There's that word again. Aloof. Schmidt's critics used it. Kashatus addressed it at the end of his biography of Schmidt: "Any remaining

Mike Schmidt

questions about Schmidt's 'aloof personality' or 'inability to communicate' should be put to rest as well." Why is aloofness so awful? Why should it so condemn a player that he must fear boos during his Hall of Fame ceremony, that he must express mild surprise about a "sense of warmth" he feels in a city where he once led a team to its first World Series victory?

Schmidt admitted throughout his career that he wasn't the kind of player the local fans embraced. "I'm not really a 'rah-rah' guy," he said in 1978. His approach was cerebral, his seeming nonchalance a conscious effort to stay focused on his swing. Schmidt discussed his approach to hitting in his odd little autobiography, *Clearing the Bases*: "I never met anybody in my entire major league career who was as deeply into the mental side of hitting as I was. I always needed a specific, mechanical element—a swing thought to use a golf term—to focus on to get me through an at bat. I was the Nick Faldo of baseball. See ball/hit ball? No way. To me, that would be like being lost in the woods without a compass."

That mental approach made Schmidt appear aloof to fans who expected heroes to growl, punch, snarl, and fume. It also made him an all-time great. Schmidt is universally acknowledged as one of the two or three best third basemen in history, if not the greatest. He led the Phillies through one of the most successful periods any Philly team ever experienced: a World Series victory, another loss, four other playoff appearances.

For this, he was booed relentlessly. When he won the MVP award after the 1980 World Series, fans argued that Bob Boone or Bake McBride deserved it more. When he went 1-for-20 in the 1983 World Series, a school bus full of children made choke gestures when they saw him on the streets of Center City.

And when Schmidt dared to protest, it only got worse. At the start of the 1985 season, the *Montreal Gazette* interviewed Schmidt. Schmidt had just moved from third to first base. He was slumping, as were the Phillies, and the fans were riding him worse than ever. In the interview, Schmidt called Philly fans "beyond help," "a mob scene," and "uncontrollable." He said his career would have been better in Los Angeles or Chicago, where fans would be "grateful just to have me around." Two months later, with the team still slumping, the interview was published.

News of the interview reached Philadelphia just as the Phillies were to begin a July home stand. Schmidt did his best to un-pop the balloon. "Things are beginning to go a lot better. And I hate to see something like this be made into something bigger than it is," he said of the interview in the *Inquirer*. Too late. Talk radio was buzzing. Fans were howling. "My teammates wouldn't stand near me in pregame drills; I think they were afraid of a sniper," Schmidt wrote in *Clearing the Bases*.

You know what happened next. In the clubhouse, Schmidt donned Larry Andersen's fright wig and Steve Jeltz's Porsche sunglasses. He didn't want to take the field in the disguise, saying later that he was "wound way too tight" for the stunt, but teammates talked him into it. He took warm-ups at first base in the disguise. While many fans still booed, many howled and cheered. "I guess it showed them I wanted to acknowledge the tongue-lashing I'd given them, and to show them a human side of me they'd never seen."

Revisionist history says that Schmidt got the fans on his side that day. Contemporary reports say something else. Before the game, the *Daily News* polled fans and found that 51 percent agreed with Schmidt's remarks and 85 percent were still glad he played for the Phillies. But when Schmidt struck out to end the game with two men on base, the boos began once again. "The crowd sounded unanimous," Rich Hofmann wrote.

* * *

WE'RE LEFT WITH a conundrum, an all-time great reviled in his own time for no other crime but a quirk of personality that made him less fun loving, or assertive, or *something* than we wanted. Then, we have the same player 22 years later, remembered more fondly than

Julius Erving or Bobby Clarke, at least according to a newspaper poll. Is this nostalgia? Is it some real change in Schmidt's character? Is it something else?

After the "beyond help" interview in 1985, team president Bill Giles took Schmidt aside. "He really misunderstands the fans," Giles told Peter Pascarelli in the *Inquirer.* "The fans really do admire and like Mike. But it's like when you spank your kid. You love your child. But in this case, when he pops up with the bases loaded or strikes out, they boo. But that doesn't mean they don't like or respect him." There's certainly truth to that.

Schmidt's salary was also a point of contention for much of his career. The team stayed one step ahead of the free-agent market for Schmidt, meaning that he was always one of the highest paid players in the league. Reading fan opinions of the day, you find his salary repeated like a mantra. "He's a .220 hitter making two million dollars." "He should be able to bear the criticism a little better for $2 million a year."

But there's more. I've sat in taprooms and heard the arguments, not just that Brooks Robinson was better (wrong but defensible), but that Ken Boyer or some other forgotten third-sacker was actually better than Schmidt. "Philly old-timers swear that Schmidt stank in the clutch, his 548 home runs somehow producing only 274 runs batted in," I wrote in the *New York Times* in 2009. It wasn't tough love; it was illogical, persistent contempt, not just from a handful of loudmouths but from a generation of fans conditioned to be over-suspicious of wealthy athletes who don't make a show of diving into the dirt or beating their breasts after losses.

Those old-timers, the unrepentant boo-birds who never "coziedup" to Schmidt, weren't the type to load into buses and ride to Cooperstown. They weren't the type, 15 years later, to vote in on-line polls. Without their input, Schmidt enjoyed a boo-free Hall of Fame ceremony and performed well in an exit poll. Haters and deniers tend to forget, or fade away, or move on to the next target. Schmidt's biggest critics moved on, projecting character flaws and inadequacies onto other players who dared to draw high salaries and approach the game with detached professionalism. Schmidt's championship and numbers remain for younger fans to gape at. Those who truly "got" Mike Schmidt had more staying power than those who loved to hate.

Still, those haters were too loud for too long. Giles likened the boos to fatherly spankings. That's a polite way to rationalize what was, for the better part of 15 years, heinous, inexcusable behavior toward a great player and an admirable, hard-working individual. In Schmidt's case, an entire city waited far too long to spare the rod.

4

CHASE UTLEY

The Man, and the Man Crush

Greatness: ★★★★
Toughness: ★★★★½
Eccentricity: ★★★
Legacy: ★★★★

CHASE UTLEY BECAME a fan favorite when he hit a grand slam in his first major league start. He became The Man when he scored from second base on a Ryan Howard groundout in 2008. He became a legend during the 2008 World Series victory celebration when he summed up 25 years of fan frustration with one PG-13 rated rallying cry.

Along the way, he became an All Star and one of the best players in baseball. He also became something else, something rare in Philadelphia. He became untouchable. Unassailable. A rare superstar who is never booed, rarely criticized, seldom held solely accountable for his team's misfortunes.

Julius Erving was one such superstar. Bobby Clarke was another. Chase Utley, thus far, is in that class. There may be others from the past five decades, but you can count them on one hand.

· · ·

UTLEY WAS ON A BUS from Scranton to Ottawa in April 2003 when his minor league manager got a call from the Phillies. Placido Polanco was heading for the disabled list with a finger injury. The Phillies needed Utley to replace Polanco at second base at a businessperson's special and in less than 24 hours.

The bus driver dropped Utley off at a gas station 45 minutes north of Scranton. "I was in the middle of nowhere," Utley said the next day.

To be precise, Utley was in the Endless Mountains, the name given to that desolate region north of Scranton. The Endless Mountains are a long way from anywhere. Utley hung out at the gas station and a roadside sandwich shop until a clubhouse attendant arrived to drive him back to Philadelphia.

Utley was a solid prospect, not an elite one. His march through the minors was slow, his statistics—.257 with 16 homers in Clearwater, .263 with 17 homers at AAA Scranton—nothing special. He was a lefty who couldn't hit lefties, an error-prone second baseman who flunked a tryout at third. He rode from the Endless Mountains to a Phillies team that was stuck on an endless treadmill, a team built around a few stars (Jim Thome, Bobby Abreu) that appeared destined to hover around .500 forever.

Just 16,947 fans were in Veterans Stadium when Utley, fresh from the Pennsylvania hinterlands, stepped to the plate in the third inning against the Rockies with the bases loaded. Aaron Cook's first pitch to Utley was a fastball. Utley jerked it into the bullpen in right field. He ran the bases so quickly that he almost overtook David Bell, who was on first base when Utley batted. "I was stuck in that gear," Utley said after the game. "I couldn't slow down."

The fans gave Utley a standing ovation. They demanded a curtain call. He sheepishly popped out of the dugout to satisfy the fans. "He was pretty embarrassed by that—he just got here," manager Larry Bowa said.

A star was born, one that would take a path few Philly sports legends ever traveled: a path that led straight upward.

• • •

IT WAS MID-JUNE 2010, and Utley was in a slump. His batting average, .307 on May 23, had dropped to .259. He had homered just twice since May 5. The Phillies were slumping, too, hovering in third place after winning the National League Pennant in 2009 and the World Series in 2008. Culprits for the slump were numerous: the bullpen, Jayson Werth, the organization itself for trading away pitcher Cliff Lee. Oddly, Utley was never mentioned as part of the problem, even when, for a month or so, he clearly was.

"I'm going to enroll in grad school and study psychology or sociology and write my thesis on the phenomenon that is the city of

Philadelphia's massive man crush on Chase Utley," David Murphy wrote in Philly.com. "When Ryan Howard doesn't hit, it is because he swings at bad pitches out of the zone. When Jimmy Rollins doesn't hit, it is because he is impatient at the plate. When Jayson Werth doesn't hit, it is because he is swinging for a new contract. But when Utley doesn't hit, he must be hurt."

Utley wasn't hurt then, but a few weeks later he broke his finger. He missed eight weeks. For a few days in early July, 610-WIP sounded like it was holding a wake for Utley's 2010 season and, by extension, the Phillies chances of reaching the playoffs. A few bold callers suggested that the team should try to trade Utley; those fans were shouted down and ridiculed by both hosts and other callers. "We're in the alternate universe," host Anthony Gargano said after one caller suggested an Utley trade.

Such reverence would be common in any other city. In Philadelphia, it's shocking. After a slump and an injury, in what looked like a lost season, trade talk for a superstar is almost mandatory. But Utley is immune. The World Series ring helps, but it got Mike Schmidt only so far. Utley kept hustling through his slump, but hustle is easy to overlook when the team's in third place.

Murphy couldn't quite pinpoint the reason for Utley's immunity, but the man crush is undeniable. Even the late, great Harry Kalas was swept up by it.

. . .

UTLEY'S LEGEND GREW slowly after that 2003 grand slam. He returned to the minors, then platooned with Polanco for a while. He hit 28 home runs in 2005, then went on a 35-game hitting streak in 2006, his batting average climbing to .330 at one point.

The streak ended on August 4 with the Phillies in their usual spot, just above .500 and just below the Mets and Braves in the standings. After the streak, the Phillies lost two games to the Mets, beat the Braves, then lost again. Utley's streak was fun, but Phillies baseball was returning to normal. The Phillies trailed the Braves 3–2 in the rubber match of their series. Utley stepped to the plate with the bases loaded in the seventh inning.

Utley slammed a hanging slider into the left-center gap for a three-run double. The hit was important, but what he did next was extraordinary. Ryan Howard chopped a ball off the dirt; it hung in the air to the right of the mound before pitcher Macay McBride fired to first for an easy out. But Utley started running upon contact; replays showed he was nearly at third base when Howard left the batter's box. The Braves first baseman took McBride's throw and fired home, but Utley slid hard and beat the tag.

Kalas, still commenting about the double one pitch earlier, couldn't contain himself. "Chase Utley, you are the man!" he exclaimed. It was one of Kalas's last catchphrases, and it became both a nickname and a rallying cry for the Phillies. And the win sparked a rally for the Phillies, who went 30–19 for the rest of the season to finish over .500.

The next season, with Utley batting .332, the Phillies reached the playoffs, and the season after that, with Utley hitting 32 home runs, they won the World Series. They returned to the World Series a year later, with Utley hitting five home runs in a losing effort against the Yankees.

The Man. A simple nickname, but very accurate.

*   *   *

THE PHILLIES TRAILED the Reds 4–3 in Game 2 of the 2010 Division Championship Series. Utley led off the seventh inning against Aroldis Chapman, a 23-year-old lefty prospect with a 100-mph fastball. Utley had been busy all night: he committed two errors in the second inning to give the Reds a run, but he singled in two unearned runs in the fifth. So as the old saying goes: if you're going to allow one, make sure you knock in two.

Chapman threw an 0–2 fastball inside. Utley jumped from the batter's box and ran to first. He had been hit by Chapman's pitch, except that someone hit by Chapman's fastball anywhere near where Utley claimed to be hit would be unconscious. The home plate umpire heard the ball hit something—maybe the bill of Utley's cap, maybe the tip of the catcher's mitt—and awarded him the base.

I was covering the game, and I couldn't help stifling a chuckle. Utley had the aura of a champion in October 2010. Chapman must have hit him right in the aura. The aura beat a throw to second on a ground ball two batters later, and the aura touched third as a Reds error allowed him to score. If Reds right fielder Jay Bruce had an aura that could catch, that playoff series would have been very different.

Two nights later, the series moved to Cincinnati, and Reds fans booed Utley every time he came to the plate. They called him a cheater. Perfect. A true Philly hero needs an enemy city. Bobby Clarke had Moscow. Wilt Chamberlain had Boston. Cincinnati isn't Moscow or Boston, but it'll do.

That hit-by-pitch, safe-at-second, shadow-tag-of-third sequence explains and reinforces the man crush, the lifetime pass we give Utley. He's a great player, greater than he's often given credit for (Baseball Prospectus-style analysis rates him ahead of Howard and Rollins), but in Philly, it helps to appear to be a little less than great. We remember the run from second to home on the grounder but forget the double to give the Phillies the lead. We remember the hit-by-pitch gamesmanship better than the two runs he knocked in two innings earlier (or the home run he hit to those booing fans in Game 3). We love a little hustle more than a lot of excellence.

We even forget a poor performance in the League Championship Series, or project an athlete's failures onto someone else. A man crush is a powerful thing.

. . .

HE STOOD at the podium wearing a black jacket and a black wool cap, odd clothing choices for a very warm October afternoon. But then, everything about the day was odd. It was Halloween, 2008. And a Philadelphia team had just won a championship.

It was impossible for most fans to express their feelings that day. There's no word beyond jubilation, beyond euphoria, that properly expresses the mix of pure joy and pure disbelief. Utley did his best to express those feelings, dropping the f-bomb heard around the sports world.

"World Champions. World fucking champions," he said. Bloggers nationwide chided Utley like Sunday school marms. He cursed! On television! In front of children! Some moralizing nitwits wrote it off as another example of boorish Philadelphia behavior.

For most fans, it was anything but. "Ladies and gentlemen, I present to you the greatest World Series speech in the history of sports," read the post on The Fightins Web site that accompanied a clip of Utley's speech. "Kids, make sure to cover your ears."

Kids, uncover your ears. Those five words established the link between the 2008 Phillies and the champions of the past, one good-natured cussword evoking memories of Chuck Bednarik's off-season jobs and Broad Street Bullies partying in neighborhood taprooms, of eras when sports were a little less homogenized and the fan experience, while maybe a little rougher, was far more personal. Utley's f-bomb wasn't angry or casual: it was a final exclamation of determination and exhaustion, of well-deserved, too-long-in-coming triumph. Utley earned that f-bomb, and so did we.

Utley was a fan favorite, The Man, a legend who is still growing. But in that moment, Utley also became one of us. He became humanized in a way few sports heroes are anymore. Utley may be a millionaire who loves Bentleys and Ferraris and vacations in Kona and Cabo (according to his own Web site), but the guy in the black wool cap, cussing into the microphone, was as blue collar and relatable as we could ever ask a superstar to be.

Utley won the city's heart that day. Two years later he still hasn't had to give it back. He probably never will.

5

JULIUS ERVING

The Showman We Could Not Boo. Or Could We?

Greatness: ★★★½
Toughness: ★★★½
Eccentricity: ★★
Legacy: ★★★★★

LEGEND HAS IT that Julius Erving was never booed in Philadelphia. That can't be right. It has to be some kind of whitewash.

Erving was too transcendently good on the court, and too professional and dignified off the court, to be booed. So says the inherited wisdom. Since when have those things mattered? Mike Schmidt was just as great a player and almost as respectable a human being, and we tortured him. And although Erving brought the city a championship, earning our undying gratitude, he did it only after six years of foreplay. Erving was never blamed for a playoff loss in those six years? Never accused of choking? That sounds like selective memory.

I searched newspaper archives, read biographies and *Sports Illustrated* features, and I never found a single instance of Erving getting booed. That's amazing, because *Sports Illustrated* rarely mentions a Philadelphia athlete without bring up a booing incident. Give them a 20-word photo caption about Philly, and they'll fit the word "boo" in somewhere. The Sixers getting booed? Sure. But the boos were always aimed at George McGinnis or Darryl Dawkins or the team as a unit. Some of that may have been in-the-moment spin on the part of sportswriters, who respected Erving in an era when the typical trip to the Phillies locker room across Pattison Avenue might feature a sweat sock to the face. But veteran Philadelphians can tell a player boo from a team or coach boo, and Erving was never singled out as the root cause of all our suffering.

It may have been a testament to his character. It could also have been an oversight.

. . .

IF ERVING PLAYED today, he would be a talk-radio and blog-o-sphere chew toy.

On March 13, 1977, Turquoise Erving (Doc's wife, but you knew that) wrote an open letter in the "Views of Sport" page of the *New York Times*. "We would have preferred that the Nets not sell him to the Philadelphia 76ers," she wrote, the royal "we" making her sound like Queen Victoria. "Maybe if Philadelphia had treated us differently I would have felt better and thought of Philly as home. . . . The papers said the team was 'in awe' of Julius. I don't think so. It's more like we weren't wanted. . . . Julius is happy because he's playing basketball, not because he's playing for the 76ers. . . . In New York, fans had respect for the game. . . . If you make a mistake in Philadelphia, they stand up and boo loudly."

Imagine reading that letter on Deadspin, then seeing the excerpts on Comcast SportsNite, then SportsCenter, with reaction shots from the teammates Turquoise called out. There was enough in that letter to keep WIP busy for a week. Carl Lindros and Wilma McNabb had nothing on Turquoise in that letter. In today's sports culture, that one rant could have sunk Erving's reputation.

In the midst of the 1983 Championship Series against the Lakers, Erving addressed Temple University students while receiving an honorary doctorate. "Winning has to be a goal," he said. "But the thing that must be most enjoyable is the work itself. The result cannot be your only enjoyment." Later in the speech: "There is too much emphasis on the result. . . . The meat of the matter is often overlooked, that without disappointments, hard work, and sacrifice, there can be no gain."

It's a positive message and a healthy attitude about the importance of winning, an attitude Erving often espoused. Sportswriters understood the message and respected the man, so they didn't twist Erving's words into something controversial. Allow me to write the headline any seasoned blogger would write today: "Erving Makes Excuse in Advance for Choking Against Lakers: Says There Is Too Much Emphasis on Results."

Let's do it again, this time with an interview Erving gave at the Academy of Achievement about his first season with the Sixers. "We were the second-best team in the world. If you get depressed about being the second-best team in the world, then you've got a problem." Write the headline along with me: Erving Settles for Second Best.

Search the archives, and you'll find plenty of quotes that could be twisted into an attack against Erving. He often referred to himself as an "artist," remarks that would be mocked today. He was open about basketball as a business and was always polite-but-firm in contract talks. He criticized management. He called out teammates, though gently. He could easily have been cast as too big for his britches, aloof, egomaniacal, or branded with the go-to insult for today's soft-spoken athlete: passive-aggressive.

Erving got a small taste of modern media when we learned in 1999 that he fathered Alexandra Stevenson out of wedlock and secretly supported her for 17 years. Despite relatively kid-gloves treatment from most media sites, Erving became fodder for the blogs and gossip columns. But he was long retired by the time we learned of Stevenson, a venerable elder-statesman whose infidelity was nearly two decades old. Had the timing been different, Erving would have been Tiger Woods.

It didn't happen that way. Journalists could be hard on players in the 1970s, but there were fewer outlets, smaller columns, and not as many opportunities for backspin. Erving was allowed to be articulate and honest. That was lucky for him, because he deserved better than mudslinging, micro-scrutiny of his words and gossipy indictments of his personal life. And it was lucky for us, because we needed a sports hero who floated above the petty fray, even if he wasn't quite as perfect as we thought he was.

. . .

TO RANK ERVING as a mere basketball player is to belittle him. He was a cultural figure, an ambassador for racial harmony, Gandhi-meets–Stevie Wonder in high tops.

Stories from Erving's heyday have an almost unreal quality. Joe Queenan wrote that Erving once autographed a newspaper and gave him a Cabbage Patch Doll for his daughter after Queenan "rescued Julius Erving from a bunch of gawking rubes." Charity-event sponsors tell stories of meeting Doc in the street, inviting him to a function, and getting not only hours of his time but his home phone number in the bargain. (Yes, the Stevenson incident sheds new light on a few of these tales, but let's take the high road.) Erving answered every interview question, signed every autograph. When he visited Children's Hospital, he stopped just short of performing a few appendectomies. Every chance encounter with Doc ended with some outsized expression of his largesse. It seems impossible for all of them to be true, yet there's not one that can be singled out as an exaggeration.

Most amazingly, Erving was always able to separate himself from the image. The man who brought playground basketball to the world, the savior of the ABA, the exemplar of mainstream black culture, was as good at staying grounded as he was at taking flight. Erving once spoke of Isaac Hayes, the soul singer who became wrapped up in his Black Moses persona. Erving talked about the importance of not being absorbed by a persona in the same way. "I had to fight Dr. J," he said.

The war with himself was something that we never saw, but it keeps him human to us. As memories fade, Erving becomes a Santa Claus who slam-dunked from the foul line. But he was very mortal. When he played, writers glossed over his foibles, just as today's media would poke and prod at them until half of society hated him. But Erving didn't deny his failings. He admitted that money was important. He accepted that ego drove him, was somehow modest without engaging in false modesty. He allowed himself to be marketed but not exploited; he promoted himself without boasting. "Always a showman, never a showboat," reads the blurb on the back of one biography. What's amazing is not just that he did it, but that everyone got it. It was all genuine—the boasts and the humility, the charity and the desire for wealth—and everyone somehow knew it.

Maybe that's why we allegedly never booed.

.   .   .

DR. J ARRIVED in Philadelphia a playground legend and an ABA champion. He was nervous when he took the court for his first game, missing a jumper and his first four free throws. We didn't boo.

The Sixers lost four straight games in the NBA Finals after winning their first two games. We didn't boo. The team adopted the "We owe you one" slogan. The city waited five years for the one the Sixers owed, but we didn't boo. Popular, exciting players left town so the team could build around Erving. The team stayed stuck in a rut. We stuck with Erving.

Moses Malone arrived while Erving was touring China with an All-Star team. Erving, in his measured way, questioned his role with the team, mused about his salary, hinted at miscommunications with ownership. "Looking out for myself, I'm still assessing where I fit into the picture. That will have to be clarified soon." We held our breath, but we didn't boo. The two stars meshed, as only two great men uniquely cognizant of their own egos can. The Sixers stomped through the NBA like a movie monster for a year. They won fo-five-fo. We cheered and cheered.

Then, the team slipped back to the pack. They lost in the first round of the playoffs the following year. Erving's drives to the basket grew less memorable. He relied more on his jump shot, never his strength. His shooting percentage slipped below .500. His rebounding slipped. We didn't boo. He spent three seasons as a rather ordinary small forward. He had nights that were flat-out awful. Larry Bird left him in the dust, except when they strangled each other in on-court arguments. The Celtics won the game and the fight. We didn't boo.

Before the 1986 season opener, Erving wrote a press release saying that he would retire at season's end. That season would be marked by farewell celebrations in every city, as rival teams exchanged tokens of appreciation for guaranteed sellouts. But the farewell tour came later. The night of the season opener, Sixers publicity director Harvey Pollack quietly distributed Erving's release in the press box after the tip. In the third quarter of a close game, announcer Jim Wise decided to inform the crowd. Erving would soon be gone. The entire Spectrum learned about it at once.

For a few seconds, the Spectrum crowd booed. Then they gave a standing ovation.

We were booing the loss of Erving, not Erving himself, but it's only fair that Erving got one tiny taste of what every other sports star heard. Most of the greatest athletes in history were booed in Philly at one time or another. Erving didn't deserve to be left out. We owed him one.

6

WILT CHAMBERLAIN
The Babe Ruth of Backspin

Greatness: ★★★★½
Toughness: ★★★★½
Eccentricity: ★★½
Legacy: ★★★½

WILT CHAMBERLAIN SCORED 100 points in one game in 1962. He might as well have done it in 1862. He accomplished the feat in Hershey, but for all the time and space between then and now, it could have been a field house in ancient Babylon.

The sheer scope of a 100-point game invites skepticism. It has to be a fluke, a dusty relic of a record from some horse-and-buggy era. Wilt Chamberlain scored 100 points in a game? Sure, and Ed Delahanty batted .400 three times for the Phillies in the 1890s. Did the ball still have laces when Wilt did it? Was he shooting into a peach basket? Was the opposing center 5-foot-9?

No, Chamberlain scored 100 points in the real-life NBA in a sport we would all recognize easily as basketball. But he did it for a team that isn't in Philly anymore, in front of 4,000 fans in the boondocks of central Pennsylvania at a time when Philadelphia basketball fans cared much more about the goings-on at the Palestra than what was happening to any professional team. The 100-point game was very real, but its story comes to us through Bill Campbell and Sonny Hill; our fathers and grandfathers don't talk about it, because they weren't there, and the game wasn't televised.

We're left with something gargantuan but dimly remembered, beautiful, astonishing, difficult to understand, and a little controversial, something that came from Philadelphia but really belongs to the whole world. The 100-point game, in other words, sums Chamberlain up nicely.

. . .

CHAMBERLAIN BELONGED to Philadelphia. Warriors owner Eddie "Gotty" Gottlieb thought so, and the NBA agreed.

In the 1950s and 1960s, the league awarded "territorial rights" draft picks, which made it easier for franchises to acquire local college heroes. Gottlieb made frequent use of the picks, turning the Warriors into a Big Five All-Star team: Tom Gola from La Salle, Paul Arizin from Villanova, Guy Rodgers from Temple, Ernie Beck from Penn.

In 1955, Gotty used his territorial rights to select Chamberlain from Overbrook High School, even though Chamberlain planned to attend the University of Kansas. The territorial picks were supposed to apply to colleges, not high schools or home towns, but Gotty found a loophole, one that infuriated some in the still-struggling league. The Knicks coach Andrew "Fuzzy" Levane said the NBA "created a monster" by adding Chamberlain to the already-talented Warriors; Levane said this four years before Chamberlain was even eligible to take the court.

Once Chamberlain joined Gola and the others, those Warriors teams were as Philadelphian as any pro team could ever be, and the franchise's swift move to San Francisco stung both devoted fans and players. Arizin refused to move any place farther away than Camden and retired; the homesick Gola lasted just a few weeks in California before accepting a trade to the Knicks. Chamberlain stayed with the Warriors for a few seasons; meanwhile the Syracuse Nationals became the Philadelphia 76ers, a team that Philly fans ignored. "In Philadelphia, Local Boys are absolutely essential," Frank DeFord wrote in *Sports Illustrated.* "The 76ers were properly scorned."

Chamberlain soon returned to Philadelphia, making the 76ers great and helping the team develop a fan base. He belonged to Philadelphia, for better and for worse. For better, because he brought the city a championship and legitimized a franchise, and because his heroics at Overbrook High School touched thousands of fans in gymnasiums around the city. For worse, because he suffered all the ironic punishments of a Philly sports hero: he was vilified for his salary, his gifts were taken for granted, his weaknesses scrutinized. He was forced

Wilt Chamberlain
(Courtesy of Temple University Libraries, Urban Archives, Philadelphia, PA)

to spend most of his career looking up at a far superior opponent, expected to carry teams on his shoulders but castigated for not being a team player. He wore the biggest bull's-eye in professional sports in the 1960s, and he wore it in a city known for its target practice.

Yet Philly fans went easy on Chamberlain. It was the rest of the world that saddled him with unrealistic expectations.

. . .

RUSSELL VERSUS CHAMBERLAIN. It was the NBA's first great man-to-man rivalry, and it remains one of the most debated personal rivalries in all of sports history. Chamberlain first faced Bill Russell and the Boston Celtics in November 1959 when he was a Warriors rookie. Russell won the matchup, and the Celtics won the game. "What the duel proved, chiefly, is that against Russell, Chamberlain cannot get away with the few simple offensive moves he has found so effective against lesser men," Jeremiah Tax wrote in *Sports Illustrated*. A few months later, Tax noted that Chamberlain "frequently outplayed Bill Russell," though Russell had the last laugh in the playoffs, playing tight defense while his talented teammates outclassed the Warriors.

That 1960 playoff series established the pattern. The Warriors fell to the Celtics in the playoffs again in 1962. Chamberlain joined the Sixers during the 1964–1965 season, and the Sixers lost to the Celtics in the playoffs at the end of that year. The Sixers lost to the Celtics again in 1966. Chamberlain won his share of battles, but Russell always won the war. Often, Russell was better than Chamberlain in those decisive games. Just as often, they played to a draw, but the other 11 Celtics beat the other 11 Sixers, and fans wondered why Chamberlain didn't do more.

The Russell-Chamberlain debate has waged in nearly every basketball book ever written. The consensus opinion—if there is one—is that Russell was better at the little things: varying his shots, defending, boxing out, playing within the system. Chamberlain was better at the big things, like scoring 50 points per night—an awfully big thing—but was a poor foul shooter and an unskilled offensive rebounder. All of these points are true, though exaggerated: winners write history, and when Boston teams win, their sportswriters attribute all of their success to being headier, more precise, more dedicated and detail oriented than their opponents. (When Boston teams lose, it's because the Yankees bought the title.)

The Russell-Chamberlain debate is interesting, but I won't chime in, because opinions now outnumber eyewitness accounts on the matter by a 20-to-1 ratio. The 1962 Warriors averaged about 4,000 fans per night. The championship 1966–1967 Sixers drew a little over 6,000 per night. Convention Hall wasn't full for the 1967 Finals, even though the Sixers faced a Warriors team that still had a few former local guys. Television coverage was spotty at the time. It's said that hundreds of thousands of people claim to have witnessed the 100-point game, even though most couldn't even nail down what city it was played in. The Chamberlain-Russell argument has descended into similar silliness: 30-year-old men devoting thousands of words to Russell's passing touch and box-out technique, based on third-hand accounts, newspaper photos, and their own prejudices.

But why debate at all? Can't Chamberlain and Russell coexist peacefully? They were friendly rivals when they played, but they came to be recast as opposites: Russell the dignified champion, Chamberlain the egotistical scorer. No one oversimplifies it quite that much (except perhaps Bill Simmons in the *Book of Basketball*), but Chamberlain is often characterized as a stat compiler, a poor team player who lacked the ineffable "winner" magic to regularly propel the Warriors, Sixers, and Lakers past the Celtics. Some detractors take that ball and really run with it; Simmons hammers Chamberlain so hard you'd swear he's writing about Matt Geiger. For many basketball writers outside of Philly, it's not about Wilt versus Russell. It's not just about cutting Chamberlain down to size. It's about whittling him away to nothing, pecking away at his achievements until he becomes a sideshow attraction, a sullen 7-footer who disrupted team offense and team payroll. You come away from some biographies wondering what anyone ever saw in the guy.

Contemporary players are constantly subject to this kind of revisionism. No sooner does a player achieve stardom than a backlash occurs, and great players from Tiger Woods to Michael Jordan inspire legions of detractors. It wasn't always that way.

.   .   .

CHAMBERLAIN FORCED rule changes. Goaltending became a foul because of Chamberlain's ability to flick balls away from the top of the basket. Leaping-dunk free throws were outlawed. The lane grew wider to keep Wilt from establishing base camp just below the bucket.

Rules changed off the court, too. Chamberlain personally desegregated Lawrence, Kansas, when he went to school there. He's given little credit for it, because it has been recast by some as a selfish act: he was breaking down boundaries for himself, not for black America or the good of humanity. It's a double standard to which Wilt alone seems to have been held: battling segregation wasn't enough; he had to do it for the right reasons.

Chamberlain was always held to illogically high standards. He was entrusted to single-handedly enhance the image of a two-bit sports league, then resented for acknowledging he was (and wanting to be paid as) the league's biggest draw. He won "only" two championships during an era when the Celtics were the only team that ever won anything. He led the league in assists the season after the Sixers won the title, dishing to Hal Greer and Billy Cunningham to demonstrate that he really was a complete, selfless player. Yet critics said he passed to prove a point, not to help the team, and a playoff loss to the Celtics was held up as evidence. Like breaking the color barrier, averaging 24.3 points, 23.8 rebounds, and 8.6 assists for a team that went 62–20 wasn't enough; Chamberlain had to do it for the right reasons.

That's the biggest rule that changed because of Chamberlain. Forget the wider lane; Chamberlain was the innovator of illogical backlash. Before Chamberlain, extraordinary feats like 100-point games or 50-point seasons were taken at face value: they were great performances by great athletes. The instantaneous counterspin that later became the stock-in-trade of Internet journalism may not have been invented for Chamberlain, but it was perfected for him. High-scoring nights were signs of selfishness. Low-scoring nights revealed a lack of desire. Winning was not enough. Losing was unacceptable. The language of perpetual dissatisfaction, used nationally now to criticize players like Peyton Manning and Alex Rodriguez, was coined for Chamberlain.

• • •

CHAMBERLAIN IS OFTEN called basketball's Babe Ruth. He's also Philadelphia's Babe Ruth.

Philly doesn't get a Ruth who's universally loved, who wins championships by the bushel, whose numerous faults are glossed over or gentrified. We get one who's vilified, whose motives were questioned, whose championships were trivialized, whose faults were exaggerated. Philly gets a guy who scores 100 points in a game and is expected to apologize.

Chamberlain is as polarizing as a political figure. You must read his biographies with your spin detector on maximum setting, as if you are reading about Bill Clinton or Sarah Palin. Apologists explain away every argument about practice rules, every disagreement with teammates, every false retirement and playoff shortfall. Detractors hammer away at his surly reputation and his battles with coaches. Chamberlain himself mostly brags of sexual conquests. The real Chamberlain was just too big to be perceived from one viewpoint. Study him enough, and you can encircle and map him like a mountain, respect him and maybe understand him, but never quite know him.

One thing you cannot do is give him the Chuck Bednarik treatment, bronzing a few images and hanging them above the hearth. Controversies, rivalries, sexual boasts, and incomprehensible numbers keep Chamberlain alive, as do the photos in the Palestra, tales told at the Penn Relays, and re-airings of *Conan the Destroyer*. The Chamberlain who became a multimedia personality and a Harlem Globetrotter, who elevated professional basketball beyond roller derby status, belongs to the world. The Chamberlain whose name is splashed all over the Overbrook High School record books, the Goliath who grew up among us and brought us a lone championship, belongs to Philadelphia. We still own his territorial rights, and we'll never give them up.

7

STEVE CARLTON

The Haunted, Eternal Samurai

Greatness: ★ ★ ★ ★
Toughness: ★ ★ ★
Eccentricity: ★ ★ ★ ★ ★
Legacy: ★ ★ ★

FOR OVER A decade, Steve Carlton was the one constant in our lives.

America changed between 1972 and 1984, changed from bell bottoms to parachute pants, Watergate to Reaganomics. We changed; fans of my generation went from toddlerhood to adolescence, Big Wheels to stolen beers. The Philly sports scene changed, from the City of Losers to the city of Broad Street Bullies to a city where, for a brief period, championship parades were regular events.

But Steve Carlton never changed. He took the mound for the Phillies every fourth day from the Vietnam War era to the time of the Commodore 64. He never aged. The pitches never changed, nor did the results. Carlton changed by not changing. The world circled him.

Close your eyes, and you can still picture him, frozen in time. He's on the mound at the Vet, wearing those old bluish-gray uniforms with the fat red "P" on the breast, hair peeking out from under his cap. In close-ups, his face is forever contorted with all of his strange jaw-stretching tics. He's shaking off Tim McCarver, though it's hard to imagine what McCarver could be signaling except "slider, slider, more slider." Then the wind up, and of course the slider comes, starting out over the plate but tailing away into an unreachable spot near the batter's ankles. You can see Dave Parker swinging wildly, then staring at his bat, wondering what happened. You can see it as clear as yesterday, because you saw it thousands of times over more than a decade, a joyful constant amid life's turmoil.

The Carlton we saw was dependable, stalwart. The Carlton we didn't see was troubled, maybe a little crazy. We never had to worry about that other Carlton. He wasn't the guy in our living rooms every fourth day. Thank heavens.

* * *

THE LONG SILENCE, Carlton's 14-year media boycott, was a blessing for everyone involved. Carlton didn't have to deal with the distractions and dissections of the media. Fans didn't get to know the real Carlton. We were all the better for it.

Before the Long Silence, the pitcher did what other superstars do. He granted interviews. He endorsed products like MAB paint. He let the world peek into his personal life. There was more to Carlton than met the eye, and some of it was a little scary.

Maury Z. Levy profiled Carlton for *Philadelphia Magazine* in 1973. He relates how a girl approached Carlton in a restaurant and asked him if he ever went to a bar called the Rusty Nail. Carlton fired back: "No. I wouldn't go there because right away all you hippies think I'm a fag because of the way I look. I mean, just because my hair's a little long and I've got this moustache, that doesn't make me one of you." Carlton explains that he knows the girl's a hippie because she's wearing pants. "Girls wear dresses," he says.

Levy also gave a charming account of Carlton's financial handlers. "All of his salary is directly forwarded by the Phillies to a trust account in California. He never even sees the checks. He gets his spending and living allowances mailed to him, and the balance goes into savings accounts and investments." A *Sports Illustrated* profile that same year introduced us to David Landfield, a failed actor turned agent who handled most of Carlton's affairs. "When he's through playing," says Landfield, "he can hunt 12 months of the year if that's what he wants."

Before the Great Silence, we caught glimpses of the moody, suspicious Carlton, a young man who possessed an odd mix of distrust and gullibility. He didn't want to be lumped among the hippies, but his pregame meditation and talk about "eliminating variables" took him far from the mainstream. His indifference to worldly possessions sounded refreshing in 1973, when free agency loomed for baseball and the real world and sports world had achieved a détente of mutual cynicism about money. Still, there was something fishy about a 28-year-old man willing to live off an allowance, a man who often retreated into a "dark room of the mind," according to former teammate Dal Maxvill.

Carlton won 27 games in 1972, but he lost 20 in 1973. Of course, writers and fans questioned his meditation and his lifestyle (and his drinking), not noticing that Carlton battled bronchitis throughout spring training and, thanks to an anemic offense, lost a lot of 3–0 and 2–1 games. Carlton stopped granting interviews. His nightlife, opinions, and finances disappeared behind a veil, and fans got to be blissfully oblivious to everything but the facial tics, the slider, and the results. Tim McCarver, who became Carlton's personal catcher because Bob Boone's pitch choices caused "negative thoughts" (Boone's words), became our window into Lefty, and McCarver framed Carlton's idiosyncrasies in a lovable way. "Steve is a very complex person," McCarver said of Carlton in 1977. "I don't claim to have him figured out completely, but I do get along with him. That has a relaxing effect on him. Maybe we're close because he enjoys my candor. I've always been extremely honest with him. I also understand that he hates to be mentored. The more he hears, the more he rebels."

A decade later, McCarver still framed the plate perfectly for Carlton. "Steve may not be a complete recluse, but he comes close. If he hadn't wound up in the majors, he probably would have been a hunting guide in a desolate cabin in the woods fifty miles or so from any paved roads."

* * *

WE KNOW HOW the story ends. We know the guarded young man became paranoid and built a bunker in the Colorado mountains, a scenario similar to the one McCarver suggested, but darker. Like most conspiracy theorists who imagine grand alliances among secret societies, Carlton was astonishingly blind to what was happened under his nose: Landfield's investments were a sham, and by the mid-1980s Carlton was essentially broke.

Then, the man who never aged suddenly got old. In 1984, his strikeout totals dipped, but Carlton was still effective. In 1985, he could no longer strike anyone out. He won one game, lost eight, and while his

3.33 ERA was acceptable, his strikeout-to-walk ratio (48 to 53) was awful. Lefty couldn't make it out of the seventh inning anymore. He injured his rotator cuff, landing him on the disabled list for the first time in 20 years.

In 1986, he started the season with a bad outing (seven runs in four innings to the Reds), then deteriorated. By June, he routinely left games in the fourth inning, having already given up seven or eight hits. The Phillies looked into trade options. There were none. The Phillies tried to get him to retire. He wouldn't. Carlton believed he could still pitch, and while no one liked to say it, everyone knew he needed the money.

Phillies owner Bill Giles gave Carlton one last start to prove that he could pitch. The Phillies took a 4–0 lead in the second inning, ironically aided by a Carlton RBI double. (Darren Daulton scored on the play. The Carlton-Daulton battery belongs on an astral plane.) Carlton walked three straight batters in the two-run Cardinals' third. In the fifth, the Cardinals tagged him for four runs on four hits and a walk. Carlton ended that inning by striking out the Cardinals pitcher. It was his last meaningful act as a Phillies pitcher. Giles waived him soon after the game.

Carlton's sad sojourn then began. He pitched for the Giants and White Sox in 1986, ineffectively. The Phillies brought him back for spring training in 1987, then released him again. The man whose silence became legendary sounded pathetic when he finally spoke. "I'm agreeable to sign something for a modest contract that would include incentives. If I didn't think I could pitch, I would walk away from it. But I know I can still win." The Indians picked him up as a reliever, then released him. The Twins tried to make him a spot lefty, the guy who comes in to face one or two left-handed batters in middle relief. It didn't work. Carlton could no longer pitch, even for a modest contract.

Only Carlton didn't see it that way. He later claimed that the National League black-balled him, for reasons unknown. He became a relative chatterbox. When he was inducted into the Hall of Fame in 1994, Carlton mixed the usual old ballplayer saws with Zen Master quotes like "the body is the vessel of the mind." Pat Jordan profiled him in *Philadelphia Magazine* that year. He described a paranoid, unpredictable man who believed a jumble of conspiracy theories. Memorabilia was Carlton's main source of income, and he was forced to play the beloved old ballplayer role for money so he could complete his concrete, earth-covered bunker designed so "gamma rays won't penetrate the walls."

. . .

IT WAS SO SAD: the stoic forced to beg, the indestructible man suddenly fragile. The Carlton who attends alumni events and jokes around with past teammates seems engaging enough, but it's easy to wonder if it's all a mask, if the real Carlton is hiding in the dark place in his mind, eyes darting about in fear of gamma rays and black helicopters. Or if both Carltons have always been there, the fun-loving everyman and the meditative, brooding samurai, two different people uncomfortably occupying the same skin.

For 13 years, none of it mattered. There were no bunkers or conspiracies when Carlton pitched. We weren't privy to his financial woes or opinions. Carlton said that he initiated the Long Silence so he could eliminate distractions, and it worked: we were never distracted. He pitched. Sliders melted into the far corners of the strike zone. Batters whiffed. The Phillies won. Children grew up. America changed. Lefty remained Lefty.

REGGIE WHITE

The Defense of the Minister

Greatness: ★★★★
Toughness: ★★★★
Eccentricity: ★★★★
Legacy: ★★★

SOME UNUSUAL CHARACTERS have made cameos on the Philadelphia sports scene. Whitney Houston. Rush Limbaugh. Even Pope John Paul II made the sports pages when he gave Ron Jaworski a papal ring. But when Reggie White was in town, the Almighty himself got involved.

For decades Philly fans felt that heavenly forces were up to something: teasing us, testing us, leading us into frustration. But the Lord was a hands-off owner who worked through intermediaries until White arrived. Then, the deus ex machina descended onto the stage and started meddling in free-agent affairs. White was one of the best defensive players in NFL history and the most respected player on one of the city's most fondly remembered teams. But his departure from Philadelphia was a divine comedy with tragic consequences.

*   *   *

WHITE AND THE EAGLES were trying to work out a contract extension in 1989. It was month 18 of the negotiations, and signs of strain were starting to show. White held out of Buddy Ryan's "voluntary" minicamp. Norman Braman, cutting short his training camp vacation in (where else?) France, assured fans that White would remain with the Eagles despite the contract flap. Braman assurances always sounded like threats. "Reggie White's not going to be traded. Reggie

White is not prepared to give up his football career, (so) I presume Reggie White's going to be a Philadelphia Eagle."

Braman claimed that he had an offer on the table $1 million higher than the one Buffalo Bills superstar Bruce Smith had recently signed, though simple arithmetic—and White's agent—indicated that Braman was fibbing. Smith signed for $7.5 million over five years, while Braman's offers were reported at $1.51 million per year, or $7.55 million for five years. That's a difference of $50 thousand, not a million, but Braman may have been thinking in francs. "He's confusing the situation, and he's good at that," said agent Jimmy Sexton.

Compounding the confusion: White was suing his former agent, who later became an Eagles employee, for adding an option year to his contract that would pay him just $440 thousand for the 1989 season. And the Eagles and White couldn't agree on injury insurance for the voluntary camps, which were about as voluntary as breathing.

Welcome to the 1989 that we would all rather forget. We want to remember White and Ryan, the 46-defense, and Bounty Bowls. But the late 1980s were really about Braman, labor unrest, and endless holdouts. Braman never met a loophole he couldn't exploit, never met a player he couldn't vilify. Men like Braman held all the cards back then. There was no real free agency, just something called "Plan B," which gave teams the right to match any offer made by a rival for a player's services. Players like Smith earned small raises by shopping their services, but the system was little more than formalized collusion: why entertain free agents when all you are doing is running up a fellow owner's bill?

White fought the system as hard as any other player. During the 1987 players' strike, White took the midnight picket shift before the infamous Eagles-Bears replacement game, the one that featured rioting Teamsters and a phalanx of Philly cops on horseback penetrating the picket lines. In 1989, he threatened to hold out for an entire season, only to learn that the holdout year wouldn't count: contractually, he would still be forced to play through the disputed option year.

So White held out all summer. No wonder we want to forget about Braman and Plan B free agency. White was the heart and soul of the team, an All Pro and a leader. He deserved better than an owner who lied about contract offers and a turncoat ex-agent.

By 1989, fans had Braman figured out, and his attempts to portray White as greedy didn't stick. White signed a four-year, $6.1-million contract in late August and received a hero's welcome from fans when he reported for training camp. Fans roared when White took the field for the team's final exhibition game. And while White's numbers were down in 1989—he recorded just 11 sacks that year—Buddy's defense was as Buddy-like as ever.

Contract negotiations and Christianity seem to be mutually exclusive, but White saw no conflict. "Everyone thinks because you're a Christian, you're not supposed to be businesslike," he said. "Since I'm a Christian, to say I'll take a $100,000-a-year job instead of $1.6 million a year, that would be stupid on my part."

Indeed, White became a free agent four years later: a real free agent, thanks in part to a lawsuit with his name on it that legally prohibited owners from creating new forms of nod-and-wink collusion. There was no way that Braman would pay him what he deserved; Braman was still trying to sue the league to block free agency while White toured the country, dining with owners and mayors, and speaking before state assemblies.

White said his goodbyes to Philadelphia weeks before signing elsewhere, but we still hopedfor a miracle. The man upstairs couldn't be strong-armed by Braman. But alas, He had other plans for the Minister of Defense. White made it clear that his hands were tied: "I want to make sure God says, 'Go here.' If he says, 'Go to Green Bay,' then that's where I'm going."

That's where White went. With the blessings of White (and a young Brett Favre), the Packers were fruitful. The Eagles gnashed their teeth. But God wasn't done instructing Reggie White.

. . .

DOES READING ABOUT White's religious beliefs make you uncomfortable? You know where the story winds up: at the Wisconsin state legislature, where White told us which ethnicities were good at what: white folks at organization, blacks at celebration, Asians at invention, and so on. From there, it's over to faith healings and the condemnation of homosexuals. White's take on Christianity, which always sounded mainstream when he was in Philadelphia, went simultaneously hard line and buffoonish in Wisconsin. It became hard to separate the player from the demagogue.

What did you think this chapter would be about? White's on-field accomplishments? They were amazing. He was the greatest defender of his generation. The glory of Ryan's defense? That defense was almost as great as its reputation. This is a book about the relationship between remarkable players and their fans, and nothing's quite as remarkable as a 300-pound defensive end explaining to a legislative body that Asians can "turn a television into a watch" while Hispanics can "put 20, 30 people in one home."

We saw a little of that White during his long free-agent goodbye, but we rarely saw it when he played for the Eagles. His spirituality expressed itself in charitable acts and inspirational speeches. It was wholesome, old-time religion. When we wanted gospel-flavored lunacy in this town, we turned to Randall Cunningham. White was normal.

Late in life, White realized the error of his ways. He recognized that he had been used as a mouthpiece for a religious organization with controversial viewpoints, that he had been "spoon-fed" things to say, that he didn't really know the Bible and had become too quick to invoke the "God said so" justification. "When I look back on my life, there are a lot of things I said God said. I realize he didn't say nothing," White said before his death. "It was what Reggie wanted to do." He began learning Hebrew and studying the Old Testament intensely. He went to his grave a serious religious scholar who spoke humbly and questioned many of the things he once preached about.

The White who gave Archie Bunker speeches was an aberration: for a few years, this small-town minister and team chaplain got Peter Principled to the forefront of the American religious scene because he was so good at sacking Phil Simms. The results were disastrous, but White was admirable before the rise and courageous after the fall. And look on the bright side: if all of this had happened a decade later, he may have run for vice president.

. . .

IT ALL SEEMS so long ago. We were delivered from Norman Braman's evil in 1994. Free agency has become so accepted that it's difficult to remember how hard players worked to get it. White passed away in

2004, and we lost the chance to get to know this new man, the skeptical scholar who could speak to the dangers and hypocrisy of oversimplified jocks-for-Jesus rhetoric. The world could use this new White, but the Almighty intervened, this time for real.

Fans always saw through Braman's anti-White rhetoric. I'd like to think that we also saw through White's own lapse of judgment. The great man was still there, even when he sounded like a fool. White may have thought he was following God to Green Bay, but he left his soul in Philly, and we took good care of it until he needed it back.

CHARLES BARKLEY

The Role Model for the Non-Role Models

Greatness: ★★★★
Toughness: ★★★★
Eccentricity: ★★★★
Legacy: ★★★

WHEN AMERICA NEEDED an anti-hero most, Philadelphia provided one of the best.

In the late 1980s, advertisers squeezed the last drops of innocence and honesty from sports mythmaking, stripping the consumerism bare and transforming great players into corporate logos. The sneaker and sport drink companies took Michael Jordan, who was an outstanding player and non-execrable human, buffed away all faults and hints of genuine personality, and created a commercialized god: Hercules on the half-court, with moves that kill and sneakers worth dying for. It was all about the shoes. You were told that you wanted to be like him, and Mars Blackmon called him "Money," in case you didn't know what made the world go around.

Jordan was breathtaking to watch but impossible to escape: outsized hero to kids, model champion for adults, Manna from spokesman heaven falling like rain on Madison Avenue. After a few years of the Jordan jackhammer pummeling our skulls, we longed for something else: the anti-Jordan. Someone not so shiny and perfect. Someone willing to say "I am not a role model."

Admittedly, Charles Barkley's "role model" commercial was just a clever bit of counter-merchandising. But Barkley said those words long before he sold them to Nike. Barkley wrote that advertising copy himself, and he meant it, defended it, and lived it.

He cut through all of that Jordan treacle like sharp acid. Or like saliva.

* * *

IN LIFE, IT'S WHAT you do *after* you spit on the little girl that really matters. Barkley spat on 8-year-old Lauren Rose in the fourth quarter of a loss to the Nets in March 1991. Barkley claimed at the time that he was spitting at the floor, riled by a heckler who called him "every name in the book." Later, he said he was aiming for the heckler but didn't "get enough foam" and delivered the saliva equivalent of an air ball, one that rained down on a child.

The television tape shows Barkley spitting downward, as if aiming at the feet of his tormentor. It also shows the likely heckler, a wobbly drunk flexing his muscles, a guy who had no qualms about shouting racial slurs in front of children. It clearly shows that Barkley didn't "spit into the crowd," as nearly every news outlet reported. It was a disgusting gesture, but it was also sensationalized.

Now, imagine a carefully handled "role model" athlete like Mike trying to save his image after an incident like that. You can see it now: a tearful press conference, wife and children at his side. A sit-down with Oprah. Maybe some evasion: it was a sneeze, a seizure, an allergy attack gone wrong. No matter what, a Jordan type would never utter the phrase "not enough foam."

We know how media "show apologies" go, and how falsely they ring, which is why we hate them. That wasn't Barkley's style. Barkley was already in trouble over a tasteless joke about beating his wife after a loss: he said it, and America acted like he did it. He had been warned several times by commissioner David Stern and league vice president Rod Thorn about his on-court demeanor. The NBA and the media moralists were cracking down on everything from on-court obscenities to irreverent sound bites. Barkley was in the crosshairs, just for being himself, before he spat. Afterward, he was at risk of becoming some symbol of all that's wrong with society.

So he said his apologies, admitted his guilt, served his suspension, and paid his fine. But when Pat Riley interviewed Barkley for NBC, America saw something other than a made-for-television penitent. "I snapped at somebody," Barkley said. "It's not like I killed somebody or beat him to a pulp." Riley lobbed a softball to Barkley, asking if a fan who pays $75 "deserves that kind of abuse." Barkley sounded ready to back down but suddenly shifted gears. "Well, they pay the money, they can do whatever they want to. . . . No, that's not right, that's not fair to me as a person." Barkley contended that the drunken fan should have been removed, that he had a right to not be barraged with curse words. He criticized the NBA for tacitly condoning the actions of drunks, just because they bought tickets. Then, he delivered an early draft of his "not a role model" speech. "I have an ability to run and dunk a basketball. There are a million guys who can run and dunk basketballs who are in jail."

No self-flagellation. No spin control. Just straight talk, defiant honesty.

Of course, Barkley really was sorry. "I can tell how he feels, because he's not making any jokes about it," trainer Tony Harris said. "He really feels bad." Who wouldn't be sorry? But why make a public spectacle of it? Barkley turned the spitting incident right back on us. He admitted he made a mistake, then he asked us to admit to ours: growling and cursing in the stands, overreacting to minor infractions, rewarding image above substance, and making secular gods and surrogate parents out of slam-dunk specialists.

After saying his piece, Barkley bought season tickets for Lauren Rose's family and took some time to get to know her. He sometimes did a lousy job of not being a role model.

. . .

THE PROBLEM WITH casting yourself as the foil is that you're doomed to never win. Barkley should have helped the Sixers to a title before Jordan's emergence, but the timing was never right. As a rookie, he teamed with Doc, Moses, Little Mo, Andrew Toney, Bobby Jones, and the whole gang, winning 58 games but losing in the Eastern Conference Finals. That may have been the greatest team ever to miss the NBA Finals and the most squandered of all the squandered opportunities in this book.

One by one, the classic Sixers faded away. Toney's feet gave out, and the Sixers offense devolved into a Malone-Barkley tug-of-war. Harold Katz decided Malone was too expensive, and Barkley became the team's leading scorer, but replacing Moses with Tim McCormick had a predictable effect on the standings. Erving and Cheeks faded little by little, and suddenly Roy Hinson and David Wingate were playing major roles, and the Sixers were out of the playoffs. Barkley grew as the superstars receded, from a lumpy rookie with a one-dimensional game to a multifaceted low-post weapon, hustling rebounder, and clever instigator. But the Sixers eroded faster than Barkley improved. Finally, the team started building around Barkley, trading Cheeks for Johnny Dawkins, drafting Hersey Hawkins, and acquiring Rick Mahorn.

It wasn't a bad supporting cast. Hawkins was the sniper who kept defenders from collapsing on Barkley. Dawkins was a solid point guard, younger and quicker than the mid-80s Cheeks. Mahorn was a defensive thumper and surrogate center. Mike Gminski, the actual center, was a mediocre player but a good system fit: he worked the perimeter on offense, ceding the low post to Barkley, and nailed every free throw. If ever there was a team custom-built to lose to Jordan's Bulls in the playoffs, this was it.

Jordan's Bulls beat Barkley's Sixers twice in the playoffs, winning both series four games to one. They weren't epic battles; Bulls fans might not remember them. The Bulls had tremendous size advantage underneath; Bill Cartwright and Horace Grant were too strong for Gminski but too tall for Barkley. Scottie Pippen directed traffic and clamped down on defense. Jordan drove and dunked, or drove and dished, or drove and drew fouls that forced the Sixers to go to their nearly empty bench. It was systematic disassembly, though Barkley did all he could, muscling rebounds from men 6 inches taller than he was, passing when double teamed, trying to deny history with just his anger and will.

The Barkley heyday was brief. Three playoff runs, two losses to Jordan, and the Sixers spun into decline. Manute Bol and Armen Gilliam replaced Gminski and Mahorn, making the frontcourt a sideshow: an elongated curiosity, a man with the power to magically disappear on defense, and a frustrated wild man who cursed, spat, threw elbows, and picked fights. The Sixers quickly became unwatchable: Bol flailing as point guards drove and dunked on him, Gilliam scoring 18 points with the team down by 20, Charles Shackleford lumbering around for 20 useless minutes per night. Barkley was as frustrated as the fans. He demanded a trade in 1992, and by then it was easy to imagine a better life without Barkley tirades and Barkley headaches. So the Sixers traded Barkley for Jeff Hornacek, Andrew Lang, and Tim Perry, quiet guys with quiet games. And we didn't have to worry about spitting incidents, off-color jokes, or 30-win seasons for the rest of the decade.

Barkley remained Jordan's foil after he left Philly, battling him in the NBA Finals with the Phoenix Suns in 1993. Their friendly rivalry faded but never really died. Barkley still takes his shots at Jordan, criticizing everything from Jordan's efforts as a general manager to his moustache. Barkley is now more a court jester than an archenemy, but court jesters often land harsher blows than archenemies. Retirement has been far kinder to Barkley than Jordan, whose gold-embossed exterior started cracking under the weight of endless comeback attempts, self-serving Hall of Fame speeches, and ceaseless huckstering. Barkley was always cracked, so he can shrug off gambling scandals and drunk-driving arrests, give rambling interviews, and dabble in politics without tarnishing some carefully trademarked "image."

• • •

I BUMPED INTO Barkley while covering Donovan McNabb's return to Philly. Barkley was walking through the crowd in the Wells Fargo Center parking lot wearing a Redskins McNabb jersey. He wore the jersey partly as a publicity stunt (Howard Eskin won a bet with him) but partly out of support. "I'm a friend of McNabb's, and I wanted to show him respect," Barkley said of his jersey choice. "I've been an Eagles fan for a long time, but I'm a Redskins fan today."

It was an amazing scene. Some fans rushed to hug Barkley or take pictures. Others shouted and waved. No one mentioned the jersey, spitting, bar fights, trade demands, or anything else that marked Barkley's tenure in Philly. Most fans just smiled and acknowledged him, the Hall of Famer in the parking lot, an old friend who showed up for the tailgate party, past sins forgiven.

No player ever held up a mirror to the sports world like Barkley, who threw hypocrisy back into the face of those who manufactured saints to sell overpriced sneakers. Only he could exist within the system and comment on it like an outsider at the same time. Only he could make not being a role model admirable. When he walked among the tailgaters at that Eagles game, he became a mirror of us as fans: a reminder that anger is fleeting, that the snarling fan and the devoted friend are often the same person.

Being the anti-Jordan wasn't about being a villain. It was about being human and being honest, relatable, and real. That's all Philly asks of her heroes: if you can't win a championship, you can at least look us in the eye. We may still be mad at you for a while, but not mad enough to generate much foam.

10

JIMMY ROLLINS

He Called Us the F-Word

Greatness: ★★★★
Toughness: ★★★★
Eccentricity: ★★★
Legacy: ★★★½

JIMMY ROLLINS KNEW the trajectory of Philly sports disappointment. He saw it firsthand as Scott Rolen and Pat Burrell followed it. He understood it, commented upon it, and came dangerously close to tracing it with his own feet before, at the last possible second, veering onto a road less traveled.

You know the trajectory well. Half the players in this book followed it. The kid arrives to much fanfare. He has some early success, inspires a dangerous infatuation within the fan base. He peaks just short of a championship. Then, our impatience sets in, and the young star quickly inherits the toxic failures of a hundred predecessors. He says or does something stupid, or something perceived as stupid, and adulation gives way to condemnation. By the time the guy's traded, half the city is saying good riddance, while the other half gropes with how quickly things went so wrong.

Rollins took that journey. He arrived as a 21-year-old September in 2000 call-up and hit a triple in his first official at bat (he walked his first time up). He was an All Star at 21. He was the league MVP in 2007 at age 27. There was no place to go but down.

Rollins found a way to keep going up. Somehow, some way.

. . .

JIMMY ROLLINS CALLED Philly fans front-runners. Us, front-runners. "I might catch some flak for saying this, but, you know, they're front-runners," he said in August, 2008. "When you're doing good, they're on your side. When you're doing bad, they're completely against you."

There's no greater insult to a Philly fan. Mike Schmidt called the fans "a mob," but it's better to be part of a mob than a front-runner. Cowboys fans are front-runners. Philly fans? Heck, we don't even know where the front is.

One measured response, culled from the archives of TheFightins. com, read like this: "Oh, okay. So when like, our defending MVP shortstop is having a shitty season and is on pace to score about 70 less runs than he did last year—we should just unconditionally support him?" The message board responses were even more diplomatic: "get out of town then rollins, u suck this year anyways," wrote one of the more eloquent posters.

Rollins was having a bad year when he used the 12-letter f-word on a television program. He had been benched once for failing to run out a ground ball, a punishment he accepted, and another time for arriving late to a game, a punishment he bristled against. His home run totals were down, his runs scored way down. The Phillies were in the midst of a sweep at the hands of the Dodgers, one that took them out of first place.

Freeze the story right here. It's the beginning of the end, right? The Phillies fall out of the race. Rollins becomes talk-radio catnip. There's another frustrating season, in which Rollins's positive remarks are re-spun as negative, his frustration regarded as whining. Then, the team trades him for a pitching prospect, and we turn the magnifying glass on Chase Utley until he fries. That's the arc, the only formula we know how to follow.

Rollins was on that path. He went into a 4-for-46 slump. We booed. He was on the list. But then he went 3-for-3 to beat the Dodgers, 5-for-7 in a 13-inning battle with the Mets, hustling the whole time. The Phillies climbed into first place, and beyond. "If you win, they forgive," said Charlie Manuel. Manuel himself forgave Rollins for the lateness and the lapses, maintaining a positive relationship with his shortstop through the rough patches. Past managers—Larry Bowa, in particular—were almost as unforgiving as the fans.

Rollins won, and we not only forgave but forgot. Booing Rollins was something someone else did. Try to find someone who admits to booing Rollins, to calling WIP to complain about him, or to posting "u suck" messages about him today. No one ever did that. It was just some lunatic fringe. Really, we knew all along that he was different from Rolen, Burrell, Iverson, McNabb, Lindros, etc., etc.

. . .

HISTORY IS STILL happening for Jimmy Rollins. He's coming off a rough 2010 season, one in which he missed a month with an injury and labored through the summer half-healthy. There was talk of benching him in the 2010 playoffs, but he delivered one of the Phillies' few signature moments in the League Championship Series: a three-run double to break open Game 2. As a player, Rollins really did peak in 2007, but a World Series ring and another World Series appearance have bought him legend status and a rare opportunity to gracefully decline. He's already the greatest shortstop in Phillies history and may go down as one of the 10 greatest Phillies ever, depending on what Utley, Ryan Howard, or a few other teammates do over the next half-decade. The final section of this chapter won't be written for a while.

So Rollins's ability to transcend the arc of frustration leaves us with two questions.

Question 1: What does Rollins's accomplishment mean to the next generation of stars? Did Rollins merely save himself in 2008, or did he blaze a new path for Jrue Holiday, Domonic Brown, or Claude Giroux to follow? Maybe it is now possible for a Philly sports star to rise, stumble, and rise again, without every misstep sending him tumbling down a garbage chute. It's hopeful to think that should DeSean Jackson someday run his mouth in the midst of a slump, talk-radio callers and Eagles bloggers will pause and remember how hard they went after Rollins, how foolish it was, and how much better it is when superstars get an extra year or two instead of rushing out of town a step ahead of the tar-and-feathers brigade.

Question 2: Are we front-runners? No, not in that preening Cowboys-fan way, but in the sense that Rollins meant? We are fickle to a fault. We can be bipolar. We may not rush after every winning team, but we anoint heroes at first blush, worship them slavishly, and then abandon them suddenly. We ridicule people who buy Miami Heat LeBron James jerseys, who suddenly grow silent about football when the Cowboys are 5–11, but how is it better to turn against a player after a bad year or a dumb comment?

If you want to get rank-and-file Philly sports fans mad, criticize them about criticism. We act like it's our right as fans, our obligation as fans, to go after the players with both barrels. The people who don't are Pollyannas, or they don't care. It's in the blood. It comes with the price of the ticket. If you don't like it, go play in St. Louis.

Whatever. That's not passion, it's petulance. Rollins struck a nerve, because he called the worst of Philly fandom—the fair-weather fawning, the sudden scorn, the often calculated efforts to set up failure—by its true name. He called us front-runners, he meant it, and in a way, he was right.

It took a miracle—a World Series-caliber miracle—for him to survive it.

11

MOSES MALONE

He Brooded Back at Us

Greatness: ★★★★
Toughness: ★★★★★
Eccentricity: ★★★ ½
Legacy: ★★

THE BEST WAY to deal with the Philly sports media is to growl at it.

Silence is golden, but it isn't enough. Steve Carlton tried that, and it worked for a decade. Eventually, we pierced the silence and found something strange lurking behind the curtain. Moses Malone added snarl to the silence. He hid his true self behind a barbed wire fence and a "Keep Out" sign. He was so scary that he was lovable, like a movie monster. He earned our respect by winning championships and MVP awards, but also by being his own man, even if that man was unapproachable and slightly terrifying.

. . .

RAY DIDINGER COULDN'T get a personal interview with Malone. Coach Billy Cunningham couldn't persuade Malone to do the interview. Nor could team owner Harold Katz or Malone's own lawyer. It was 1983. The Sixers were about to win their first NBA title in 16 years, and no one knew anything about the team's leading scorer except that he was (a) very good, and (b) menacingly quiet.

Didinger wrote a Malone profile for the *Daily News* without Malone's input; the article is among the best reprinted in Didinger's book *One Last Read*. The reporter's interviews with Malone's friends, family, and ex-coaches reveal a likeable yet guarded young man. Malone grew up in abject poverty and was exposed to coarse exploitation as soon as his basketball gifts manifested. College recruiters made illegal promises. When Malone became the first basketball player to skip college, political pundits decried the downfall of society and questioned Malone's intelligence. Malone chose a crumbling American Basketball Association over college, and he bounced from Utah to St. Louis to Portland. The Salt Lake City press called him Mumbles. A coach in Buffalo shipped him off after a week, saying that Malone couldn't play.

"Is it any wonder the Malones became cynical?" Didinger asked of Moses and his mother, who watched scouts pile $100 bills on the kitchen table. All of the turmoil occurred before Malone turned 22. The film footage of his ABA signing shows a skinny, grinning, wide-eyed youngster with a bow-tie and an afro, a child who looks nothing like the grizzled, thick-muscled superstar we came to know. The kid wasn't ready to be a vagabond, or a recruiting trophy, or a political symbol before his 22nd birthday. He became all three. Then he became defensive.

By the time he arrived in Philly, Malone was already an MVP, and Philly was Philly, notoriously tough on its sports heroes. Of course Malone kept his guard up. He could afford to let his play do the talking for him because Erving did most of the talking for the team.

When he did speak—Malone didn't maintain Carlton's cloistered silence, instead grunting a few post-game observations, focused solely on the night's action—he became part of our folklore. No one knows exactly when Malone said "fo' fo' fo'," which is what "four, four, four" sounds like coming from a deep bass with a thick Virginia drawl, but everyone agrees that he said it. Malone later explained that it was more of a wish than a prediction: after a long season, he had no interest in a 21-game playoff, and he hoped the Sixers would make life easier for themselves by sweeping three straight opponents.

Of course, the playoffs actually went four-five-four, with Malone averaging 26 points and 15.8 rebounds per game throughout the postseason, moving the Sixers past the Knicks, Bucks, Lakers, and all the demons that had boxed them out of the championship in the 1970s and 1980s. One of the quietest men this city has ever seen made the boldest prediction, or wish, we ever heard and then backed it up with a ferocity that defied words.

. . .

OFFENSIVE REBOUNDING requires technique, timing, and tenacity. It's an unglamorous job, jockeying beneath the basket, establishing
position, anticipating when and where missed shots will bounce. It's a
task like grinding for the puck in hockey or taking on the fullback in
the hole in football, the kind that wins games but disappears from the
highlight reel, the kind that some superstars don't have the backbone
or stomach for.

Moses Malone grabbed 7,382 offensive rebounds in the NBA and
ABA. No other player has more than 5,000. Shaquille O'Neal, the best
center of this generation, is nearing retirement with 4,161. Malone's
record will not be broken for a long time.

Malone's highlight reels are filled with offensive boards and put-
backs. He's always in perfect position, just under the basket, as a shot
by Erving or Mo Cheeks bounces off the rim. Instead of boxing him
out, the Celtics or Bucks defenders flail at him as he scores. It happened night after night, city after city, year after year. Robert Parish
couldn't stop him. Kareem Abdul-Jabbar couldn't, either. Malone was
Philly justice for four short seasons, outmuscling, outworking, and
out-thinking flashier opponents.

The only person who dared to question him was the man who
paid him.

. . .

HAROLD KATZ HAD many infuriating traits as a meddlesome
owner. One was to accuse injured players of not trying hard enough.
Another was to constantly harp on players' salaries. In March 1984,
less than a year after Malone led the Sixers to a championship, Katz
unleashed his dubious motivational skills on one of the most dedicated players in the history of basketball.

"Is Moses a $2 million player the way he's playing right now? No.
Absolutely not," Katz said of Malone. "Watching him now, you could
say he's not the same player he was last season."

Malone was slumping at the time and taking the Sixers with him.
He was averaging only 18.5 points and 11 rebounds per game over
an eight-game stretch, and the defending champions had lost five of
their last six games. Malone was also playing with a brace on his left

ankle, having sprained his ankle in December, and his wife was pregnant. Katz acknowledged that the slump and the ankle brace might somehow be related, but he had other axes to grind the night after an ugly 112–100 loss in Phoenix. He wasn't happy with Malone's offseason conditioning. He didn't like Malone's decision to film a Nike commercial instead of resting during the All-Star break. He didn't like the attitude of the Sixers—these are the Erving–Cheeks–Malone–Bobby Jones Sixers, mind you—because "every guy on this team acts too cool and doesn't show enough enthusiasm."

Erving and others defended themselves against their boss's tirade. "If my style's been cool, it's been cool for 13 years," Erving said. Malone had no comment.

Before the ankle injury, Moses was Moses. In November 1983, he spoiled the return of Bill Walton, scoring 28 points, collecting 16 rebounds, and blocking nine shots in an overtime win against the Clippers. His numbers were down in the early going—"down" meaning 23.5 points and 15.5 rebounds per game in mid-November—but teams were harassing Malone constantly in the paint, taking advantage of a referees' strike to engage in extra rough stuff.

After his ankle healed and his wife delivered a healthy baby, Moses was Moses again, scoring 25 points to avenge a loss to the Suns, breaking Jeff Ruland's tooth in a victory over the Bullets, scoring 32 points and 27 rebounds in double overtime against the Celtics . . . you get the idea.

The scandal blew over, but Malone remembered. Two years later, when the Sixers traded him, he cited the "no way" quote as the beginning of the end of his relationship with the team. "Harold criticized me when I was hurt," Moses said. "Harold just doesn't treat the team like family, even though he thinks he does."

But Moses said little about his frustration during the 1983–1984 season, or the 1984–1985 season when he averaged 24.6 points per night and led the league in rebounds, or the 1985–1986 season when Katz stalled through contract extension talks and the Sixers offense got bogged down in Malone-versus-Barkley custody battles for the low post. Malone suffered a severe eye injury at season's end, the Sixers had a brief hot streak without him, and Philadelphia sports history changed for the worse. Katz traded Malone for Ruland and a first-round pick, then traded the first-round pick for Roy Hinson. "I'm glad to be coming to a great organization, not like the one in Philadelphia," Malone said of his move to the Washington Bullets.

"They traded Moses!? Is Katz crazy?" asked one fan in a newspaper reaction piece. *Daily News* staff writer Leon Taylor answered the fan himself. "Yes, the 76ers traded Moses to the Washington Bullets. The question of Katz's sanity won't be revealed until the next NBA season begins or until the 1987 championship series ends." With the benefit of hindsight, we can answer the fan's second question with a definitive "yes."

. . .

MALONE SAID he had "five or six good years left" when the Sixers traded him, and he was right. After six great years and a seventh season lost to back surgery, Malone returned to the Sixers. "I didn't really want to leave the first time," he said. Malone's new job: backup and mentor for 7-foot-6 Shawn Bradley. Malone's first advice to Bradley? "Get an attitude. Get a mean attitude." Good luck with that.

The Sixers, built now around the likes of Dana Barros, Jeff Hornacek, and Clarence Weatherspoon, were hopelessly inept. Katz was now a hands-off owner, claiming he was tired of the media criticism, if you can imagine. Malone was slow and creaky, but he was still crafty about drawing and avoiding fouls, and he could still rebound.

One night in December 1993, Bradley got into early foul trouble against the Bucks, and Malone came off the bench for 10 points and 6 rebounds in a 10-minute span. He finished the game with 18 points and 12 rebounds, earning his 16,000th career NBA rebound along the way. The man who rarely spoke said what we knew he would say: "It's about winning, I come to get a win, and this was a great opportunity for me to play like I think I can play."

That win lifted the Sixers to 6–12. What would Katz have given to see the "too cool" Sixers again instead of that team populated with veteran journeymen and draft-day mistakes? What would we have given to see Malone be cool with Doc and Little Mo for another year or two? Bob Ford summed it up in the *Inquirer*. "Malone's big nights may be more widely separated than they used to be, but, then again, so are Sixers' wins. You take them where you find them and enjoy them while they last."

. . .

MOSES MALONE WAS sensitive to criticism, as sensitive as we ever accused Mike Schmidt of being. That was clear from the two-year grudge he nursed against Katz. His conditioning really did lapse after the championship season, and out-of-town papers took note of his distended belly, which may have contributed to his ankle sprain.

These facts don't take away from Malone as an all-time great or as one of the most dedicated players ever. They do remind us that he was mortal, that not every game was a 25-point, 20-rebound win over the Celtics. Malone escaped the worst of our scorn. The championship ring saved him, as did Katz, who made an easy villain in those days.

But Malone's silence and his scowl were his real saviors. He never delivered the quote that turned toxic, and he never gave anyone but Katz the impression that he was giving less than his all. He appeared to be angrier than any of us after losses, and he didn't look too thrilled after wins, for that matter. You don't criticize someone who is madder than you are. You give him his space and let him get back to work. Once he created some space, Malone always found a way to rebound.

12

BRIAN DAWKINS

The Idiot Man, Hallelujah

Greatness: ★★★★
Toughness: ★★★★★
Eccentricity: ★★★
Legacy: ★★

THE *DAILY NEWS* called it Dawk Day Afternoon.

The Eagles were 18-point favorites against the expansion Houston Texans, but they started the game flat. The Texans scored a touchdown on their first series. Donovan McNabb, who signed a huge contract extension during the week, threw an interception on the next possession. The Eagles were scuffling, trailing 7–3, when Texans rookie quarterback David Carr tried to scramble up the middle on third down. Darwin Walker stripped the ball, and Brian Dawkins recovered. The Eagles drove 42 yards to take the lead.

The Eagles led 17–7 late in the second quarter when Dawkins intercepted a Carr pass and ran it back 27 yards, putting the Eagles in field goal range.

The Eagles led 20–7 in the third quarter when a drive stalled at the Eagles 43-yard line. During the week, the coaches installed a fake punt and gave special teams ace Brian Mitchell permission to call the play if he thought the Texans return units were napping. Mitchell called the fake, took a direct snap, head-faked, then shoveled the ball to Dawkins, who raced 57 yards for a game-icing touchdown.

Late in the game, Dawkins sacked Carr, making him the first player ever to have a sack, an interception, a forced fumble, and a touchdown reception in the same game.

Dawk Day Afternoon wasn't Dawkins's breakthrough game—he was already a two-time All Pro—but it was his signature game. The

Eagles had a lot of great safeties through their history, from Bill Bradley and Irv Cross through Randy Logan and Wes Hopkins. But Dawkins showed on Dawk Day Afternoon that he would eventually be the best ever.

The Eagles were fun to watch in those days. They were still a team on the rise. They lost in the NFC Championship game the previous year, but they were underdogs to the mighty Rams, and they had not yet conditioned us for inevitable playoff heartbreak. They ran trick plays all the time, regularly smothered bad opponents, always fought well against tougher foes. McNabb criticism had not yet become reflexive, and Dawkins could be called the "Donovan of the defense" without anyone thinking it an insult. In the weeks before the Texans game, the Eagles beat the Redskins 37-7 and the Cowboys 44-13. We still found fault—one *Daily News* headline demanded "We Want More!" after a third-straight blowout victory—but those Eagles really gave us little to fret about.

But something happened on Dawk Day Afternoon. The Eagles became Dawkins's team. Dawkins was angling for a new deal in the wake of McNabb's extension, and it was clear that he deserved it, as much for his dedication as his play. "The attitude is perfect. The player is a prototype," Rich Hofmann wrote. Dawkins carried the team on his shoulders and didn't grouse about money. Well, maybe he did, just a little. "I play this game for the love of it but I do play it to help my family," he said about his negotiation efforts.

Dawkins had to wait until the following April to get his new contract. By then, the Eagles had lost another NFC title game, one they were expected to win, and doubts had crept in about the team, the coaching staff, McNabb. Doubts about everyone but Dawkins.

. . .

WE REMEMBER the hit, not the interception. Michael Vick dropped to pass, looked over the middle, found Alge Crumpler running up the seam. Crumpler caught the ball in stride, but Dawkins, playing deep, gathered his body and launched himself at the tight end. Crumpler somehow held on, but he doubled over in pain after the blow. It was called "The Shot Heard 'Round the Linc" on the highlight video. Dawkins called it business as usual. "That's just what I do as far as hits go. I'm trying to send a message to you that it's not going to be just flag football when you are coming across the middle," he said after the game.

It may have sent a message, but it was a 31-yard gain for the Falcons. They scored a touchdown on the next play to cut the Eagles' lead to 4.

The interception occurred late in the third quarter. Vick sought Crumpler again, this time along the left sideline, but Dawkins read the play, stepped in front of the tight end, and took the ball back to the Falcons 11-yard line. He ran to the orange end-zone pylon, held it high over his head, and electrified the crowd. An Eagles field goal made the score 20–10, but the Falcons were finished, Vick rattled by cold, sacks, and a defense too disciplined for his Mad Scrambler tactics.

Dawkins also forced a Vick fumble that day, but the Falcons recovered. Derrick Burgess had two sacks. McNabb hit Chad Lewis for two touchdowns. Dorsey Levens dragged half the Falcons roster across the end zone for the Eagles' first touchdown. When prompted, we remember all of it. But when we close our eyes, we see the hit. A play that should be on the Falcons highlight reel (their biggest gain of the day) got co-opted and repurposed as one of the greatest plays in Eagles history.

The Eagles were difficult to watch in those days. Blowout victories in the regular season had become expected. The fall schedule was an extended undercard. The Eagles won 13 games, but the only games that mattered were the NFC title game and the Super Bowl. Thanks to Dawkins, we finally won the former and were going to the latter.

"Hallelujah!" Dawkins screamed into the television microphone after the game. He took a lap around Lincoln Financial Field, fans cheering, confetti flying. Our memories of this are dim, because we were celebrating ourselves, lighting fireworks in the icy streets or calling long-lost friends to share the news. We remember the hit, because the Falcons were driving and we were glued to the screen, muscles tensed, hearts braced for a pain worse than anything even Dawkins could deliver to Crumpler.

The hit sent a message to us as surely as it sent one to the Falcons: it was okay to believe again. Even it was just for a few weeks.

. . .

NEWS LEAKED ACROSS the Internet in February 2009. Dawkins, a free agent, had visited the Denver Broncos. Then he signed with them. Or maybe he didn't. An unconfirmed report here, a hastily posted Internet rumor there. Dawkins wasn't really leaving; he was just frustrated with the Eagles' glacial contract talks and wanted some leverage.

Then, he was gone. "It's unthinkable. Unimaginable. Incomprehensible. Simply unbelievable," Andy Schwartz wrote for CSN Philly.

Every Eagles fan felt the sting, even those of us who understand that business is business, that overpaying 34-year-old safeties is a bad idea, that Dawkins had (yes) lost a step in coverage. Dawkins had been with the Eagles from the lowest lows of the Ray Rhodes era to the Super Bowl. When the Eagles offense devolved into a soap opera, when the once reliable team ran from icy-to-torrid, even when Dawkins was playing at less than peak ability—his wife's pregnancy complications slowed him down in 2007—Dawkins's passion and preparation, his tenacity and desire, were constants. "It's amazing how, even the fans from the 50-yard line to the nose bleeds—when he comes out of that tunnel, they feel his energy," teammate Shawn Andrews said. "It's like everybody has a piece of Dawk on their shoulder."

The Eagles were frustrating to watch in those days. Many fans had soured on McNabb, and Reid grew intractable. The Eagles had just reached another NFC Championship game by the most improbable route possible, finishing 9–6–1 but springing to life in the postseason, but they were far more infuriating than fun. About the only thing that really touched us, besides the uniforms themselves, was Dawkins the warrior, Wolverine, the Idiot Man who psyched himself into a berserk marauder before taking the field.

Now, Dawkins was leaving, taking his all-important leadership with him. The "leadership" card is always overplayed in the sports media, and the handwringing after Dawkins's departure grew particularly ripe: in Football Outsiders, I lampooned the situation by joking that the Eagles were trapped in their own locker room, unable to find the door without Dawkins's aid. The "leaderless" Eagles finished 10–6 and reached the playoffs. Safety play fell off, as replacement Sean Jones was a flop, but while the Eagles missed Dawkins, we missed him more, because we cling to the personas that capture our imagination and bring us hope.

We'll miss him more as the years pass. McNabb is gone now, as are most other links to that frozen day at the Linc, and the Dawkins Eagles are passing into mythology. They left without a championship, but they did not leave without joyous moments. None was as joyous as that thundering tackle, a play that resonates like Wilbert Montgomery's touchdown run or Randall Cunningham's non-sack touchdown against the Giants. Dawkins was one of those few players who possessed the power, not just to chase away sports demons, but to scare them with his own ferocity.

Hallelujah.

13

JOE FRAZIER

Better Than the Greatest, If Only Briefly

Greatness: ★★★★½
Toughness: ★★★★
Eccentricity: ★★
Legacy: ★★★

PHILADELPHIA WAS ONCE a boxing city. America was once a boxing nation. Joe Frazier was once champion of the world.

It's easy to forget all three of those facts. Boxing is about as relevant to contemporary American culture as silent film. The Philly fight scene, what's left of it, has gone retro-chic. When Hollywood made the movie Ali, the boxer who played Joe Frazier appeared 27th in the credits, turning the title character's greatest nemesis into a glorified prop.

But Frazier wasn't a footnote in the Muhammad Ali saga. He wasn't a champion by technicality. He was one of the greatest ever, representing a city that was once crazier for boxing than for football or hockey.

. . .

"PHILADELPHIA HAS ALWAYS been suspicious of those who represent it in sports," Mark Kram wrote in *Sports Illustrated* in March 1968. "Its cynicism, for the most part, is justified. It has suffered Joe Kurharich and the Eagles far too long; it has been bored frequently by the Phillies and disappointed by a hundred fighters who came within a punch—and one too many nightcaps—of being champions."

The son of a South Carolina sharecropper, Frazier came to Philadelphia and immediately became heir to the city's sports legacy. He inherited the failures of Gil Turner and Sugar Hart, boxers who galvanized the "Philadelphia Fighter" reputation with their tenacity, their less-than-scientific style, and their ability to come up short in title bouts. It's remarkable how irrelevant the particular sport is to Philadelphia's sports heritage: no matter what the endeavor, from boxing to basketball, Philly is always fully stocked with palookas who can't quite win. If Philly joined a national curling league, we'd find the toughest curlers around, intimidate opponents with our brooms, then lose in the semifinals.

Frazier didn't just typify the Philly style of boxing. He also typified the classic Philly work ethic. "He is an honest workman, and if he is ever remembered at all it will be because he is such a fighter," Kram wrote. "He comes to work, and he gives the last measure of himself, however unaesthetic the workmanship may be."

Frazier was a contender in a boxing world with no champion: Ali was in exile, banned from boxing for draft dodging. Frazier defeated Buster Mathis (avenging a loss to Mathis before the 1964 Olympics) at Madison Square Garden in 1968 in typical Smokin' Joe fashion: he started slowly, taking too many punches in early rounds, before wearing Mathis down with blow after blow to the kidneys. For his efforts, Frazier earned a title as worthless as a tin sheriff's badge and a chance to fight Jimmy Ellis for an even bigger cereal-box prize.

Without Ali, there would be no real championship. Frazier knew it, so he lobbied for Ali's reinstatement and stayed out of the World Boxing Association tournament that Ellis won to earn Ali's title. "I earn what I win," Frazier said in Kram's article; he was speaking about Mathis, but he might just as well have been speaking about the championship itself. Frazier beat Ellis, then trained specifically for Ali, who once reinstated was eager to reclaim the title he never lost.

It set the stage for the greatest series of bouts in boxing history: international superstar versus unaesthetic Philadelphia workman, with all the world watching a sport that no one watches anymore.

. . .

BOXING'S SAD IRONY: it's easier to watch the 1971 Joe Frazier–Muhammad Ali fight than it is to watch a current heavyweight championship. The Greatest and Smokin' Joe are waiting for you on YouTube. David Haye and Vidali Klitschko are available only on Pay-Per-View, at midnight, in the VIP room of your local strip club.

That's an exaggeration, of course. You can find Haye and Klitschko on YouTube. But you shouldn't have to: they should be in your living

Joe Frazier
(Courtesy of Temple University Libraries, Urban Archives, Philadelphia, PA)

room on your high-definition television. They aren't, because boxing did everything possible to sabotage itself over the last 40 years.

Boxing refused to change with the times, staying a late-night, limited-access, premium-priced luxury while other sports generated billions of advertising dollars by making their product as widely available as possible. In the 1970s, fans could watch *Wide World of Sports* to see an Ali-Frazier fight a few weeks old; that made sense in a world with three channels and just a handful of sports viewing options. By the 1990s, ESPN streamed round-the-clock slam dunks and touchdowns straight into our frontal lobes, but all the network could show of Pay-Per-View championship bouts were stills, which looked as anachronistic as something out of the 1948 *New York Post* even when the images were only a few hours old. All the while, Mike Tyson was biting and growling, making an already violent sport even more gruesome. While football and basketball took over the world, boxing made itself a dirty thrill and a square, outdated one, like watching stag reels on a 16-mm projector in the basement while smoking stogies.

But boxing was beautiful in Frazier's time; it takes only a short trip through the old footage to see it. In the Fight of the Century, Frazier wears sherbet-green trunks with gold trim, Ali wears cherry-red trunks with white trim, and both appear bathed in light, as if they themselves are glowing. Ali dances, Frazier ducks and weaves. Frazier smiles after landing a punch, Ali shakes his head no-no-no after breaking a clench. At one point, Ali rakes his knuckles across Frazier's face as if swatting away gnats; at another, Frazier grabs Ali under the shoulders and rips him from the ropes. It's all action, all the time, breathtaking athletes doing amazing things. It looks choreographed, like a movie, with a crowd full of Frank Sinatras and Woody Allens gasping and cheering from the opening bell.

As the rounds go on, Frazier lands left hook after left hook, aiming for the spot where Ali likes to bob his head while throwing an uppercut. Finally, Ali goes down in the 14th round, just for a moment, and we are witnesses to history: not sports history, not Philadelphia history, but American history.

Ali-Frazier II—the fights, like Super Bowls, demand Roman numerals—finds both fighters without a title and dressed in white trunks with white robes, like bishops at some cultish ceremony. Howard Cosell calls Frazier a "terribly grim man" where Ali is concerned: Frazier took Ali's poetic trash talk seriously, and he had no patience for it. Ali, fitter and more prepared, shuffles and clowns, while Frazier lunges. By mid-fight, Ali lands flurries, while Frazier clenches and swings left hooks with nothing behind them.

Ali-Frazier III is world history: Ali in white, Frazier in black, battling beyond exhaustion in the strife-torn Philippines. Ali is three-fourths of the way up the ladder to immortality, an international icon of religious tolerance and conscientious objection. Frazier has one foot out of the sport, a brawler who took too many beatings from George Foreman and chafed too long as Ali's comic foil. Frazier stuns Ali with his tenacity and brutality, but Ali answers with unearthly talent and unyielding perseverance. There's no more dancing and taunting by the middle of the Thrilla in Manila: it's all flat-footed thuds, titans staggering toward each other to land thunderclaps. Words don't do it justice, and words don't have to, because you're a few clicks away from watching it on your laptop right now.

Between the Ali-Frazier battles, there were Foreman-Frazier I and II ("Down Goes Frazier! Down Goes Frazier! Down Goes Frazier!"), and Smokin' Joe wouldn't truly be a Philly guy if he didn't go 1–4 in those bouts. You don't have to listen too carefully to hear Cosell rooting against Frazier. Philly fans often think that national broadcasters pick on us; believe it or not, Joe Buck has nothing personal against the city or our players. But Cosell had a personal stake in Ali, and Foreman started earning "poet of the ring" headlines in 1968, so the legendary announcer had fewer positive things to say about the "grim" man who didn't find it charming when Ali called him a gorilla. Watch the Ali-Foreman fights in sequence, and it's a long downhill; even during Frazier-Ali I the announcers remind us that Ali isn't in fighting trim, as if to cheapen the accomplishment Frazier worked so hard to validate. By the end of the five fights, Frazier had lost so often and been needled by announcers so much that his greatness was hard to recognize.

To recalibrate after watching these giants shatter mountains, load up Frazier versus Jerry Quarry or Jim Ellis or some other mortal. Watch Frazier absorb punches and draw blood in the first round. Watch him duck, weave, and unload that left hook. It's like watching the Eagles win 12 games or the Phillies conquer the NL East, all in just 36 minutes.

*   *   *

JOE FRAZIER'S GYM, a landmark on North Broad Street, is now shuttered and boarded up. For 40 years, Philly fighters trained there with one goal: to be the next Joe Frazier.

The Blue Horizon still hosts four or five nights of boxing per year about 3 miles south of Frazier's gym. Visit the Blue Horizon, and you'll see a cross-section of the city: boxing diehards from the North Philly neighborhoods, well-wishing families and friends of the fighters, old-timers who look like they haven't left their seats since 1974. You'll also find a lot of suburbanites on ghetto safari: something draws them away from their HDTVs and the comfortable luxury of the Linc and Citizens Bank Park into a crumbling old "arena" (more of a repository theater with a ring) with no air-conditioning in a fringe-of-disaster neighborhood.

Philly lost something when boxing went underground, late night, and off the air, just as we lost something when Connie Mack and later the Vet closed. We lost grungy immediacy. We separated ourselves from the visceral experience of sport. So we lock the car doors and head for the Blue Horizon to get it back, so we can see Philadelphia fighters again the way they were meant to be seen.

Ali, Foreman, and Frazier are three legends from the last truly great age of boxing, but two of them were destined for bigger things. Ali is now something mythological. Foreman is a trademarked lovable-lug spokesman, an affable shill who is almost unrecognizable from his brutal early-career matches. Together, they teach us about religious tolerance and healthy dinners, representing 1960s radicalism and grills that cook on both sides at once.

All Frazier represents is boxing. He is remembered because he was such a fighter, an unaesthetic workman who earned what he won and defended it for three years, only to become a cameo player in another man's epic.

But he was a champion, one of our few. Even if it takes a pilgrimage to North Broad or a trip through the archives, we owe it to Frazier and ourselves to remember him, even if we forget his sport.

14

DAVE SCHULTZ

The Reluctant Enforcer

Greatness: ★★
Toughness: ★★★★★
Eccentricity: ★★★
Legacy: ★★★

I F YOU'RE LUCKY, you'll be remembered for one thing in your life. It may not be the thing you want to be remembered for, but you can't be picky, because most people are simply forgotten. Only the titans of history—Augustus Caesar, Napoleon, Julius Erving—stay well-rounded figures forever; mere mortals must be satisfied with the hook, the niche, the catchphrase, or the caricature.

Dave Schultz the hockey player is long forgotten. Dave "the Hammer" Schultz, enforcer, goon, and bully, will live forever. That's a shame, because Schultz was a solid all-around player and a reluctant fighter. But it could be worse.

Everyone knows that Schultz set a record with 472 penalty minutes in the 1974–1975 season. Most people also know that he scored 20 goals in 1973–1974, but only because everyone who writes about Schultz takes pains to remind readers that the Hammer was more than just Bobby Clarke's bodyguard. He could skate, he could pass, he could play defense. He wasn't a great player, but he wasn't a Hanson brother from *Slap Shot*, either.

But oh, the fights.

Schultz checks Garry Howatt of the Islanders as he crosses the blue line, Howatt retaliates, and suddenly Schultz has Howatt against the glass, landing about 20 blows while Howatt tugs at his hair and a fan tries to reach onto the ice to grab Schultz's jersey. Schultz then surrounds the pinned Howatt, grabbing the glass on either side of his opponent, head-butting and mashing him as about a dozen security guards fail to maintain order in the seats. Leon Stickle (yes, *that* Leon Stickle, the guy who legalized offsides for a few moments in 1980) breaks up the fight, and Schultz throws his pads in disgust, skating to the locker room before Stickle tells him he isn't ejected and guides him to the penalty box.

Schultz takes on Keith Magnuson, top goon of the Blackhawks, at center ice on January 18, 1975. Magnuson lands the first punch, and the two trade blows for a few seconds, but then Schultz drops a few right-handed hammers. Magnuson's head lulls back, his legs buckle, he starts to wobble, but the blows don't stop. "He's getting beaten to a pulp!" Gene Hart shouts as Schultz switches from haymakers to uppercuts. By the time the referees converge, Magnuson, his sweater long gone, cowers behind them for protection.

Tiger Williams of the Maple Leafs slashes Clarke, and Schultz appears, fists flying, to pin Williams to the glass. While they grapple and trade blows, Bob Kelly challenges Dave Dunn in an undercard. Wild group thrashing ensues: it's like a 1970s key party, only stag, and it lingers for several minutes. Referees whisk Kelly and Dunn from the ice, but Schultz and Williams still wrestle, too tired to land any real blows, until Schultz, holding his nose in disgust, gets escorted to the dressing room.

And so on. YouTube preserves dozens of Schultz brawls, which look more like Viking melees than hockey to modern eyes. Schultz won many of the fights and lost a few. He fought to protect Clarke and others, fought to intimidate opponents and establish dominance, fought to tactically force key opponent scorers to spend time in the box.

But he never enjoyed it. "I love hockey, and I wish reckless violence wasn't part of it," he said in his autobiography. "The fighting gave me notoriety," he later said. "That part I loved, but [it] never came naturally to me. I had to think about it all the time. I would sit there the afternoon of every game thinking about who I was going to fight and visualizing the fight. It was nerve-wracking. I was always afraid of that one punch, the one that would knock me out of my career."

That's a Schultz we never imagined: a Mike Schmidt of brutality, meditating and visualizing in preparation for a confrontation with Magnuson or Terry O'Reilly. Schultz often said that too much was made of the fights, rejecting the notion that some of his fights "set the tone" for this or that playoff series. There's no question that some teams were intimidated, but it was supposed to be about the hockey, the hard checks and the battles in the corner, not the fights.

For purists, it was about the hockey, but most of us aren't hockey purists: we're not on the edge of our seats in November or glued to the draft in June. For us, there was Schultz singing "Penalty Box," Schultz bloodying noses, Shultz slugging it out night after night like he was defending our regional honor. Even the guy who hired him remembers the Hammer, not the player. "Chicago came into the Spectrum, and Schultz kicked the shit out of Magnuson," Ed Snider once said, recalling a famous brawl with a smile. As our generation ages, that's the perception younger fans inherit of those old Flyers: there was a great center named Clarke, a great goalie named Parent, and 14 bloodthirsty knuckle-draggers named Dave Schultz. It's a warped perception, but it's better than none at all.

· · ·

SCHULTZ BECAME a Flyers Hall of Famer in 2009. He became an American citizen in August 2010. Both honors were at least two decades overdue.

Schultz has been one of the Philadelphia area's favorite immigrants for decades, a respected South Jersey businessman whom everyone seems to have met and liked. When Senator Bob Brady asserted that Schultz and three other ex-Flyers were "not terrorists, though they were terrorists on the ice," we could chuckle despite the horrible taste of the joke. Schultz is a neighbor, just like any other, except that he used to kick the shit out of people.

And that's the happy ending to this chapter. Schultz the hockey player, while good, was forgettable. Schultz the Hammer is a fun folk hero for the YouTube age, but a guy who does nothing but pick fights on the ice is ultimately a thug, not a role model. But Schultz the citizen still lives here, strong but humble, a working-class kid from Saskatchewan turned Camden County limo service operator, a regular guy who had to literally fight to keep his job for a few years. We got to watch him for only 5 years, but we got to know him for 30, and we're glad that we did.

15

ERIC LINDROS

The Once and Future Captain

Greatness: ★★★★
Toughness: ★★★½
Eccentricity: ★★★
Legacy: ★★★★

THE FLYERS TRIED to make Eric Lindros disappear. Bobby Clarke stripped him of his captaincy. He removed Lindros from the team's television commercials. In a particularly Orwellian move, he had the captain's "C" on Lindros's sweater airbrushed from the cover of the team's *Media Guide*.

It was May 2000, and Lindros was somewhere between Concussion 4 and Concussion 6. He had questioned the team doctors, decried the team's play-through-pain culture. Clarke retaliated by ripping Lindros, questioning his toughness, even insulting his manhood, and by rewriting history, deleting Lindros from the team's database like a Pharaoh chiseling away the cartouches of a fallen rival. "The mere mention of his name left players, coaches and even the team's broadcasters feeling uneasy," wrote Rob Maaddi of the Associated Press at the time.

And yet, Lindros played. Doctors cleared him before Game 6 of the Conference Finals against the Devils, two months after Concussion 4, three weeks after Concussion 5. The Flyers threw him right back into the starting lineup. In a 2–1 loss, he was the team's best player, serving up 3 of the team's miserable 13 shots, winning six of nine face-offs, scoring the Flyers' lone goal in the waning moments.

"He came remarkably close to making fools of his critics, the biggest of whom sat in the general manager's suite and looked a lot like

Bob Clarke," wrote Helene Elliott in the *Los Angeles Times*, though team doctor Tom Gormley, who sat next to Clarke during the game, said that Clarke cheered for Lindros throughout the game. "I never saw Clarke root harder for somebody than for Lindros that night," he recalled. Flyers fans, despite the accusations and acrimony, rooted just as hard. Flyers fans who made the trip to Newark for Game 6 gave him a standing ovation. "They can't win the Stanley Cup without him," one fan told the *Trenton Times*. "Anybody who says they don't need him is nuts."

Two days later, Lindros suffered Concussion 6 from two brutal collisions, first with Scott Stevens, then with the ice. His career appeared to be over. "I don't know what the future holds," Lindros said a few days later, his eyes still glassy from the hit. A few months later, he announced that he would play hockey again, but not for the Flyers. Whatever fences were mended during Game 6 were permanently burned. "I don't give a crap whether he plays again or if I ever see him again. All he ever did was cause aggravation to our team," Clarke said, once again trying to rewrite history.

. . .

THE ERIC LINDROS tragedy is a story with no heroes, only villains and victims: Bob Clarke, the legend turned autocratic, cavalier about the health of his best player and all too willing to carry his fight to the public; Carl Lindros, Eric's father and agent, the Airwolf of helicopter parents, an overprotective meddler who took a personal feud with Clarke too far; 610-WIP, the sports-talk station, overeager to smear Lindros's name in an effort to boost ratings, to accuse him of drunkenness and mafia connections, to feed and fuel the Clarke-Lindros flap for two years. Then there was Lindros himself, the greatest player in hockey for a few short seasons, but a young man too tied to his parent's apron strings, one who too often let others do his talking for him.

To say Lindros caused "nothing but aggravation" was ludicrous. It was Clarke the general manager venting like a taproom malcontent. The Flyers had been out of the playoffs for three years when they made their historic trade with the Quebec Nordiques to acquire Lindros in 1992. Three seasons later, the Flyers won the Atlantic Division, with Lindros winning the Hart and Lindsay trophies. Two years later, they reached the Stanley Cup Finals. Lindros was the leader of the Legion of Doom, flanked by John LeClair and Mikael Renberg. He was Philadelphia's biggest star at a time when Allen Iverson was a rookie, Scott Rolen was an enigma, and the Eagles' starting quarterback was Ty Detmer. He was the guy who sold season tickets when the CoreStates Center replaced the Spectrum. Lindros brought the Flyers success, prestige, and money.

On the ice, he was brutal yet beautiful, an overpowering presence who could win with power or finesse. Off the ice, he was hard to pin down. Depending on whom you believe, he either dumped beer on a fan's head in an Ontario bar or was falsely accused of doing so. Depending on whom you believe, he was either a casual acquaintance of Joey Merlino, or he knew the mobster well enough to date his sister. Depending on whom you believe, he missed a 1997 game with either back pain or a vicious hangover.

In the early years, Clarke and team owner Ed Snider stuck by Lindros; Snider even sued WIP over the hangover rumor. Lindros was a big target, practically the only Philly sports figure worth talking about, and the incidents that weren't simply fabricated were blown well out of proportion. Carl Lindros inserted himself into every story, sometimes speaking on his son's behalf, sometimes pushing his own anti-Clarke agenda through the media. He was quick to call beat writers and columnists with his own interpretation of events. "Carl could be oppressive," WIP and ESPN personality Al Morganti once said.

Ultimately, the Clarke-Lindros united front crumbled, not because of mobsters or off-field incidents but because of a hard-to-diagnose injury that old-time athletes never took seriously enough: the concussion. Because in the tough-guy days, you sniffed smelling salts, got back on the ice, and didn't worry about potential brain damage.

* * *

CONCUSSION 1 OCCURRED on March 7, 1998, after a violent collision with a Pittsburgh defenseman. No one doubted that the injury was serious. "He was in a fog," team doctor Jeffrey Hartzell said. "He did know that he had left a bag on the bus, but he didn't know that there was a hockey game going on." Lindros missed 18 games.

Concussion 2 occurred on December 29, 1998, after back-to-back hits in Calgary. "It's not anything as bad as what I have had before,"

Lindros said. "It's a bottom-level concussion." He returned to the ice after two games.

Concussion 3 occurred on January 14, 2000, after a minor scuffle in Atlanta. The collisions that caused the injuries were becoming progressively less severe. Lindros missed four games.

Between Concussion 2 and Concussion 3 came the collapsed lung. Lindros complained of soreness during a game in Nashville. Trainers iced him, and he stayed in the game. That night, the pain increased, and he grew pale. Team trainer John Worley tried to get Lindros ready to fly back to Philadelphia, then quickly reconsidered. He took Lindros to the hospital, where doctors performed emergency surgery, removing three liters of blood from his chest cavity. "They stuck that tube in me and we hit a geyser," he said from his hospital bed. "This should put to rest anyone's doubts about Eric and his courage," Ed Snider said of Lindros.

Ironically, it only increased the doubts. Carl Lindros became suspicious of the team's motives. He claimed that the team was trying to rush Lindros back to the ice in time for the playoffs. Lindros himself mulled such a return, but the Flyers were swept out of the postseason before Lindros could come back. Snider, Clarke, and the Lindros family all denied there was undue pressure, but a mutual distrust developed, or intensified.

Concussion 4 occurred on March 4, 2000. Lindros tried to play through it. Teammates could tell he wasn't himself. "I noticed that in between periods lately he seemed to be rubbing his head a lot," Adam Burt said. Hartzell diagnosed a migraine. A specialist diagnosed a grade II concussion.

The team went to comical lengths to downplay the severity of Concussion 4. At one point, Hartzell suggested that Lindros's headaches were the result of teeth grinding, perhaps when Lindros chewed gum. Clarke accused Lindros of hiding his symptoms. Lindros accused the Flyers of creating a "wacky" culture in which he was afraid to admit his injuries. It was the culmination of what CNNSI called "three years of diagnoses, denial, and accusations."

By Concussion 5, which he suffered in a minor league skate-around while rehabbing from Concussion 4, Lindros was no longer a team captain. Clarke had the captain's "C" stitched onto Eric Desjardins's sweater in a televised pregame ritual that would have made Nathaniel

Hawthorne proud. Lindros was clearly under pressure to silence critics, to preserve a legacy.

By Concussion 6, he was curled up on the ice, a broken man.

. . .

IT WASN'T ALWAYS that way. In the 1997 Eastern Conference Finals, the Rangers wanted to get under Lindros's skin, get him off his game or into the penalty box. They knew he liked to retaliate after hits, sometimes recklessly: he had earned a two-game suspension against the Rangers in the regular season for a pair of high-sticks, one of which broke Shane Churla's nose.

So the Rangers unleashed the goons, sending Churla, brawler Ulf Samuelsson, and other maulers onto the ice whenever Lindros took a shift. Early in the series, it seemed to work, with the Rangers baiting Lindros into numerous scuffles.

Then, Lindros stopped retaliating and started scoring. He had a hat trick in Game 3, then scored the game-winning goal in Game 4. The Flyers easily won the series in Game 5. In postgame press conferences, the 24-year-old praised his teammates and spoke of the hard work that lay ahead. "He said all the things a captain and leader is supposed to say," Ray Parrillo wrote in the *Inquirer*. He refused to accept the Conn Smythe trophy, symbolically reminding the team that the Stanley Cup was their ultimate goal.

After the game, Rangers star Mark Messier told Lindros it was his turn to take home the Cup. "He had a great series, right from the first game on," Messier said. Mario Lemieux expressed similar sentiments a few weeks earlier, after the Flyers beat the Penguins. Many fans felt that a torch had been passed, from Wayne Gretzky to Lemieux and now to Lindros, that he was destined to be the game's premier player and a perennial champion.

The Red Wings swept the Flyers in the Stanley Cup Finals. Lindros had one meaningless goal in the series. Coach Terry Murray was fired after the series. His "choking situation" remarks before Game 4 forced Clarke's hand, but many thought Lindros pulled strings to get Murray fired. As usual, someone else spoke for the Flyers' captain. "Don't blame my son," Carl Lindros told reporters.

It took only one series: from high to low, glory to suspicion, heir apparent to shadowy clubhouse politician. Lindros couldn't have changed that much in four games. It had to be some other force throwing that switch that moves a player's career inexorably from upside to downside.

Seven months later, Lindros collided with a Penguins defenseman and collapsed to the ice with Concussion 1.

The torch was never passed.

. . .

THE FLYERS PLAYED a final preseason game at the obsolete Spectrum before the arena was shut down in 2008. The team invited all of its past captains to attend. Despite Clarke's efforts to burn the archives and tear down the obelisks, the fact remained that Lindros was once a captain and one of the best. Would he attend? Would he take the ice alongside Clarke?

Lindros didn't go, citing an important personal engagement. But he recorded a message that played on the jumbo screen. He called Philadelphia fans "the best fans, in my eyes, in professional sports."

There are no heroes in the Eric Lindros tragedy. Clarke's staff callously shrugged off postconcussion headaches, legitimizing Carl Lindros's claim that the team was willing to risk players' long-term health in the name of victory. Carl Lindros set his son up to fail, making Eric a league-wide target with his bigger-than-the-game trade demands and constant machinations. Sports-talkers irresponsibly stoked controversy in the name of ratings. And Lindros, just 25 when Concussion 1 struck and his career began to unravel, was too immature to be all he was asked to be.

At the end of the drama, only the fans looked good. "Philadelphia cheered Eric Lindros on his first day and his last," Rich Hofmann wrote in the *Inquirer*. Fans cheered for Lindros, even as the media tried to bury him and the organization tried to excise him from history. Most fans never bought the "lack of heart" argument because they saw him play through injuries, some of them life-threatening. They saw a true Philly kind of player: a scorer with a mean streak, a potential all-time great whose intensity was too much for his own body.

Flyers fans feared that Lindros would be shunned from that final Spectrum game. Some writers feared a three-ring media circus if he attended. Ultimately, Lindros's brief video was perfect. His message was simple. The fans' response was warm. The Flyers even added an introduction to Lindros's message: a clip of Lindros scoring a playoff goal against the Devils.

The black "C" was clearly visible on Lindros's sweater, never to be airbrushed away again.

16

DARREN DAULTON
The Pan-Dimensional Catcher

Greatness: ★★★
Toughness: ★★★
Eccentricity: ★★★★★
Legacy: ★★

DARREN "DUTCH" DAULTON isn't sure how many dimensions there are. But he'll "bet dollars to donuts there are 11 or 12."

It's inaccurate to say that Daulton has a unique cosmology. You simply have to leave the sports aisle of the bookstore and wander over to the New Age aisle. There, you'll find books about other dimensions, higher states of consciousness, a universe of vibrating energy frequencies, strange mélanges of Christianity and occultism, and numerous other scientific/philosophical/theological mash-ups. You may even find Dutch's book, *If They Only Knew*. Reading it is like reading the whole New Age aisle in one sitting, then washing it down with a Jayson Stark column. In the sports aisle Daulton is an eccentric, but in the New Age aisle he's downright mainstream.

I point this out because I'm not qualified to talk about Daulton's theories. He says as much in the introduction to his book. "The people that make derogatory remarks about something they know nothing about are the ones who aren't ready for answers." Count me among them. I know nothing of the fifth dimension (Dutch has *been*), and I made derogatory remarks about Daulton when he spoke at a Phillies rally before the 2009 World Series. "The Phillies wanted multiple personalities to speak at the rally," I wrote in the *New York Times*. "Thanks to Daulton, they only had to make one phone call."

So I won't comment on Daulton's cosmology, except to express my awe at his ability to shift from the Bible to chakras to Kundalini energy to Jewish merkabah mysticism and back to the Bible in the course of two pages. If he could have taught Mitch Williams to paint the corners so effortlessly, the Phillies would have won the 1993 World Series.

. . .

THE PHILLIES ADDED Daulton to their Wall of Fame in August 2010. Mike Schmidt, Jim Bunning, Steve Carlton, and others were on hand to honor the three-time All Star. The man has experienced the fifth dimension, but he's still amazed by Phillies fans and their love of the 1993 team. "It's kind of neat," he said that night. "Some of the towns I go to, the kids were 7–8 years old back then, and now they're 25–26 and they say, 'I don't want to make you feel old, but my mother had a crush on you back in '93.' And I'm like, 'You made me feel old.'"

Daulton now co-hosts a sports-talk show among his other business ventures. On the air, there are no chakras to be heard of; Daulton is the old jock, full of stories of his glory years and insights on the current Phillies. At the Wall of Fame ceremony, he was the stereotypical baseball hero, blowing kisses to the crowd and cracking jokes. "Not sure if I'm quite worthy to be next to some of those names up there. But that's what you get when you stuff the ballots every day, about 10,000 votes a day." Daulton is one of the first ex-Phillies off the bench when the team needs a beloved alumnus. He never fails to deliver or to thrill crowds who couldn't care less about a player's philosophy so long as he hit 27 home runs and guarded the plate like it was a national treasure.

. . .

DAULTON SPENT 14 seasons with the Phillies, 3 of which were actually good. The 1993 season we remember well: 24 home runs, 105 RBIs, 117 walks, 147 games behind the plate. Daulton was excellent in 1992 (27 homers, 109 RBIs), great before the strike in 1994 (a .300 average, 15 homers). For the rest of his career he was injured, buried in the minors, or stuck on the bench because of his inability to hit left-handed pitchers and the Phillies' strange Lance Parrish fixation.

Daulton was on the pennant-winning 1983 Phillies, though only for two September call-up games. He was a farmhand in 1980, cracking the 40-man preseason roster the year Phillies won the World Series. He was still around in 1997, batting cleanup and playing right field before the Phillies shipped him to the Marlins. Daulton backed up Bo Diaz and tutored Mike Lieberthal. He was a teammate of Pete Rose and Scott Rolen. He survived a generation of Phillies baseball, most of it forgettable. There were years shuttling between AAA Portland and the majors, years platooning with John Russell or subbing for Parrish, years of .196 batting averages. There were knee injuries and shoulder injuries, and of course there was criticism, enough to make Daulton guarded and defensive by the time he finally turned things around in 1992. "I am probably not as kind a person as I once was," Daulton said near the end of the 1992 season. "I am not as open with people as I once was because of what has happened. I still read the papers, but I stopped listening to the radio talk shows. Hell, up until this season, I used to be a daily topic of conversation."

All of this is forgotten, because we remember 1993.

• • •

DAULTON'S DRIVING RECORD is as long and baffling as his career and his cosmology. In 1988, he refused a breathalyzer test and was arrested for DUI in Florida. He lost his license in the late 1990s because of a series of speeding tickets, some for speeds exceeding 100 miles per hour. In 2001, he caused $20,000 in damages to his BMW, refused a sobriety exam, and was again charged with DUI. He claimed at the time that the government was involved in the accident. In 2003, he was charged with DUI and driving with a suspended license yet again.

Daulton was a passenger in May 1991 when Len Dykstra's Mercedes SL500 crashed between two trees after John Kruk's bachelor party. Daulton suffered a severe eye injury and missed a month of the season, but the accident caused Dutch to take his life and his gifts more seriously. Manager Jim Fregosi said he became "a smarter hitter" after the accident; batting coach Denis Menke said Daulton "came of age" as a hitter and leader. The record shows that he didn't come of age or become smarter as a driver.

He had myriad other problems, some comical, some inexcusable. There were domestic violence charges, failure to meet the terms of his divorce, a 2009 interview in which he claimed "there's probably no one in any sport that has taken more drugs than I have and I think people still respect me." There was a punching match with a water cooler in 1988 and a probation arrest at an airport in 2004.

We forget all of that. It's no wonder that Daulton is amazed by the adulation. A city intolerant of the failures of some of its most respectable superstars somehow embraced a man who mistreated his wife, caused terror on the roads, and spent most of his career battling injuries, a few of them self-inflicted, all because he came close to winning a World Series.

It's a mystery that all the New Age philosophy in the world cannot explain.

. . .

EVERYTHING RETURNED to status quo after Daulton joined the Wall of Fame in the summer of 2010. The Phillies kept battling injuries and stayed on course for another playoff appearance. Daulton went back to his radio gig, his personal life and cosmological mysteries compartmentalized while he talked about Brad Lidge and Roy Oswalt.

Daulton has stated that the world will end on December 21, 2012, the last day of the Mayan calendar, but he doesn't act like anything is about to change. He doesn't tell fans that the Wall of Fame will soon crumble, or that outfield prospect Domonic Brown's career will be cut short by cosmic calamity (to date, the only thing that hasn't cut a Phillies prospect's career short).

The New Age guru doesn't connect well with the sports hero, who doesn't connect with the hard-driving, hard-living reprobate, and none of them connect with the journeyman catcher who had a handful of standout seasons. Still, they somehow come together in Daulton, a man who will tell you that everything is connected on some intangible level.

There are many dimensions to Darren Daulton; I'm not sure how many, but I'll bet dollars to donuts that there are 11 or 12.

17

BERNIE PARENT

He Left Us So He Could Stay with Us

Greatness: ★★★★
Toughness: ★★★★
Eccentricity: ★★
Legacy: ★★★

WHAT WOULD YOU say about a player who abandoned his team, a Philly team, during the playoffs over a financial dispute? Of all the unforgivable sins in sports, that has to be the greatest. Philly sports fans have seen some cads over the years, but none of them—not Dick Allen, not Terrell Owens—walked out on his team in the heat of the postseason.

Except Bernie Parent, one of the most beloved sports figures in Philly history.

Sure, the team he walked out on was the Philadelphia Blazers of the World Hockey Association, a forgotten, rinky-dink rival to the NHL. And Parent's beef was legitimate enough: the team was losing money and cutting salaries, and Parent left after the second game of the playoffs because the Blazers refused to guarantee the remainder of Parent's $600,000 contract.

Still, it happened: a Philly team in the playoffs, a starting goalie skating off the ice, never to return. "Money is not everything, but it sure helps if the security is there," Parent said at the time. Parent was worried that the Blazers would fold or, just as bad, relocate to some outpost city; the team drew only about 4,000 fans, even for playoff games. Parent's coach, John McKenzie, accused him of being "selfish"; Dick Olson, Blazers president, told Parent's lawyer that the goalie "would never play for the Blazers again."

True enough. Without Parent, the Blazers were swept from the playoffs, then swept out of Philadelphia. The team moved to Vancouver, then to Calgary. The franchise dissolved in 1977, and the WHA surrendered to the NHL in 1979. The Blazers are less than a footnote, ranking somewhere between the USFL's Philadelphia Stars and an indoor soccer team on the irrelevance scale.

Parent, meanwhile, rejected an offer from the WHA's New York franchise, then took a pay cut to return to the Flyers, the team that had drafted him in 1967 but traded him to Toronto in 1971. "I never wanted to leave here in the first place. I love Philadelphia . . . the fans . . . and even though I've been away I've always considered myself a Flyer."

Money is not everything. Parent left a Philadelphia team because he didn't want to leave Philadelphia. So began a love story that continues to this day.

. . .

THE FLYERS HADN'T beaten the Bruins at the Boston Garden in seven years when the teams faced off for the Stanley Cup in 1974. Even during the 1973–1974 season, when the Flyers won 50 games, they were 0–3 in the Garden. After Game 1 of the Finals, they were 0–4 in Boston, and the Bruins took a 2–0 lead in Game 2. But the Flyers rallied. Bobby Clarke deflected a Bill Flett shot for one goal. Defenseman Andre DuPont scored on a 15-footer in the waning seconds. Then, in overtime, Bruins scorer John Bucyk had a one-on-one opportunity against Parent, a chance to give the Bruins a two-game advantage in the series and reaffirm Boston's home supremacy.

"I saw Bucyk coming and I stayed on the edge of the crease," Parent said after the game. "I waited for his shot and I got it."

Parent stoned Bucyk, and a few minutes later Clarke rebounded his own shot and scored the game-winning goal. The series was tied, and the Flyers were suddenly believers. "Now that we've won here, I surely believe we're going to do it," coach Fred Shero said.

Parent's overtime save in Game 2 was just the beginning. In Game 3 he stopped 24 of 25 shots, including a power play drive by Wayne Cashman in the first period that would have given the Bruins a 2–0 lead. And then came the decisive Game 6: 30 saves, including a slap shot by Ken Hodge in the third period that Parent kicked away, and a last-second prayer by Bobby Orr that started in the Bruins zone and ended just a few feet wide of the net. "Parent in that particular game played the best game any player's ever had for the franchise," Clarke later said.

Parent won the Conn Smythe Trophy that day, and the everlasting affection of the Philly fans. Thirty years later, he admitted to *Philadelphia Magazine* that he didn't see Orr's desperate last-second shot because he was watching the clock tick down to zero. "I didn't know where the puck was, man!" he says. "If his shot is on net, it's a goal. Who knows what happens then."

• • •

PARENT'S MASK APPEARED on the cover of *Time* magazine in 1975. It was stark white, with small Flyers logos on the side. It was simple, elegant, and terrifying. "When wingers were bearing down on Parent they saw nothing of cartoonish personality, just ghostly intimidation," wrote Regan Fletcher on the Tenders Lounge Web site of that mask.

It was also an old-school mask, with no helmet or crossbars, nothing to stop a stick from smashing into the eye.

"Most of the young goalies are using these new masks with the helmet and the bars," Parent told Ray Didinger from the hospital in February 1979. "They're probably better. If I was wearing one of those, I don't think this would have happened."

Parent had been trying to protect a one-goal lead against the Rangers. Flyers defenseman Jimmy Watson threw Rangers forward Dave Maloney to the ice in front of Parent, and Maloney's stick slammed into Parent's eye. The blow caused internal bleeding and weeks of blindness. It ended Parent's career. It nearly ruined his life. He became a drinker. A few years later, when his wife gave him an Alcoholics Anonymous quiz, he answered "Yes" to 23 of the 24 questions. "The 24th I lied about," he told *Philadelphia Magazine*.

Parent sobered up, and after a few years of coaching (he mentored Pelle Lindbergh) he grew into the role as natural for him as Stanley Cup goaltender: retired sports hero. Parent learned to use his name and credibility as a promoter and motivational speaker. When not engrossing crowds with Broad Street Bullies lore, he can be found on his boat. Visit his personal Web site, and you'll find that both the Flyers and speaking engagements take a back seat to the fishing report.

"The best fishing is at night. The night bite has been good on eels. The daytime striper fishery has become very quiet statewide," he reported from the coast of Wildwood in July 2010. His maritime blog is the perfect antidote for anyone forced to read Curt Schilling's on-line pontifications.

Parent still enjoys the rare, unequivocal admiration of Philly fans, something he earned during the Stanley Cup Finals and never relinquished. When he missed most of the 1975–1976 season with a neck injury, backup Wayne Stephenson played well enough to make the All-Star game. But Shero reinserted Parent into the lineup against the Maple Leafs in the playoffs, and when Parent made two tough stops in the second game of the series, the crowd erupted in a chant of "Bernie, Bernie, Bernie." The still-hurting Parent and Stephenson traded goal-tending chores in those playoffs, and Parent had to take himself out of the lineup at one point.

The Flyers lost to the Canadiens in the Finals, and a long, injury-riddled decline took Parent from those Finals through the meeting with Maloney's stick. But Parent remained a hero, a player whose throwback jersey is worn by teenagers and whose face on the Jumbo-Vision can still draw a raucous ovation at any Philly sporting event.

. . .

PARENT'S CAREER is full of "what ifs." What if he had worn a modern helmet in 1979? The Flyers reached the Stanley Cup Finals in 1980 with Pete Peeters and Phil Myre in goal. Both played well enough, and perhaps Parent, who was 34, would have played a backup role that year. Still, could he have won Game 3 of the Finals, in which Myre gave up six goals in a spot start? Might he have kept his guard up when Goring crossed the blue line and referee Leon Stickle decided to legalize offsides for a few seconds?

What if Orr's prayer found its target, and the Bruins forced overtime in Game 6 of the 1974 Finals? Maybe the Flyers would have lost and become the 1964 Phillies. Maybe the Broad Street Bullies would have been forgotten.

What if Parent did what good soldiers are supposed to do: honored his contract, played out his Blazers career, skated out to Vancouver with the team? Flyers history would look very different, and Parent would be thought of as a great player we never got a chance to root for, a Ferguson Jenkins or Ryne Sandberg, traded away by a shortsighted franchise.

Legends are built upon these fragile foundations. Parent embraced Philadelphia by abandoning it, helped teach the city how to win, then left the ice blinded and battered but not forgotten. "Only the Lord saves more than Bernie Parent," the old bumper sticker proclaimed, but Parent is one of the few Philly sports heroes who can do something even the Almighty would find challenging. He can get Philly sports fans to agree, and he can get them to smile. Parent said 40 years ago that he always considered himself a Flyer. He always was a Flyer, and he always will be.

18

RYAN HOWARD

The Baby Brother We Could Not Pick On. Yet.

Greatness: ★★★★
Toughness: ★★★
Eccentricity: ★★
Legacy: ★★½

RYAN HOWARD, MVP and home-run champion, was batting .198 with five homers. It was May 8, 2007, and the Phillies were already four games under .500 and six and a half games out of first. Howard was out of the lineup: a thigh injury he suffered in March, after an offseason filming commercials and making public appearances, was bothering him so much that Charlie Manuel gave him three days off from playing the field. Howard could still pinch hit; a day earlier, he fouled out to end a 4–3 loss to the Diamondbacks.

Sure, his thigh was bothering him. Was there something else? "I think he's trying too hard," GM Pat Gillick said. "It looks like the pitchers have him inside conscious," Dusty Baker said, noting that pitchers weren't throwing the ball outside, fearing Howard's opposite-field power. Howard acknowledged the injury, the pressure, and the adjustments but assured fans not to worry. "You've watched me grow," he joked in the *Inquirer*. "You've watched me blossom from the caterpillar to the butterfly."

If you've watched Philly sports long enough, you can pinpoint the moment when things go wrong for a young player. This appeared to be that moment for Ryan Howard. The nagging injuries, the sudden fame, the crushing expectations . . . the early birds prepared to leap off the bandwagon. Howard was on the Rolen Express to Burrellsville.

But not so fast. Howard's thigh required a trip to the disabled list, but not before he pinch hit with the bases loaded in the seventh inning of a game the Phillies trailed 3–0. Howard pulled the first pitch he saw over the right-field wall for a grand slam.

Maybe Howard was different. Or maybe it was the Phillies that changed.

* * *

HOWARD IS PERHAPS the luckiest great player in Philly sports history. He arrived when there were many other local players—great, controversial, and both—for fans to obsess over. He helped his team to the World Series relatively early in his career. He has taken his share of criticism during slumps, but he's never been subjected to the full assault of the local media.

Howard won Rookie of the Year in 2005, the season after the Eagles lost the Super Bowl. He rose to promise while Terrell Owens did sit-ups in a driveway and Allen Iverson wore out his final welcome with the Sixers. He hit 58 home runs in the summer that Brett Myers assaulted his wife and Gillick shipped Bobby Abreu out of town. Pat Burrell provided a little lineup protection, but he was much more valuable as a criticism magnet: if Howard wasn't seeing hittable pitches, it was because opponents could pitch around him with no fear of Burrell. As big as he was, Howard got to grow up in the shadow of other people's scandals and failures. There was little negative to say about him, and there was always someone else to criticize if you had the itch.

The scandals of others couldn't save Howard in 2007. You could argue that he saved himself. He batted .280 with 10 home runs in June, .323 with 10 homers in July. He finished the season with seven home runs in the final 10 games, and they weren't ordinary games. They were the games that propelled the Phillies into first place and into the playoffs, the games that set the stage for 2008.

And there's the rub. Howard didn't save himself. Chase Utley saved him by batting .323. Jimmy Rollins saved him with 30 home runs. Cole Hamels saved him with 15 wins. Howard survived an "off" season because the Phillies surprised everyone by finally becoming a great team.

Imagine if they hadn't. Some Philly fans just don't understand sluggers. They don't recognize that 48 home runs come with a price: strikeouts, a mediocre batting average, slumps. If Howard batted .251 with 48 homers and 199 strikeouts for a third-place team, he'd be in the crosshairs. The doubters would harp on his strikeouts, accuse him of "laziness" when he drew walks in close games, gripe about his defense and conditioning, and complain about "meaningless" home runs. If you don't believe that, then you haven't lived in Philadelphia in the last four decades.

Luckily, Howard batted .251 with 48 home runs and 199 strikeouts for a World Series champion, so we got to see his great season for exactly what it was.

. . .

HOWARD HAS ALWAYS been philosophical about the Philly sports media because he could afford to be. After the 2010 NBA draft, he offered 76ers rookie Evan Turner some advice. "He said you gotta' compare Philly to, like, a big brother," Turner said of the conversation. "Some days he's gonna like you and some days he might not like you, but he still loves you, and it's all about what you do and how you do things . . . but it's always having the support, no matter what."

Howard used the "brother" analogy on other occasions, and it's a label that puts the best face on the worst elements of fandom. We're the City of Brotherly Love, and brothers squabble and bicker, so that's why we boo some players every time they come to the plate. It's an appealing justification for sometimes appalling behavior. Unless you're the Marquis de Sade's kid brother, you have probably never experienced anything like our fan base at its worst. We're nothing like brothers to our best players. We're more like histrionic, manic-depressive girlfriends who smother them with kisses for a while, then put a cinder block through their windshields when they let us down.

But Howard could be forgiven for thinking otherwise in the summer of 2010, when the Phillies were coming off a pennant and the Flyers off a Stanley Cup near-miss and the pressure was off. Fast forward to the 2010 National League Championship Series. Howard may soon discover exactly what kind of temper Big Brother has.

. . .

HOWARD STRUCK OUT 12 times in the 2010 National League Championship Series against the Giants. After a few of the early strikeouts, a strange sound rattled through Citizens Bank Park, like a loud muttering, 40,000 people grumbling under their breath at once. Writing for the *New York Times*, I called the sound a "Proto Boo," a transitional form that evolves into a regular boo if conditions are perfect.

The Phillies weren't playing well, and while Howard batted .318 with four doubles in the series, he kept making outs with runners in scoring position. There was no one for him to hide behind. The Phillies were alone in the spotlight, and he was alone in not having a signature playoff moment, not having a no-hitter (Roy Halladay) or three-run double (Jimmy Rollins) or hit-by-pitch rally starter (Chase Utley). Eagles fans cheered Donovan McNabb just two weeks earlier, symbolically releasing him from bondage. It was someone else's turn at the bottom of the well.

In the bottom of the ninth inning of Game 6, with Rollins and Utley on base and the Phillies trailing 3–2, Howard struck out looking. We didn't boo. We gasped. A gasp is an inhale, a boo an exhale. The 2010 season was over, so we didn't have time to exhale. We will exhale in April. I am not sure how it will sound.

Howard's luck may be running out. We now get to decide what kind of brothers we are. We can harp on Howard's shortcomings or focus on his strengths. We can enjoy his upbeat personality or we can repurpose him as "soft." There are a hundred labels we can hang on him, or we can let him keep the ones he best deserves: former champion, former MVP, man who deserves the benefit of the doubt. Every butterfly doesn't have to end up pinned under a piece of glass. If we keep watching Howard grow, without all of our patented tough love, maybe he'll surprise us one more time.

19

DONOVAN McNABB

The Haters' Favorite

Greatness: ★ ★ ★ ★
Toughness: ★ ★ ★
Eccentricity: ★ ★ ★ ½
Legacy: ★ ★

O F ALL THE absurd experiences I have had as an Eagles fan and sportswriter, nothing prepared me for October 3, 2010. That was the day Donovan McNabb returned to Philadelphia as quarterback of the Washington Redskins. It was a circled date on the media calendar, a homecoming that promised to be worth the hype. The 610-WIP morning show talked about almost nothing else for two weeks before the game; they were planning an anti-McNabb rally, a reunion of the Dirty Thirty with jugglers, midgets, and stilt-walkers. The national media was also buzzing, and not just about the game. Dozens of articles appeared the week before the game. Will the Eagles fans boo? Should they boo? Will they riot? Should they riot?

I was on the beat as well. I sold the *New York Times* on a "man on the street" story about the crowd. I covered Terrell Owens's return for Fox Sports in 2006, and I saw tailgaters running over TO dummies with golf carts. I expected burning effigies for the McNabb return, to say nothing of midgets and jugglers.

So on a damp, chilly October afternoon, I laced up my best sneakers and walked the parking lots, from the Holiday Inn to Lincoln Financial Field, through the Wells Fargo Center, up to FDR Park, then back to the stadium. I walked alone, searching for the heart of Philly fandom on the Sunday afternoon when the symbol of our regional neurosis returned to lead an enemy into battle.

. . .

DONOVAN McNABB DID not throw up during Super Bowl XXXIX. There's no footage of it, there's no evidence of it, and there's no player who said it happened at the time. It didn't happen, and claiming over and over again that it happened doesn't change the fact that it didn't happen.

The facts: McNabb scrambled for no gain with 3:28 to play in the game. Tedy Bruschi drove his helmet into McNabb's ribs on the play. The hit rattled McNabb, who was slow to get back to the line. He started coughing and gasping in the huddle. Receiver Freddie Mitchell called one play because McNabb couldn't get the words out. During this gasp-and-wheeze sequence, McNabb completed a 3rd-and-10 pass to Mitchell, then a 13-yard pass to Brian Westbrook. The Eagles offense may have been moving at a less-than-optimal pace, but it was moving. After the two-minute warning, a refreshed McNabb threw a 30-yard touchdown to Greg Lewis. The score gave the Eagles a slim chance to beat the team of the decade, but of course it didn't happen.

Go back and read accounts of the sequence. "He gave it his all. He was almost puking in the huddle," Hank Fraley said. "One play had to be called by Freddie Mitchell because Donovan was mumbling because he was almost puking." Here's the account from Mitchell, who wasn't a guy who toed the company line: "You could see that he was dealing with some kind of complication. . . . I don't know if it was breathing or what. . . . He always coughs a lot, trying to get something out. . . . I don't think he was physically hurt."

I needed to put these facts in writing because they will soon be lost. We have a habit of rewriting the past, retrofitting it to the official Philly story line. In a few years, all we'll remember of Super Bowl XXXIX is that Donovan McNabb puked. Then he spat on a little girl. On Scott Rolen Day. The stiff.

In most other cities, coming back from a severe hit, gutting through pain, and throwing a touchdown pass to keep a game within reach would be considered an act of heroism. In Philly, it was instantly recast as a sign of weakness. McNabb suffered from that kind of in-the-moment revisionism since the day he was drafted, when a talk-radio gadfly decided to make a name for himself at the expense of both a young athlete and the reputation of a whole city's fans.

. . .

THAT GADFLY WAS still on the job over a decade later. In mid-July 2010, Angelo Cataldi sounded like a baby without his binky. Talk-radio discussion is always slow in summer, even when the Phillies are very good, but Cataldi sounds lost. In the absence of anything substantial to say about Philadelphia or national sports, all discussions on 610-WIP travel back to McNabb.

The subject of basketball Hall-of-Fame speeches comes up, and the morning team muses about whether Michael Jordan will launch into another self-serving rant before introducing Scottie Pippen. Cataldi jokes that McNabb would give a similar airing-of-grievances speech. "Boy, that's our only chance of getting mentioned in a Hall of Fame speech," Cataldi muses, inflating his importance as McNabb's primary off-field antagonist. A few days later, a caller just back from Washington reports that he saw McNabb's image painted on a city bus. "Was it the same bus he threw his teammates under?" Cataldi asks, referring to an incident that never occurred.

Angelo Cataldi: clown prince of Philly sports-talk, legitimate football writer turned funnyman, Ivy League-educated Boston millionaire masquerading as a South Philly everymook. Cataldi's show can be hysterical at times, informative at others, occasionally even poignant. Unfortunately, Cataldi and his talk-radio colleagues often mistake glib character assassination for ornery humor, and their nonstop barrage of criticisms and barbs starts to sound like truth to those who listen for hours each day, days each week. This isn't WIP's first intrusion into the Philly Fan's Code story, and it won't be the station's last. The contributions are rarely positive. No, WIP didn't invent Philly sports negativity, but they legitimized it. They gave it a loud, incessant voice and made a name brand out of it.

Back in 1999, Cataldi assembled the Dirty Thirty, a collection of stereotypical angry-fan scoundrels, to take a charter bus to New York to boo the Eagles if they selected anyone but Ricky Williams. Many people were on the Williams bandwagon at that point. Even governor Ed Rendell loved him. But most of us weren't willing to make a scene when the Eagles chose McNabb. We weren't willing to devote an entire day to booing and screaming and making sure the cameras saw the "Philly fans" in action.

According to the McNabb Deniers—the people who think he puked in the Super Bowl, that he was never very good, that he brought us nothing but misery—McNabb never forgave or forgot the incident. In fact, McNabb rarely mentioned it, usually downplaying it when asked. It was Cataldi and the talk-radio crowd who never forgave or forgot. Cataldi doesn't like being accused of setting up a strike force to boo McNabb that day: he was booing the pick, not the person. In the days before McNabb's return with the Redskins, he brought up the incident constantly: how it was really an example of the national media picking on Philly fans, how McNabb could never let the incident go, and on and on.

That this self-serving self-victimization found an audience shouldn't be surprising anymore. That's how talk radio works. At least the WIP talkers only told people whom to boo, not whom to vote for. They were as effective at deflecting credit and assigning blame as any pundits on the airwaves. By 2009, McNabb could have a three-touchdown game against the Giants, and after four hours of talk radio you would swear DeSean Jackson and Jeremy Maclin must have thrown those passes to themselves, because surely no one else deserved credit for the effort.

As October 3 drew closer, the anti-McNabb rhetoric on talk radio grew more shrill. So I walked the parking lots and talked to tailgaters, fellow reporters, and cops, searching for fans as consumed by hate as they were told to be.

.   .   .

I COINED THE term "McNabb Denier" at Football Outsiders because "hater" wasn't strong enough. Critics didn't just hate McNabb, they tried to erase him, plastering his legacy with labels: choke artist, momma's boy, passive-aggressive, hypersensitive, inaccurate, not serious about winning, out of shape, not a leader, not a winner. They called him "an athlete, not a quarterback," a company man, a poor fit for the offense, and on and on. According to the McNabb Denier agenda, he was a third-rate passer good only at scrambling. They claimed the Eagles were successful only because of their defense and players like Westbrook, that McNabb choked in every pressure situation and had terrible personal qualities, but Andy Reid kept protecting McNabb because he wanted to justify the decision to draft him.

This is loopy, flat-earth stuff, but admit it: you know people who believe all of that, or 90 percent of it. And it's not just the Dirty Thirty types who believe it, but girlfriends and maiden aunts and casual fans, people who picked up the negativity in the air. My 75-year-old aunt once yelled at me for writing positive things about McNabb. The Deniers did a fine job of pushing their agenda to the forefront of the debate.

And yes, McNabb was often inaccurate with his passes. He made some dopey remarks about race and didn't know overtime rules. He had slumps and frustrating games, running hot and cold from 2005 to 2009. But the criticisms were mostly recycled: the Deniers weren't attacking McNabb, they were just going after the man of the moment. They borrowed "sensitive" from Schmidt, "momma's boy" from Lindros, "passive-aggressive" from Scott Rolen, and "just an athlete" from Randall Cunningham. They swirled in some of the casually racist potshots that every black quarterback endures, then put a cherry on it when the Eagles couldn't beat the Patriots, relabeling the inability to erase a 10-point deficit in the fourth quarter as a "choke."

For that angry faction of us—those perpetually dissatisfied, loud, pessimistic, hypercritical, mob-minded fans we too often let speak for the rest us—McNabb was simply the latest target for a pain that's far too deep to be sports related. He was just the latest phase in an evolution that began long ago, even before Dick Allen, and morphed to fit Schmidt, Lindros, Rolen, and others. With McNabb, the angry faction of Deniers skipped the step where they pretended to like him. They booed early and avoided the late-career rush.

On that drizzly October afternoon, I searched South Philadelphia for that angry faction. But I found something else.

· · ·

I SPECULATED in the *New York Times* that the crowd would make a noise "like the dinosaurs going extinct" when McNabb took the field for the Redskins. Instead, you cheered. You shocked the seasoned reporters in the press box. You shocked the national media, which printed the story of McNabb's standing ovation before the first quarter was over. You may have shocked yourselves.

I wasn't shocked, because I walked the lots, talked to you, watched and listened. I saw Cataldi's furtive, half-hearted little rally, saw a few

McNabb jersey burnings, talked to few surly drinkers with "McNabb can go to hell" attitudes. But I also saw Eagles and Redskins fans walking side by side, talked to out-of-towners in maroon jerseys who could joke around with the locals, met guys with Eagles trailers who remembered all the good times and looked forward to an exciting, competitive game. Most of the tens of thousands who showed up that Sunday were more interested in loving the game than hating those who played it. The slobbering, snarling contingent was shouted down, drowned out, marginalized, and exiled back into the dark corner where it belongs—for once. Maybe we can start making a habit of it.

So instead of burying my fellow fans that day, I was able to praise us. "Philly Fans Tell McNabb How They Really Feel," read the headline, and while it would have been easier and funnier to write about lunatics and jugglers, I was proud that I could write the truth. McNabb is back in our memories, not quite as a hero but certainly not as a villain. It's as much as any Philly sports figure can ask for.

20

RANDALL CUNNINGHAM

The Ultimate Something or Other

Greatness: ★★★½
Toughness: ★½
Eccentricity: ★★★★
Legacy: ★★★

THE RANDALL CUNNINGHAM story is a tragedy and a comedy, an absurdist epic, a romance about the doomed love triangle between a city, a player, and himself. It's an opera filled with overblown emotions: the tale of an orphan prince, a prodigious man-child, a character you simultaneously want to hug and strangle, assuming you get a grip on him. It is filled with events you would never believe if you didn't witness them. It's a story that inspires awe, laughter, pity, anger, frustration, and remorse. But at least it inspires.

Highlight montages don't do Cunningham justice. You can watch him leap over defenders for a touchdown, see him duck beneath Bruce Smith in the end zone and throw deep to Fred Barnett, enjoy all of the spin moves and ball fakes, the escape-artist routine from the collapsing pocket and the runs to daylight. You get the image of the breathtaking athlete, but you lose the substance or, rather, the understanding of how little substance there was. The highlight reels make you think that Cunningham's great plays were rare events, a dozen signature dazzlers cherry-picked from 10 years of game film.

They weren't. Cunningham's highlights were business-as-usual Sunday afternoon romps. Cunningham generated a half-dozen stop-your-heart highlights every week, whether they were scrambles, passes, or punts that rolled forever along the Meadowlands turf. The Buddy Ryan Eagles were a team of highlights that were occasionally organized into victories. Cunningham's Plastic Man routine permeated the memories of those of us who watched him. For a few years after he left, it looked odd when a quarterback faced a rush and didn't duck, pirouette, and razzle-dazzle his way to either safety or an even worse predicament.

Adjectives fail to describe Cunningham. Merrill Reese called him "Rambling Randall" early in his career, and those of us who heard his first games on radio—his starting debut against the Rams wasn't televised—had to use our imaginations as Reese tried to catch up. Angelo Cataldi, then an *Inquirer* reporter, used every verb he could find in the thesaurus to describe a Cunningham touchdown in a 1985 preseason game. "He charged out of a collapsing pocket, dodged a rush by former Eagles defensive end Carl Hairston and danced down to the 2-yard-line, where he knifed between linebackers Chip Banks and Ernie Johnson and sprawled across the goal line."

That was Sunday in Philadelphia: charging, dodging, dancing, knifing, sprawling. Trying to understand Cunningham from a highlight reel is like trying to learn about Led Zeppelin from a three-song mix tape. You get a few impressions, but you barely scratch the surface.

. . .

FROM THE BEGINNING, Cunningham was a little odd.

In his rookie season, Paul Domowitch called him "an interesting blend of brashness, arrogance, chutzpah and self-confidence. He's a cross between Joe Cool, Joe Namath and Don Cornelius." Cunningham was brash, cocky, brimming with nascent hip-hop sensibility. His backstory undercut the arrogance: both of his parents died when he was a freshman in college, but he overcame the shock to become an all-conference quarterback and punter at UNLV. The boasts and designer clothes were a defense mechanism; a closer look revealed a frightened child, wary of riches and fame.

Years later, that child was still there, cowering beneath the façade. Cunningham existed on a planet all his own. "Being confused has a lot to do with my personality," he said in Mark Bowden's *Bringing the Heat*. "Randall's soft voice emerges from the labyrinth of his psyche in constant lamentation," Bowden added. When things were going well, Cunningham cuddled with Whitney Houston and appeared on the Arsenio Hall show wearing outfits of his own design. When things went poorly, he retreated into his faith: not the grown-up religion of a man drawing strength to face his problems, but the fairy-tale faith of a little boy whose prayers are wishes. He talked about his talent after wins, his rewards in heaven after losses.

In 1990, Cunningham tore his ACL in the first game of the season. "I've always had faith that God would protect me," he later told *Sport* magazine. "But last year, I had my doubts. I remember thinking that He only blesses you for so long." The gentle-soul Cunningham had a crisis of faith; the media-idol Cunningham designed and wore hats with the slogan "I'll be back, scramblin'." Both Cunninghams missed the point: ACL injuries are part of life, not challenges from on high, and Eagles fans, weary of scrambling highlights, craved some good old victories instead.

. . .

FANS STRUGGLED to keep up with all of this. Cunningham is often called the first ESPN creation. His rise coincided with the network's growth and the development of the highlight-driven sports culture, where slam dunks killed set shots and leaping touchdowns made pocket passing look quaint and obsolete. He was also a talk-radio creation. WIP started toying with its sports-talk format in 1986, and by 1990 the station was all sports, with Cataldi co-anchoring the morning drive. Cunningham's daffy quotes, star-studded social life, and utter self-absorption, mixed with his talent, made him a talk-radio gold mine. So while one new media form showcased him as football's Michael Jordan, another lambasted him as the sport's Howard Hughes. And both had valid points to make.

Coverage of Cunningham changed over the years. Our perception of him changed. He didn't. He essentially had six rookie seasons. He was comically raw in 1985. "He took a very sophisticated position and narrowed it down to one receiver. If the receiver is covered, he just takes off and runs," John Spagnola joked after one of Cunningham's spellbinding scared-squirrel performances. Buddy Ryan famously told Cunningham not to worry about the finer points of passing, and when quarterback coach Doug Scovil passed away, Cunningham took Ryan's advice to heart.

So by the 1990 playoffs, the Rams could execute an all-zone game plan, order their pass rushers to contain instead of attack, and baffle Cunningham into a 24–7 loss. The next postseason, the Redskins could blitz the house, shake off a few scrambles, and hold the Eagles to six points and just one completion (a 9-yarder) to a wide receiver. By that point, Ryan realized that his starting quarterback had become Peter Pan. He briefly benched Cunningham for Jim McMahon, but the move proved to be an embarrassment to everyone and a bruise to one of the world's most fragile egos. "It was kind of insulting when I thought about it," Cunningham said after the game.

When Cunningham got hurt in 1991, the three forces that propelled his life were headed for a collision. The public Cunningham (as seen on television) was confident, the private one (as talked about on radio) was more oblivious than ever, and the mortal Cunningham was slowing down physically more rapidly than he was growing up emotionally.

Rich Kotite propped Cunningham up behind a power-running offense and made him look like a real quarterback for a season in 1992. But Cunningham broke his leg in 1993, and when he returned in 1994, he went from deluded to delusional. He criticized Kotite's offense, criticized teammates, blamed the media for blowing his issues out of proportion. An anonymous teammate said he had become "a cancer on this team" who wants to "bring us down with him." Kotite benched Cunningham in favor of Bubby Brister for the final two games of the 1994 season, even though the Eagles were still mathematically alive for the playoffs. Cunningham cleared out his locker and campaigned to join Ryan in Arizona. He agreed to tell his side of the story in a carefully controlled television interview, but only if his wife could sit beside him on a sofa "like President Clinton and Hillary on '60 Minutes.'"

But even that wasn't the end of the story. Kotite left, Ray Rhodes and Jon Gruden arrived, and Cunningham retained his starting job, stumbling through four games while trying to run a West Coast offense that must have been differential calculus for him. Rodney Peete replaced him and took the Eagles to the playoffs. When Peete was hurt against the Cowboys, Cunningham entered the game unprepared, completing just 11 of 26 passes as the Cowboys rolled. Cunningham's son was born during the week before the game, so Cunningham didn't bother studying the game plan. He tried to scramble, improvise, dodge, dance, and knife, but he was 32 years old, banged up, and rusty; older but still not really grown up. He couldn't pretend to be the Ultimate Weapon anymore. It was heartbreaking to watch him try.

. . .

WHEN CUNNINGHAM WAS inducted into the Eagles Hall of Fame, he carried his youngest son, Christian, onto the field with him. A year later, Christian died in a hot tub accident.

After he left Philly, Cunningham became an announcer, a stone mason, a Pro Bowl quarterback and Comeback Player of the Year winner, and eventually a minister, albeit of a church that conducts baptisms in Jacuzzis. He became a fond, faded memory. With the loss of his son, he became a tragic figure, though in some ways he always was one. He was a simple man in a complex situation. He courted the limelight instinctively, perhaps thinking that was what he really wanted, but he was better suited to the life of a quiet family man. In retirement, he finally got the warm, spiritual life he always deserved, and it's sad to know a large part of that was taken away from him.

That's where the saga ends, though there may still be another chapter. Younger fans sometimes advocate Cunningham for the Pro Football Hall of Fame; he has already become a stat line and a highlight reel for many people too young to remember his baseball caps, gold-tipped shoelaces, and playoff meltdowns. If voters have a weak moment, Cunningham could wind up on the podium someday, delivering a speech that will no doubt have us scratching our heads for weeks.

Cunningham isn't really a Hall of Famer. But he's a player you will likely remember long after most of the guys in this book are forgotten. You will tell your grandchildren about the touchdown pass to Jimmie Giles and the Fog Bowl, and they won't believe you until you show them the highlights. And even then they'll never know what the Cunningham experience was really like, because those of us who lived through it are still trying to figure it out.

Intermission
Coaches and Executives

PHILLY FANS EXPECT the same attributes from their coaches, managers, and team presidents and owners as they demand from their players: excellence mixed with lots of toughness and a dollop of unpredictable craziness. Unfortunately, the offbeat intensity that makes some players great also makes them poor management material. Toughness gets you only so far when you are drawing up plays or writing lineup cards, and eccentricity wears thin when you are trying to lead groups of disparate millionaires through a 162-game summer or an 80-game winter.

Guys Who Screamed

Larry Bowa almost cracked the Philly Fan's Code as a player. As a manager, he spent four years raining down angry Chihuahua rants on a Phillies team trapped in second place. Amazingly, fans never blamed Bowa; one by one, Scott Rolen, Pat Burrell, and Bobby Abreu were singled out as the "soft" element that had to be eradicated so the team could emulate their manager's competitive fire. Somehow, Bowa's tantrums and mood swings failed to make anyone a better hitter, and after Charlie Manuel took over, we heard a lot of quotes about how nice it was to go 0-for-4 in a game and know you would still be treated like a professional the next day instead of getting the silent treatment. Many fans still think Bowa was dealt a bad hand of stiffs. It's more likely that Charlie Manuel would have gotten the Phillies to the playoffs by 2004.

Ray Rhodes was another tough guy fans loved for a few years, but his fire-and-brimstone speeches grew stale pretty quickly, and it was obvious they were all he had. Mike Keenan took the Flyers to two Stanley Cup Finals, but players hated him so much they would give him Nazi salutes behind his back. To keep his job, Keenan had to either win a Cup or prove he could play nice with someone in the organization, whether above or below him. He did neither. Keenan's shtick was more effective than Bowa's because hockey is not baseball: riling up a hockey player will make him check an opponent through the Plexiglas, while riling up a baseball player just makes him swing through the slider.

It's hard to give much credit for the Sixers' 1982–1983 success to Billy Cunningham's tough-guy demeanor because Julius Erving and Moses Malone probably didn't need anyone screaming at them to play hard. Like Bowa, Cunningham nearly cracked the Philly Fan's Code as a player. Unlike Bowa, Cunningham usually backed up his on-court

rants with off-court man-to-man honesty. Fans could also relate to Cunningham's Howling Man routine at courtside. Who among us wouldn't scream "Andrewwwww," when Andrew Toney ignored a play call, waved off Erving and Malone, and decided to drive the basket by himself?

Billy Cunningham
(Courtesy of Temple University Libraries, Urban Archives, Philadelphia, PA)

The ultimate tough-guy-turned-executive in Philadelphia history is Bob Clarke, and he's a fine example of how a player's sustaining fire can be a manager's Achilles heel. Sam Donnellon summed up the problem when writing about the fates of Scott Rolen and Eric Lindros in 2001. "Saying 'Lindros' three times to Clarke is like saying 'Beetlejuice.' He is immediately transformed from a serene, thoughtful, even-keeled general manager to a guy with blood flowing from his mouth and a stick in his hand. At this point, it is 1976 again, and Lindros is a Russian."

Donnellon was comparing Clarke to Dallas Green, who led the Phillies to the 1980 World Series and earned carte blanche to go on radio shows and criticize players like Rolen for their lack of passion-desire-competitiveness for all eternity. Green, "a screamer and a yeller and a cusser" by his own opinion, screamed and cussed his way out of favor in Chicago and New York, but the Phillies kept him around as a "consultant" at the start of the 2000s, figuring that Bowa didn't provide enough dysfunction. Clarke's greatness and unassailable work ethic as a player gave him a great deal of benefit of the doubt when he was publicly clashing with Lindros, Keenan, or someone else: while he did some counterproductive things as an executive, he never criticized a player as a form of self-promotion or self-aggrandizement. The same can't be said for Green, who still pops up in the media and sounds like he's saying things just so people will pay attention to him. Clarke and Green gave us great memories, but their inability to relate to anyone who didn't spit nails, and their willingness to criticize those players

Dallas Green
(Courtesy of Temple University Libraries, Urban Archives, Philadelphia, PA)

publicly and personally, made it too easy for us to turn on some of our best players of the 1990s and 2000s.

Guys Who Mumbled

Just as Philly fans love a coach who froths at the mouth, many of us are suspicious of a coach who comes across as laid-back, measured, or (heaven forbid) corporate. Ironically, the city's most successful coaches have been mild-mannered, almost introverted personalities, at least when dealing with the public.

Fred Shero was called "the Fog" because he was often lost in thought and had a habit of quietly disappearing from social gatherings and press conferences. Shero wrote Dag Hammarskjöld quotes on the locker-room board—everyone knows "Win today, and we walk together forever" from the first Stanley Cup Finals—but he scrawled Hammarskjold's "Only he deserves power who every day justifies it," during the 1975 playoffs to get the team over a Game 7 hump. Imagine Bowa or Rhodes saying, thinking, or comprehending the phrase "only he deserves power who every day justifies it" and you get a sense of the chasm between this group of coaches and the last.

Shero's eccentricities evoked skepticism right up until the Flyers won their first Cup, and his departure was typical of his "vanishing act" reputation: he resigned in 1978, saying that he didn't want to coach anymore, then took over the Rangers a few weeks later. When the Rangers came to the Spectrum for an exhibition in 1978, fans brought signs that read "Rangers Beware: He Lies," and "Win Today and Renegotiate Forever." Shero's coaching had much more to do with the Flyers' success than Cunningham's did for the Sixers or Green's for the Phillies: he was a tactician who channeled the team's fisticuffs into a strategic advantage. But he has nearly been erased from the Philadelphia sports story line, because Broad Street Bullies and Swedish philosophers just don't mix.

Charlie Manuel, like Shero, is a hard man to read, in part because his speech is nearly incoherent. Manuel came across like a teddy bear after years of Bowa the saber-toothed porcupine, and there was a loud contingent of Phillies fans who were convinced Manuel would coddle the Pat Burrells of the world into last place. Instead, he won the loyalty of players, instilled the kind of calm demeanor a team needs to survive 162 ups and downs, and got a team of All Stars to play like a team of All Stars. If you think Manuel had little to do with the Phillies success (it doesn't take a genius to write Rollins-Utley-Howard on a lineup card to win games), consider how Bowa or Green would have handled Jimmy Rollins's mini-mutiny in 2008. Manuel's drawl hides a lot of personnel management savvy and, yes, a desire to win as intense as Bowa's, Cunningham's, and Clarke's. After four division crowns, fans have figured that out.

Andy Reid and Larry Brown never won championships in Philly, but both led their teams on successful runs while infuriating fans with their unwillingness to scream, yell, and cuss when things went wrong. Brown came across as downright dour, a sourpuss who sometimes looked like he hated his job, which was understandable when his job was figuring out a way to get Allen Iverson to show up for practice. Brown was generally respected by fans because (a) we knew putting up with Iverson wasn't easy, (b) he made the Sixers winners by getting them to play team-oriented and defense-oriented basketball around Iverson, which was a relief after a decade of watching guys like Shawn Bradley and Derrick Coleman, and (c) someone else in the Sixers front office hogged much of the limelight, allowing Brown to work in relative peace.

Reid grunted and mumbled through interviews, making Eagles press conferences the least informative part of the sports week, and his corporate "no comment" comments made him an easy target for nonstop second-guessing. The warm-hearted yet firm persona he presented to players—and the effect it had on their development—was rarely seen and appreciated by casual fans. At this writing, Eagles fans are convinced that Michael Vick miraculously changed from an animal abusing pot smuggler who never read a playbook into a smart quarterback and a well-adjusted citizen all by himself, never guessing that the spiritual, paternal, detail-oriented coach might be having some effect on the quarterback. Instead, we complain about time-outs before halftime.

Guys Who Took It Hard

Two of our most respected coaches gave so much of themselves to the team that it was detrimental to their health. Gene Mauch was as intense as Cunningham and as detail-oriented as Reid. He was smart

Gene Mauch

(Courtesy of Temple University Libraries, Urban Archives, Philadelphia, PA)

enough to invent strategies like the double-switch, tough enough to slug Mets catcher Jerry Grote for venturing into the dugout after a foul ball, and patient enough to keep Dick Allen from diving head first off the deep end. But he overworked himself and his players, and long after his career was over he admitted to waking up at night and reliving heartbreaking games from 1964 (and 1986, when his Angels lost the League Championship Series on a ninth-inning home run).

Like Mauch, Dick Vermeil asked for everything from his players and even more from himself. Mauch earned criticism for running Jim Bunning and Chris Short to the mound on two days' rest (a bad decision, to be sure). In fairness, Vermeil should be taken to task for getting the Eagles so pumped up to beat the Cowboys that they had nothing left for the Raiders in Super Bowl XV. Vermeil's almost neurotic passion was inspirational to fans, but it was ultimately as detrimental to his team as Mauch's flop-sweat micromanagement. Both coaches were accomplished leaders and admirable men, but Manuel would have reached the playoffs in 1964, and Reid would have won Super Bowl XV.

Guys Who Signed Checks

Leonard Tose and Harold Katz were sports owners of a bygone era: Tose, the tipsy small-time businessman operating on a shoestring; Katz the diet-plan millionaire who tried to be a tin-helmet George Steinbrenner. Tose gambled away fortunes, tried to move the Eagles to

Dick Vermeil

(Courtesy of Temple
University Libraries, Urban
Archives, Philadelphia, PA)

Phoenix, and died penniless, but he's fondly remembered because he was kind to players, generous to a fault, and bubbly when dealing with the public. Katz assembled a dream team, then tried our civic patience as he slowly pulled it apart, picking fights with one outgoing legend after another while carping constantly about money.

Like any fans, we want our owners to spend money, and it helps if it looks like they are enjoying it. That's what made Tose fun and Katz grating: owners should give waitresses $100 tips and not grouse about having to actually pay for the services of Moses Malone. Ed Snider has become so rich and powerful that criticizing him is like criticizing Big Government or the weather, so most of us don't bother. Phillies owners and execs, from the Carpenter family through Bill Giles to Dave Montgomery, are branded as cheap no matter what they do, though to their credit they rarely muddle into individual player controversies. Jeffrey Lurie and Joe Banner make tidy scapegoats for Eagles failures because they can so easily be characterized as a Hollywood dilettante and his bean-counting assistant. Grudgingly, many fans have accepted that their approach to salary management has worked, especially since most fans can remember how much worse the alternatives were.

Norman Braman was vacationing in France and therefore unavailable to appear in this chapter.

Guys Who Defy Categorization

During an interview for a "Top 10" program on NFL Network, I compared Buddy Ryan (who arrived in Philly when I was 16) to the wild-and-crazy uncle you called when you needed someone to buy beer. You thought he was cool at the time, but years later you realized that he was irresponsible and a little creepy.

A huge percentage of fans still think Ryan was cool, because hazy nostalgia softens or rearranges the most frustrating moments from Ryan's tenure (the House of Pain Game, for example, occurred the year after Ryan was fired but is still sometimes lumped among his successes). Ryan re-created the brutality and controversy of the Broad Street Bullies without worrying about details like winning a play-off game. He's sometimes hailed as a master motivator and a player's coach, but he treated Ron Jaworski and other offensive players badly at the start of his tenure, then fostered an adversarial relationship between the offense and defense that was detrimental to Randall Cunningham's fragile psyche. He sided with the Players Union in the 1987 players' strike, which was laudable at a time when men like Mike Ditka and Tom Landry were willing to destroy careers in the name of union busting. But he wasn't a very good coach, and his talents as a personnel evaluator are overrated: Cunningham and Reggie White were already here when Ryan came to town. No individual in Philly sports history got so free a pass for doing so little.

But while Ryan left his mark, no non-player stomped all over Philly sports history as thoroughly as Pat Croce. Croce rose from Flyers fitness trainer to Sixers team president and co-owner through a series of events so unlikely that Croce needed to write a half-dozen motivational books to sort it all out. Croce found a way to become a central figure in both the Lindros and Iverson sagas, and always hung around the edges of smaller controversies. Croce's rah-rah press appearances made him popular, and he reveled in his role as the face of the Iverson Sixers. Some people may have even believed that he was doing something for the team besides cheerleading and using the team's success to plug his self-help books.

Croce forgot about Philly sports when the Sixers declined; he's now a Jimmy Buffett wannabe who writes about pirates. We've started to forget about Croce too, but it took about 20 years for us to realize how little substance there was to his shtick. That crazy tough-guy routine really does work.

21

BILL BARBER

The Forever Flyer

Greatness: ★★★★
Toughness: ★★★½
Eccentricity: ★
Legacy: ★★★½

BILL BARBER WAS angry at the Flyers and thinking about quitting hockey. The Flyers had demoted their rookie forward to Richmond in October 1972 so he could improve his checking. Barber didn't think he deserved the demotion. Fuming, he hopped in his car and drove south, earning a speeding ticket for doing 90 in a 70 mile per hour zone. When he reached his Richmond hotel, someone smashed into his parked car in the parking lot.

He thought briefly about returning home to Callander, Ontario. Instead, he focused on his game. He had nine goals and five assists in 11 minor league games. He returned to Philadelphia a better checker and a mentally tougher player. "Going to Richmond did me a world of good, even though I didn't think I needed it at the time," Barber said later that year. "I just had to make up my mind not to carry a grudge and work to come back and show I belonged."

Barber showed he belonged, first as a runner-up Rookie of the Year, then as a member of two Stanley Cup teams, then as the team's all-time leading scorer, and finally as a Hall of Famer.

· · ·

FANS YOUNGER THAN 40 tend to merge the Broad Street Bullies into one entity, a rampaging horde of interchangeable Visigoths who didn't win two Stanley Cups so much as plunder them. Local lore en-

Bill Barber
(Courtesy of Temple University Libraries,
Urban Archives, Philadelphia, PA)

courages this: writers played up the team's feistiness to comical proportions, and older fans seem to revel more in the fights and penalty minutes than in the goals and victories (which is why Dave Schultz's chapter came earlier in this book). For many of us, the 1973–1975 Flyers exist as a childhood memory, a blurry DVD transfer, a laugh-out-loud Simpsons reference, and folklore. Sure, there were Bobby Clarke and Bernie Parent, but after that everyone was a Hammer or a Cowboy, brutish and bloody-knuckled.

Of course there were goons, Schultz and Andre Dupont and Ed Van Impe. But there was also Reggie Leach, the precision sniper waiting on the wing. And there was Rick MacLeish, the clutch-shooting puck-handler teammates called "Cutie." In our regional rush to lionize their thuggery, we forget that those Flyers had skaters, scorers, finesse players, and cuties.

And then there was Barber. He was the technician, the two-way player, the penalty killer. "He skated up and down the ice with the reliability of a metronome, and by dedicating his NHL career to blending in, he stood out," Jay Greenberg once wrote. "He had the soul of a grinder, but the talent of an artist." He was also a dive specialist who could draw penalties on a team known for causing them.

Barber's versatility gave the Flyers a unique chemistry. "Reggie had the cannon of a shot," Barber said in *The Good, the Bad and the Ugly.* "I complemented in the sense of playing more detailed in all three zones and making sure I was accountable defensively." Factor in Clarke's tenacity and passing, and the Flyers were able to do so much more than bully opponents.

For 12 years, Barber stood out by blending in, finding a dozen different ways to contribute: scoring 50 goals one season, leading the league in short-handed goals the next, suiting up for 80 games per year like clockwork. After retirement, he found a new way to bring notice to the unnoticed: he drew our attention to a minor league, then gave us the closest thing to a championship parade that we'd had for 20 years.

.   .   .

FOR A FEW YEARS, minor league hockey mattered in Philadelphia.

It was the mid-1990s, and Philly sports fans were in their usual state: championship-starved and miserable. The Phantoms arrived on Broad Street with low ticket prices, a bruising, throwback playing style, and a chance to win a cup, even if it wasn't a Stanley Cup. They also had legitimacy, thanks to Barber.

Barber became a Flyers lifer after retirement. He was an assistant coach, then a scout who logged 1,200 to 1,400 miles per week on the road. He then became a minor league head coach, first with the Hershey Bears, then with the Phantoms when the Flyers purchased them. There were rumors of a feud with Clarke, rumors that kept Barber away from the Flyers' head coaching job. When Clarke demoted Wayne Cashman as Flyers coach, he promoted Roger Neilsen over Barber. Barber, hoping for a chance to coach at the NHL level, hid his feelings. "When you're dealing with what your assignment is, you can't let your feelings go to the guys you're dealing with. I could not allow my guys to see, feelingswise, me express disappointment," he said. He denied any rift with Clarke, then went about the business of developing players and trying to win the Calder Cup.

The Phantoms won games. They sold out the Spectrum. Phantoms fans even got the "Philly fan" treatment, with Canadian small-city reporters warning their fans about those hooligans in the stands. (One writer called Phantoms fans "a different breed" and said he was "slack jawed" by our behavior.) Barber coached the Phantoms to a Calder Cup in 1995, led by Mike Richards, who would later take the Flyers to the Stanley Cup Finals. A sellout crowd watched the series clincher.

Barber had brought the city one more championship. It wasn't much, but when you are dying of thirst, you drink out of any cup you can get.

. . .

TWELVE SEASONS is a long time in hockey and an eternity in Philadelphia. Barber is linked with many of the greatest moments in Flyers history. There were the two Cups, of course. He recorded 13 points in the playoffs for the 1975–1976 team that fell just short. He played a huge part in the team's 35-game unbeaten streak in the 1979-80 season. When referees blew the Leon Stickle call in Game 6 of the 1980 Conference Finals, Barber was one of the players to speak out. "My God, the play was two feet offside," he said after the game. When the Flyers defeated the Russian National Team in 1976, Barber, rarely a brawler, delivered two hard checks before Ed Van Impe delivered the blow that sent the Soviets to the locker room. And in the early 1980s, with the Broad Street Bullies fading into legend, Barber kept skating, a veteran on a team populated by Pelle Lindbergh, Tim Kerr, Mark Howe, and Brian Propp, a mentor for a second generation of hockey stars.

He's also linked with one of the saddest moments in Flyers history. Barber finally got his chance to become the Flyers head coach midway through the 2000–2001 season. Soon after earning the job, his wife was diagnosed with lung cancer. Barber coached through her illness, even through her death in December 2001, taking the Flyers to a second-place finish in 2000-2001 and a first-place finish in 2001–2002. But the team fell apart in the playoffs both years, and the young players turned on Barber, whose mind and heart certainly were not fully in the game at that point. After nearly 30 years with the team, after working through heartbreak and personal tragedy, Barber was fired.

That 2001 players revolt is a small speck on a marvelous legacy. Barber is beloved because he won, because he played hard, because he subsumed his ego to the team. He is also loved because he chose Philadelphia as his city, because he did everything he was asked and more, and because he dedicated himself to Philadelphia hockey, even when the front office took him for granted.

It was an amazing run for a guy who couldn't wait to get out of town in 1972.

22

DARRYL DAWKINS

The Man from Lovetron

Greatness: ★ ★ ½
Toughness: ★ ★ ★ ½
Eccentricity: ★ ★ ★ ★ ★
Legacy: ★

DARRYL DAWKINS wasn't really an alien from the planet Lovetron. He was, however, a time traveler, a man years ahead of his time.

Dawkins shaved his head (briefly, in the late '70s) at a time when no one but Curly Neal thought bald was beautiful. He wore an earring when only pirates and Mr. Clean wore them. A decade before Michael Jordan, a generation before King James, Dawkins understood that he was more a brand name than a player. "I'm an entertainer," says Dawkins. "I got a wild imagination. I do whatever I think is going to make me known, to make me marketable so that I can do commercials, appearances, whatever. If you're interesting, people come to you."

So Dawkins gave us Planet Lovetron, later renamed Chocolate Paradise, the home world of Chocolate Thunder and all things funky. He gave us named dunks: the Rim-Wrecker, the In-Your-Face Disgrace, the Spine-Chiller Supreme. He gave quotes so outlandish that they snapped you to attention. He was an unhinged mix of George Clinton and Muhammad Ali.

If only he was a better basketball player.

. . .

TAKE AWAY THE QUOTES and shattered backboards, and Dawkins was just another frustrating Philly disappointment, another example of talent without discipline, an athlete unable to cope with nearly unachievable expectations. He signed a million-dollar contract with the Sixers straight out of high school, then sat the bench for two years as the team tried to win with Julius Erving and a bunch of ball hogs. The bench time bothered Dawkins. "When I walked into the league, they wanted me to be Wilt Chamberlain right away—without one minute of college ball," he told the *Daily News*.

When he reached the starting lineup, Dawkins was often breathtaking, often infuriating. He had the size to overpower most opposing centers, and his range as a shooter made him a multidimensional offensive threat. But he was soft as a rebounder and sloppy as a defender. He sometimes got into early foul trouble and spent games shuttling back and forth from the bench. Newspaper accounts of his games would list his dunks—six one night, seven the next—but they also noted that forwards Caldwell Jones and Bobby Jones easily outrebounded Dawkins. Coach Billy Cunningham and owner Harold Katz met with Dawkins regularly to get him focused on defense and aggressive on the boards. It usually worked for a game or two, then Dawkins would lapse into old habits, sleepwalking around the court in between rim-wreckers and spine-chillers.

But oh, the dunks! The first backboard smasher came against the Kansas City Kings; Dawkins made headlines, but tellingly, the Sixers lost the game. Dawkins called it "The Chocolate-Thunder-Flying, Robinzine-Crying, Teeth-Shaking, Glass-Breaking, Rump-Roasting, Bun-Toasting, Wham-Bam, Glass-Breaker-I-Am-Jam." The second dunk came at the Spectrum in a Sixers victory, just three weeks later. "It was the power of the Chocolate Thunder," he said. "I could feel it surging through my body, fighting to get out. I had no control over it." Spectrum fans gave a standing ovation. The league summoned Dawkins. Glass-shattering dunks were banned.

And then there were the quotes. In the Sixers locker room, little-used subs Bernard Toone and Jim Spanarkel dressed on either side of Dawkins; that way, there were fewer log jams as reporters pressed Dawkins for quotes. "I have to dress in the shower," Spanarkel once joked about the crowds. When not pioneering hip-hop and presaging slam poetry to describe his jams, Dawkins could be more contemplative. He coined an aphorism worthy of Yogi Berra: "When it's all been said and done, there's nothing left to say or do."

It was all an act, part defense mechanism, part calculated effort to get rich. He openly mused that the backboard incidents would attract crowds, and "the more people I bring out, the more money I might get." He believed that flamboyance would get him farther than discipline. If he had come along a decade or two later, he might have been right. The Time Traveler was once again a decade or so too early.

. . .

A *SPORTS ILLUSTRATED* column once predicted that Dawkins's destructive dunks would "follow him for the rest of his career, marking him as indelibly as the midget pinch hitter did Bill Veeck."

They followed him far longer. Dawkins became more disciplined after he left the Sixers. He never became a great defender, but he played five competent, mostly distraction-free seasons for the Nets. After retirement, Dawkins tried to enter coaching, but no one wants a coach from Planet Lovetron. He spent 15 years in the basketball hinterlands, playing briefly for the Globetrotters, coaching low-level teams in cities from Allentown to Winnipeg. The man who still ranks sixth on the all-time NBA shooting percentage list (dunks, after all, are high-percentage shots) was last seen coaching a community college team in Lehigh, hoping to work his way all the way back to the NBA by a route almost interplanetary in length and improbability. He knew his past antics hurt his current chances. "People always remember me as 'Chocolate Thunder,' the entertainer," Dawkins said. "No one forced that on me. I brought that on myself."

Philly fans loved the dunks and the laughs, but shtick goes only so far when you can't be bothered to box out. There were few complaints when the Sixers traded Dawkins, and even those voices went silent a few weeks later when the team signed Moses Malone. Dawkins turned down a chance at greatness to be a clown prince, a flashy, one-man spectacle. He's a minor character in Philly sports history, but he left a lasting, regrettable legacy in the NBA. The league is so full of one-dimensional dunk artists that you don't notice them anymore; you just expect that 20 points per night and nod-and-wink defense earns a league-maximum contract and a sneaker deal. At least Dawkins was funny and his dunks fascinating. He worked at the wrong thing, but at least he worked on something, unlike too many of his acolytes, who just make themselves marketable so they can do commercials, appearances, whatever.

23

PETE ROSE

He Taught Us to Win, and Laid Off the Action

Greatness: ★★★½
Toughness: ★★★½
Eccentricity: ★★★
Legacy: ★★

SOMETIME BETWEEN EPITOMIZING all that was good about sports in America and epitomizing everything that was evil about sports in America, Pete Rose played five noncontroversial seasons for the Phillies, helping the team win one World Series and reach another.

Rose was already a legend when he arrived, an MVP, two-time champion, and 12-time All Star fresh off his 3,000th hit. He was as legendary for the way he played as for his production: he was Charlie Hustle (a derogatory nickname coined by Whitey Ford, which Rose embraced), the guy who sprinted to first base after every walk. Rose was spikes flying into the second baseman on a double play, collisions at the plate in All-Star Games, gracious interviews with reporters, and tireless autograph sessions with fans. He was a team-first pepper pot who also happened to be able to bang out 200 hits per year, the role model for how baseball should be played.

Baseball fans love "intangibles," and they'll tell you never to underestimate hustle, teamwork, leadership, and moxie, not realizing how grossly overestimated those virtues are. Hitting behind the runner and legging out grounders is great, but batting .330 is far, far better, though the traditional baseball school of romanticized wisdom loses sight of such obvious facts. The Phillies of the 1970s were short on intangibles. They were a talented but surly team that always fell short of the pennant. "He is more than just a player, he is an attitude," Ray

Didinger wrote when the Phillies were wooing Rose. The common logic was that the Phillies needed someone who "knew how to win." Rose, fresh from The Big Red Machine that won the 1975 and 1976 World Series, fit the job description.

But those Phillies needed tangibles, too. Their lineup was long on sluggers and free swingers, short on on-base guys. Bake McBride and Larry Bowa batted first and second for the 1978 team; their batting averages weren't bad, but their on-base percentages (.315 and .319) led to a lot of bases-empty home runs (which were blamed on Mike Schmidt's inability to drive in nonexistent runners). Their regular first baseman was power hitter Richie Hebner, "The Hacker." The Phillies had too many hackers; they needed someone on base when Schmidt and Greg Luzinski started hacking.

The skeptics and the statisticians claimed that the Phillies needed Rose the Player, but the old diamond romantics claimed they needed Rose the Attitude, who always got better press. The team acquired both in a package deal after a month of negotiations, for a four-year $3.2 million contract in December 1978.

Rose batted .331 for the 1979 Phillies, but the team took a step backward. He started the 1980 season slowly, batting .203 as of May 6. At age 39, every slump looks like a sign of the end. "Like a landmark skyscraper, he has been standing tall for years, but has age started to erode the base?" Bill Lyon asked in the *Inquirer* that May. The Rose experiment appeared doomed: the Player was nearly finished, and the Attitude could carry only a .203 average so far.

Rose was unconcerned. He did everything he could to get on base, including things no one else would think of, like drawing catcher's interference calls on four teams during the season. The slump ended. He batted .307 in July, .318 in August. The Phillies climbed slowly into first place. Rose had eight hits in the League Championship Series. In Game 5, he drew a bases-loaded walk in the eighth inning to chase Nolan Ryan and ignite a five-run, game-winning rally.

And of course, he provided one of the signature highlights of the World Series, shadowing Bob Boone as the catcher chased a Frank White foul pop, watching as the ball hopped from Boone's mitt, and scooping it before it could fall into the dugout. Phillies playoff games of the 1970s were filled with improbable blunders, unlikely errors, and bad calls. A Boone error in Game 6, with runners on base and the top of the Royals lineup due up, was par for that awful course. Rose the Player wasn't great in 1980—he was a singles hitter with a mediocre batting average, a banjo first baseman who made a lot of overaggressive outs on the base paths—but Rose the Attitude, with his hustle and attention to the smallest elements of the game, changed Phillies history.

Rose rebounded with a fine season in 1981 and a passable one in 1982. The Phillies returned to the World Series in 1983, but by then Rose was a .245 hitter with no power at all. The Phillies released him in October 1983. *Inquirer* editor Edwin Guthman thanked Rose for his contribution to the city, writing that Rose "demolished the Phillies' torturous reputation of faltering in the clutch. . . . Gone is the certainty that Philadelphia teams are destined to blow the big games."

. . .

ROSE, OF COURSE, later got too involved with bookies and lowlifes, became a gambling addict, probably bet on baseball games while he was a manager, possibly on his own team. The Lords of Baseball have only two modes for assigning punishment—arbitrary and vindictive—so they banned Rose for life, stopping just short of blaming him for the death of commissioner Bart Giamatti.

Rose has now spent a generation in exile, the embarrassing uncle whose name is never brought up at Thanksgiving dinner, an easy target for every moralizing columnist climbing onto his sanctity-of-the-game soapbox. Most young fans have only a vague idea of what Rose did wrong, and they would be shocked that baseball's unforgivable pariah reigned as the embodiment of sportsmanship and competitiveness for over 20 years.

Luckily for us, the story of Rose's rise and fall isn't a Philadelphia story. We can satisfy ourselves with a meaty, noncontroversial bit in the middle: a player, an attitude, some hits, a catch, and the demolition of a tortuous reputation. Paul Owens once said that Rose would "show us how to win." The Phillies may have needed that, but the city of Philadelphia needed it more. Rose showed us all how it was done.

24

DICK ALLEN

The Origin of the Booed Species

Greatness: ★★★½
Toughness: ★★★
Eccentricity: ★★★★
Legacy: ★½

NTHROPOLOGIST JOSEPH CAMPBELL popularized the term "monomyth" to describe the similarities that exist among the myths and heroic epics of cultures all around the world. Every heroic epic starts with an ordinary hero, who meets a wizard/sage/Jedi Master, then travels to a mysterious realm/galaxy far away, where he must face awesome challenges for the greater good of humankind. The monomyth explains everything from Navajo legends to Greek mythology to *Star Wars*. It suggests that there's something innate in human nature that makes us relate to these universal themes.

Dick Allen personifies the Philly sports monomyth. He created the template that framed the careers of dozens of players who came after him, many of whom are in this book. The Allen monomyth can be broken into eight chapters:

1. The Sudden Arrival: The player has an amazing rookie year or early career, dazzling the fans with memorable moments. In Allen's case, those moments were tape-measure home runs delivered with a 42-ounce bat.
2. The Brief Honeymoon: For a few months or years, all is well, and media coverage is lauding. Here's what Larry Merchant wrote in the *Daily News* in the summer of 1964: "It is fairly obvious by now that the Phillies have something more substantial at

third base than noise, tape, a glover and a prayer. . . . They have Richie Allen. He is something special."

3. The Disappointment: The player's team comes up short in the playoffs or championship game. After that, the player is labeled a "non-winner." Allen sped through the first three stages in the 1964 season.

4. The Misunderstanding: The player has a public feud with a popular teammate, coach, or general manager. The player is usually in the right (or at least has a justifiable beef), but for varying reasons public opinion favors the other guy. Allen got into a fight with first baseman Frank Thomas, who liked to call black players "boy" and bend their fingers backward when shaking hands. Allen punched Thomas for picking on Johnnie Briggs during batting practice, and Thomas swung his bat at Allen in retaliation. Fans sided with Thomas.

5. The Unraveling: The player spends years enduring ceaseless criticism, boos, and, in Allen's case, showers of pennies and fruit from the stands. At the start of the unraveling, most of the criticism is unfounded and unfair, but by the end the player has often become what he was branded, because of either bitterness or a calculated effort to force a trade. By the late 1960s, Allen arrived at games with beer on his breath and made sure Gene Mauch smelled it.

6. The Final Departure: The player is finally traded, often in a blockbuster that causes the collapse of the Philly team while the player goes on to great things in a new city. Allen fell to his knees and kissed his glove on the final day of the 1969 season, knowing he would be traded. The Phillies went from losing 75 to 85 games per year in the late '60s to losing 90 to 95 games per year in the early '70s. A few stops later, Allen won an MVP award.

7. The Strange Return: The player comes back to Philly for a "bygones are bygones" period once he's nearly washed up. He has a few brief moments of glory, but the bad feelings from his previous tenure still linger. Allen played two seasons with the Phillies in the mid-1970s, but when he missed a line drive down the first base line during the League Championship Series (he was running in the opposite direction for a pick-off play, but never mind), the old criticism returned.

8. The Revision: The player retires for a decade, then fans and sportswriters rewrite his story to say that he was secretly loved by all but a few loudmouths. Allen was named to the Philadelphia Sports Hall of Fame in 2010. As an added perk, the sportswriters who insisted on calling him Richie for six years acquiesced to using his preferred name of "Dick."

Not every Philly star experiences all eight stages of the monomyth, and the handful that win championships can even steer clear of the whole cycle. As a class exercise, apply the myth to the following athletes: Ron Hextall, Allen Iverson, Scott Rolen, Eric Lindros, Randall Cunningham, Donovan McNabb. Even championship-winners like Moses Malone, Steve Carlton, and Ryan Howard fit many elements of the monomyth. It's a story that repeats itself, time and again. Worst of all, we have seen the tale's enemy, and he is us.

. . .

BASEBALL HISTORIAN Bill James once said that Dick Allen "did more to keep his teams from winning than anyone who ever played." He also called him the "second most controversial player in baseball history, behind Rogers Hornsby" and a talent equal to Willie Mays who "lost half of his career or more to immaturity and emotional instability."

James is usually right on the money, and it's true that Allen feuded and sulked, drank and played horses on game day, played bad defense, and disappeared or threatened retirement when things weren't going his way. So maybe he did keep his teams from winning. But no city did more to turn Allen into a malcontent than Philly did.

When you send a 21-year-old black kid to Little Rock, Arkansas, in 1963, when you ask him to integrate baseball in one of the most racially backward regions in America, then leave him with no support network as fans picket games and leave threatening notes on his windshield, you're tempting fate. Allen spent a season in a segregated city, living separate from his teammates and enduring racial slurs while sitting in the dugout. Many black players suffered the same fate, but by 1964, most could count on things getting better when they came north to play in the majors.

Dick Allen
(Courtesy of Temple
University Libraries,
Urban Archives,
Philadelphia, PA)

Allen came north and learned that things were just as bad. Fans booed Allen even before the 1964 collapse. They booed when he booted a ball, booed the official scorers if they called a close-call Allen bobble a single instead of an error. Arnold Hano of *Sport* magazine overheard coaches accusing "colored" players of being bad clutch players. "Maybe it meant nothing," he wrote of the boos and criticism of a player on his way to a Rookie of the Year award. "The time of its occurrences makes you suspect, however."

By the time of the Thomas incident, all was laid bare. The fans in Connie Mack Stadium were prepared to believe the worst—immediately—about a young black superstar, and none of the few who were in a position to correct them—team ownership, coaches, sportswriters—felt compelled to do any heavy lifting.

In Little Rock, the *Arkansas Democrat* refused to mention Allen's race before the 1963 season: the newspaper lost advertisers and subscribers when it backed desegregation and didn't want to risk another profit-killing controversy. Here in the enlightened North, *Delaware County Times* columnist Ed Gebhart wrote, "Frank Thomas shouldn't have hit Richie Allen in the shoulder with a baseball bat. He should have hit him in the head." Thomas told his story to the sympathetic media, called himself "a victim of circumstances," and painted "Richie" Allen as sensitive because he didn't like being compared to "Muhammad Cassius Clay." The Phillies didn't allow Allen to tell his side, and no one bothered digging, because Thomas's story was good enough. In some ways, Little Rock was better than Philadelphia: at least the newspapers there stayed silent. They didn't go out of their way to make matters worse.

Today, we can read accounts by authors such as Joe Queenan who consider Allen their favorite ballplayer. Obviously, the people who grow up to write books today aren't the same people who threw tomatoes and shouted racial slurs at the left fielder. Modern writers offer their hazy reflections on the 1964 Phillies, and while they usually recount the tensions on the team and in the nation, race is "out there," deep in the past, a sin of the father, somehow even tangential to the Allen story.

You can't have it both ways. You can't paint Allen as an underachiever without noting what he endured; you can't talk about the booing after the Thomas incident without acknowledging how many fans came to the park looking for an excuse to boo. That's why James's criticism of Allen was unfair. Allen was immature, unstable, and controversial because he had little choice. Maybe Jesus or Gandhi could have endured what Allen did without getting worn down. Under the circumstances, it's amazing that Allen managed to be a great hitter, year after year, despite an absolute lack of local support. Forget Willie Mays; it's a miracle he didn't turn into Mike Tyson.

. . .

THE CITY HAS COME a long way in terms of race relations, but we're still under the sway of the Allen monomyth, and it still does damage to players of all races, as well as fans. Allen is our Original Sin, proof that fans really can run a player out of town, tarnish an image, turn a decent apple rotten. Yet we keep shuttling players through those stages, repeating the same mistakes again and again. We keep turning our heroes into Dick Allen, then turning them away, then embracing them again when they are old and the damage is done.

There's something innate in Philadelphia fandom that makes us do it. We need to eradicate it, not just for the players but for ourselves.

25

BERNARD HOPKINS

The Other Fighter

Greatness: ★ ★ ★ ★
Toughness: ★ ★ ★ ½
Eccentricity: ★ ★ ★ ½
Legacy: ★

O SCAR DE LA HOYA was finished. The Golden Boy, boxing's savior, the only active fighter the average sports fan could name, couldn't pull himself off the mat. A left hook—the calling card of the Philly Fighter—slammed into his rib cage in the ninth round of a title bout in 2004, damaging his liver. He could barely breathe. De La Hoya was forced into retirement by the punch, but the purse from the bout yielded a $30-million parting gift. The Other Guy, the guy who won, earned only $10 million.

It must be noted that De La Hoya, despite a myriad of titles and international fame, was the challenger. The Other Guy was the champion: a holder of other, more prestigious titles with 19 defenses on his résumé. The Other Guy battled his way from the streets of Philadelphia to prison, to the center of controversy, and finally to the top of what was left of the boxing world, only to earn one-third as much money as the promotion-savvy superstar he knocked out.

Meet Bernard Hopkins, The Other Guy, from the other sport.

. . .

YOU WANT CHAMPIONSHIPS? Hopkins has them. He earned his first in 1995 and defended it for a decade, collecting others along the way. Philadelphia has never had a champion like Hopkins.

You want toughness? A childhood in the projects. Five years at Graterford Prison.

You want eccentricity? How about a man who earned $10 million per fight but told reporters that he kept two different wholesale club cards in his wallet? ("If he'd just mentioned the one, I could have done him a deal," promoter Bob Arum once said.) How about a guy who threw the Puerto Rican flag on the floor during press conferences . . . twice? How about a stereotypical ex-con bruiser who is really a cerebral ring tactician, one who breaks down tendencies, watches hundreds of hours of tape, and lives off defense and counterpunching? Hopkins is like Joe Frazier seasoned with sprinkles of Jack Benny, Cosmo Kramer, and Andy Reid.

You want Philly props? Hopkins was born in the Ramsey projects, fought at the Blue Horizon, the Spectrum, and in Atlantic City. In true Philly fashion, he was always overshadowed nationally by Roy Jones, Jr., and by De La Hoya, and had to box well into his 40s. He is still fighting, for money and for respect. "I'm tired!" he said after a 2008 victory at Boardwalk Hall. "I'm tired of proving myself."

Hopkins is everything we could want in a champion. All he needs is a sport. In Joe Frazier's chapter, I lamented the current state of boxing. Hopkins is a victim of the greed, corruption, and mismanagement that destroyed a great sport.

Look at the titles he has won: USBA, IFC, WBC, WBO, WBA, WTF. He became a "super champion" by beating Felix Trinidad (instigator of the flag tosses) to win a sampler platter of the titles just listed. Super champion? Why not Super Duper Double Deluxe Champion? "Champion" shouldn't need modifiers; if it does, then the achievement is diminished.

The alphabet soup of governing bodies leaves the casual fan mystified and suspicious. We wonder just how meaningful some of these belts were. Sure, they were hard earned, but so is the Calder Cup. So is the Arena Football League Championship. Is winning the IFC harder than winning the NFC East? If there's a need for a "super champion," are all of those other titles like pennants, college basketball conference titles, Little League participation trophies? Hopkins is one of the greatest middleweights in history, but boxing is splintered into so many factions, crowning so many champions at micromanaged weight classes, that it's hard to sift Hopkins's accomplishments out of the mess.

The multiple titles underscore the anarchy of boxing in the last 20 years. The sport operates on an outdated model: no schedule, no tournaments, no easy mechanism to ensure that the best fight each other, minimal sport-wide promotion. Boxers promote themselves, like De La Hoya, or turn to slithery carnival barkers like Don King. Sure, that's how they did it in the 1970s—King organized the Thrilla in Manila—but the sports and entertainment worlds had evolved by Hopkins's time. The only quasi-sport that still operates like boxing does is professional wrestling, and stars like De La Hoya and Felix Trinidad, while great athletes, borrowed more media-manipulative shtick from the World Wrestling Federation than they did from Muhammad Ali. Even Hopkins wore an executioner's mask to the ring that would make an old school-wrassler proud.

Initially, Hopkins wasn't interested in promotion. He wanted to box. As a reward, he made less money than his contenders. When Hopkins fought Trinidad, he earned $2.8 million to Trinidad's $9 million. Hopkins always admitted that the flag tosses were premeditated acts, efforts to throw Trinidad off his game. They were also barely concealed efforts on Hopkins's part to make himself more marketable, even if he had to be the villain: when the first altercation didn't draw enough attention, he did it a second time in Puerto Rico. Interracial grudge matches make more money.

After beating De La Hoya, Hopkins joined him, becoming the East Coast president of De La Hoya's Golden Boy Promotions. Hopkins then switched weight classes, bulking up in pursuit of new opportunities at the light heavyweight level. He provoked an entourage melee against Winky Wright in 2007, placed well-publicized side bets with Antonio Tarver before their bout in 2006. He challenged heavyweight champion David Haye in 2010, but Haye declined to fight because he thought Hopkins just wanted "a big payday," as if there were any other reason to endure a beating in front of an audience.

Any resemblance between these goings-on and an actual sport is almost accidental. It would be like the Phillies brawling against the Devil Rays during batting practice just to boost television ratings while Chase Utley chuckled about his $250,000 side bet with Carlos Pena and Jimmy Rollins challenged Smarty Jones to a footrace. This is modern boxing: spectacle, wrapped in prefab controversy, smothered in sleaze.

Little of this should be held against Hopkins. It's just business. Acting like Joe Frazier isn't good for the bottom line anymore. And whatever the shenanigans outside the ring, Hopkins has always been beautiful inside it, a technician who took boxing seriously and could beat opponents a hundred different ways.

He is the champion of a sport that doesn't deserve him.

.   .   .

ALEX TRINIDAD was finished. The overhyped 28-year-old with the 40–0 record and one good punch—a Philly-style left hook—tried to climb to his feet after absorbing a thundering right cross with one minute left in the 12th round. Trinidad's father climbed into the ring to stop him from fighting. The Other Guy won.

Hopkins beat Trinidad on September 29, 2001, in a fight that was delayed two weeks by the 9/11 terrorist attacks. Boxing writer Michael Woods set the scene: "The Garden hummed with a mixture of antic-ipation and lingering sadness; this was the first major sporting event held in Manhattan after the Twin Towers collapsed. The 10-bell salute to the fallen prior to the fight hit the hearts of the 20,000 in atten-dance." Trinidad wore an NYPD cap, Hopkins his executioner's mask. Woods noted that the mask meant "there would be no capitulation to political correctness because of the immense tragedy 18 days before. There was business to take care of."

Hopkins took care of business, but he took care of family first. He was training in Manhattan when the World Trade Center attacks oc-curred. His first thought was that he wanted to return to Philadelphia. Hopkins was an executioner with well-placed priorities. But he was still The Other Guy, underpaid and overshadowed by the Trinidad spectacle, one he fueled when he took a flag from Trinidad's hand and threw it to the ground.

Woods wrote of the "copious holdouts" who only came to accept Hopkins as a great fighter after the Trinidad fight. Three years later, Richard Hoffer wrote in *Sports Illustrated* that the De La Hoya vic-tory gave Hopkins "the attention he deserves." By 2008, he was tired of proving himself. He was still climbing into the ring when this book was being edited in December 2010, preparing to face Jean Pascal to win three light heavyweight titles.

Maybe the big purses keep him going. Maybe it's the love of box-ing that he discovered in prison, the discipline that saved him from a life of street violence. Or perhaps this is the fate of the one Philly sports hero who wins championships by the bucketful and successfully defends them again and again. Maybe he cannot stop. The hunger for respect is insatiable. He must silence every last doubter, defeat every Golden Boy, keep winning until the whole world climbs into the ring and stops him.

If so, Hopkins can never win. Boxing will never be as popular as it once was. Hopkins's championships are like a sidebar in the Philly sports saga, something from another category. Even in this book, Hopkins is The Other Guy. That's boxing's fault, not his.

26

TERRELL OWENS

The Man Who Spoiled Memories

Greatness: ★★★
Toughness: ★★½
Eccentricity: ★★★★
Legacy: ★★

TERRELL OWENS WAS supposed to be a Moses Malone or a Pete Rose. His job was to fill a well-defined niche in the Philly sports universe: the hired-gun free agent acquired to make a good team great and push perennial bridesmaids up to the altar. Instead, he was a divider and a destroyer, a man who not only tore the Eagles apart but tarnished our memories of what they accomplished.

Owens played 22 games for the Eagles, though he created enough controversy to last a lifetime. He was outstanding nearly every time he took the field, yet he caused so much instability that it's hard to look back fondly on anything he did. For all of his athletic gifts, his most unique accomplishment was to turn a 13–3 season and a Super Bowl appearance into a black hole in our consciousness.

We were always on edge with Owens. Even acquiring him was a long, convoluted drama involving voidable contract years, missed paperwork deadlines, an apparent trade from the Niners to the Ravens, confusion about free agency, and finally a smoky-room deal that scattered draft picks and an obscure defensive lineman (Brandon Whiting, making his first and only appearance in this book) all around the league to appease the interested parties. With Owens, nothing was ever what it seemed, not even simple free agency.

Once he arrived, we fretted about his relationship with Donovan McNabb, in part because WIP was already pinning the "sensitive" label on the quarterback, in part because Owens hinted in *Playboy* that

Jeff Garcia was gay, which isn't the kind of quote that makes for good receiver-quarterback relations. But McNabb assured us that he and Owens were besties, and they hooked up again and again on the field during their Golden Era, which lasted seven games. Eight receptions and three touchdowns in a rout of the Giants. Six catches and a touchdown in a rout of the Lions that was over in the first quarter. It was a fun early autumn.

Then the Steelers blew the Eagles out, with Owens shouting at McNabb on the sidelines and McNabb turning away. They hooked up for three touchdowns the next week, lampooning their argument for the cameras, and we assured ourselves that all was well. A few weeks later, the Eagles hosted the Cowboys, and Owens tore his ACL after a typically dirty hit by Cowboys safety Roy Williams. We held our breath, but McNabb led the Eagles through the playoffs without Owens, and when Owens ran onto the field for Super Bowl XXXIX, most of this city felt we really had a chance to win.

Can we stop the story there?

What happened next has been simplified into an Owens-versus-McNabb feud, which shows just how well Owens understood media manipulation. Owens wanted a new contract, but he couldn't stage a holdout just one year after the Eagles rewrote the rules of free agency to obtain him. So he dogged it in practice, showed up the coaching staff, did sit-ups in the driveway of his suburban mansion to maximize his photo opportunity. He knew that fans had a latent distrust of McNabb, who incurred blame for the Super Bowl loss (Owens's heroic comeback and nine catches made him blameless). So he took shots at McNabb's conditioning, perpetrated the "puke" myth, and effectively deflected much of the criticism he deserved.

Once the season started, Owens caught a lot of passes as McNabb threw to him with an almost spiteful regularity. McNabb was playing through a sports hernia, but Owens told ESPN that the Eagles would be better with Brett Favre at quarterback. It was another calculated attempt to get out of his contract, but Owens had the perfect foils in McNabb and the Eagles: McNabb responded with flummoxed professionalism, which made him look weak, and the Eagles suspended Owens, which made the team less competitive while embroiling them in a long squabble with the union.

Owens's negative impact went beyond the 2005 season. Before Owens, the Eagles were the smartest team in the NFC, if not the whole league. The Eagles were known for winning games with precision and handling off-field affairs with restraint. Guys like Todd Pinkston and Reno Mahe weren't really talented enough for the roles they played, but they avoided mistakes and played within the system, and the Eagles went 12–4 like clockwork. McNabb was a heady game-manager who knew when to throw short to Chad Lewis, when to throw deep to Pinkston to draw pass interference (or, by some miracle, a Pinkston completion), and when to run.

But after the Owens eruption, the Eagles were bumbling slackers, a team that lost games because they couldn't field punts properly and went into frustrating November slumps where nothing went right. McNabb became less of a ball distributor and more of a bomber, all the while dealing with lingering allegations hurled at him by a man who would say anything for a few dollars and a little attention. Owens generated enough chaos to undermine the whole organization, creating an environment where nobodies like Fred Mitchell felt comfortable running their mouths instead of studying their game plans. The Eagles could no longer march in step once Owens turned the team into supporting characters in his personal drama.

But the worst thing he did was retroactively ruin 2004. Watching highlights from those games is like watching the wedding video after a divorce. The Eagles spent an autumn plowing through the NFL like a thresher, but the fact that we can't enjoy the memories has nothing to do with what happened in the Super Bowl. Mitch Williams didn't take 1993 away with one pitch. Herm Edwards didn't spoil 1980 by letting Kenny King run past him. It's not about one pass, one mistake, one out-of-breath moment after a kidney shot reframed as a character flaw.

It's about a player who salted the earth behind him, a selfish showboat who was as unlike Pete Rose or Moses Malone as a human being could possibly be. That's who Owens was, and it's who he always will be in Philadelphia.

27

TUG McGRAW

The Slaphappy Workhorse

Greatness: ★★★
Toughness: ★★★
Eccentricity: ★★★½
Legacy: ★★

I F SOMEONE DIDN'T crack a joke once in a while, the pressure of 1980 would have crushed us.

The Phillies spent that summer and early autumn rising and falling from first place to third and back again, oscillating between two games up and three games back for four endless months. They played 60 one-run games in the regular season that year, 22 extra-inning contests, and it only felt like every one of those nail-biters occurred after September 1. Then came the greatest, must grueling League Championship Series in history, against a team good enough to call Nolan Ryan their number 2 starter. Then, the World Series, which had been terra incognita for 30 years.

It was all tension, all the time. Those 1980 Phillies were a tightly wound bunch: Mike Schmidt, with his raindrop analysis and batting mantras; Steve Carlton, moody, mysterious, and silent; Larry Bowa, always a bang-bang play away from apoplexy; brooding Bake McBride; frustrated, slumping Greg Luzinski. "Until this year . . . the Phils have been cursed by being the best players in baseball who always battled two teams in October—the opposition and themselves," Ken Denlinger wrote in the *Washington Post*. Dallas Green tried to spur the Phillies to victory with a whip and a branding iron, and summer was an exhausting forced march, the Expos shadowing the Phillies' every win and loss, the defending champion Pirates lurking in the brush, the Astros waiting at the end in their cavernous sweat lodge with their pitching staff of flamethrowers and knuckleballers and a center field fence in the next time zone.

Through the ordeal, Tug McGraw kept us laughing. After a narrow escape against the Expos, he explained his pregame preparation: "I spent the day thinking about the Expos. What's a synonym for 'hate'? Something stronger than disdain. Contempt! That's it. I was working on my contempt for the Expos. . . . I had a good fast ball tonight, but even better contempt." After Game 1 of the NLCS, he named his pitches: the Jameson ("That's the one that goes straight. I drink my Jameson straight"), the Peggy Lee ("the hitter asks if that's all there is"), the Cutty Sark ("it sails"), and the Bo Derek ("it's got a pretty good tail on it"). And after the NLCS, when the failures of 1976–1978 and a hundred years before were washed away with a straight shot of Irish whiskey, he said, "I feel like I've just gone through an art gallery on a motorcycle."

That's the Tug McGraw we remember: the comedian-philosopher, the inspirational poet, his glove slapping against his thigh after a win, his arms stretched to the stars after a World Series save. McGraw was funny, he was a stabilizing presence in an unstable locker room, and he was inspiring. But his efforts in 1980 had more to do with perspiration than inspiration.

.   .   .

JUST READING McGRAW'S box scores from September 1980 is enough to tire anyone out. Relievers in that era didn't saunter out of the bullpen in the ninth to protect two- or three-run leads the way Brad Lidge does today. Two-run leads were Ron Reed's job. Three-run leads belonged to Dickie Noles. McGraw usually entered the seventh or eighth inning of a tie game, often with runners on base. His job: stay perfect until help arrives.

There were nights like September 8 against the Pirates, when Bob Walk gave up back-to-back doubles to start the seventh inning. McGraw stopped the rally, then pitched a scoreless eighth, then bunted home a run on a squeeze as part of a four-run rally, then picked his way through hitters like Bill Madlock and Dave Parker to earn a win.

And there was September 24, when the Mets battled the Phillies to a scoreless tie through nine innings. Larry Christenson was finished after eight, so McGraw pitched a scoreless ninth, then a scoreless tenth, before Pete Rose finally singled home the immortal Jay Loviglio to give McGraw the win.

Two days later, in the September 26 game against the Expos—the contempt game—Dick Ruthven left a 1–1 game in the seventh and McGraw gutted through two innings before McBride sparked a celebration with a solo home run in the bottom of the ninth.

And in the final game of the regular season, with the Expos needing a win to force a one-game playoff, McGraw entered a tie game in the ninth and pitched three scoreless innings, striking out Andre Dawson, forcing Gary Carter to pop up, and waiting past eternity for Schmidt to deliver an 11th inning home run.

McGraw's record in September and October 1980: 5–0, 0.34 ERA, five saves, no home runs, three walks, and 22 strikeouts in 26 and a third innings, all of them with the game, the postseason, and Phillies history in the balance.

For an encore: five appearances in five NLCS games. A save in Game 1, thanks to the Jameson, which flew straight past Astros bats; a torturous loss in Game 3, where McGraw entered a scoreless tie in the eighth and was still there in the 11th, when Joe Morgan tripled and Denny Walling singled a pinch runner home; a 10th inning save in Game 4; an averted disaster in Game 5, with McGraw coming so close to our scrap heap when he failed to hold a two-run lead in the ninth, Garry Maddox doubling in the 10th, and Ruthven making a relief cameo to save McGraw when he was less than perfect.

For a second encore: four more appearances in the World Series— another win, another loss, two more saves, bases loaded in the ninth in Game 6, the heart of the Royals lineup around the corner, Bob Boone and Pete Rose playing hot potato near the dugout, a .326 hitter at the plate, strikeout, celebration, the motorcycle rolls to a stop before smashing through the Picassos.

I'm tired just writing about it, and I left three-quarters of it out.

. . .

"YOU GOTTA BELIEVE" is a Mets slogan. McGraw coined it—if such a simple catchphrase can really be "coined"—in 1973, two years before he joined the Phillies. You Gotta Believe made a snappy title for McGraw's inspirational segments on Channel 6 news, and it's a worthy name for his charitable organization, devoted to helping those with brain tumors and brain trauma. But it's a New York slogan, one the Mets took back when they embroidered it onto their jerseys after McGraw's death in 2004.

New York can have it. It's one of McGraw's weakest quotes, anyway. Remembering McGraw for "You Gotta Believe" is like remembering Groucho Marx for one of his shopping lists. The Mets get a catchphrase. We get the courage, the memories, the laughs, the sweat and toil of that 1980 autumn, the final pitch before the implosion of the Vet, the ashes scattered at Citizens Bank Park. New York can have the words, because we got the inspiration behind the words, the feeling that it was really possible to win. With his heroics in the autumn of 1980, McGraw gave us belief. At times, it's all that has sustained us.

28

TOMMY McDONALD

The Legend We Could Love

Greatness: ★★★★
Toughness: ★★★
Eccentricity: ★★★½
Legacy: ★

TOMMY McDONALD was a line in an encyclopedia before Ray Didinger rescued him.

By encyclopedia line standards, McDonald's entry was a good one, but it takes a little statistical know-how to realize it was a great one. Unfortunately, most fans don't thumb through football encyclopedias, and those who do don't always know what they are looking at. His numbers—495 catches, 8,410 yards, 84 touchdowns—don't move the meter much anymore. When I wrote the first draft of this chapter, McDonald was 63rd on the NFL receiving list. While I was editing this chapter, Andre Johnson—an exciting player but hardly an immortal—shot past McDonald on a typical pass-happy Sunday, dropping the Eagles' only Hall of Fame wide receiver to 64th.

So you have to tease the greatness out: McDonald played in the 1960s, an era of run-heavy offenses and 14-game schedules, and he retired with the second highest touchdown total in NFL history. His 1961 season, in which he caught 64 passes for 1,144 yards and 13 touchdowns, was the equivalent of a great Randy Moss season today. Historians and old fans knew how great he was, but the sports world is more likely to humor historians and old fans than listen to them.

Luckily, Didinger isn't just a historian and an old fan; he is an influential writer and a member of the Hall of Fame selection committee. "I began a personal campaign to get Tommy into the Hall, not because he was my boyhood hero, but because I felt a player with

Tommy McDonald
(Courtesy of Temple University Libraries, Urban Archives, Philadelphia, PA)

eighty-four career touchdowns deserves enshrinement," Didinger wrote in the introduction to *One Last Read.* That's how the Pro Football Hall of Fame works: sportswriters campaign for players they think are overlooked, everyone argues, and eventually a finger comes down from football heaven and points to a few lucky old-timers from the days before satellites beamed the stats of backup running backs straight to your cell phone.

In 1998, thanks to Didinger, that finger pointed to Tommy McDonald, giving Philly something we needed: an old football legend we could truly embrace.

. . .

YOU KNOW a little about the 1960 Eagles: Chuck Bednarik played 60 minutes per game, put every opposing running back in the hospital, and doubled as the Phillies catcher. The Eagles beat the Packers for the NFL title, and Vince Lombardi was calling in favors from the Almighty to make sure it never happened again. Tommy McDonald, 178 pounds of moxie, caught a 55-yard touchdown from Norm Van Brocklin every single week. Those were slight exaggerations: very slight, in McDonald's case. McDonald caught 13 passes in 12 games and another in the championship. He was held without a touchdown just twice. He caught a 62-yarder, a 57-yarder, a 52-yarder, a 39-yarder . . . you get the idea.

The 1960 season was a wonderful fairy tale. The 1961 season was harsh Philly reality. Bednarik faded, and Van Brocklin was gone. McDonald was the star. The Eagles were as exciting as they were doomed.

McDonald scored touchdowns in each of the first two games of the 1961 season, both Eagles wins. He then caught 11 passes for 187 yards—unimaginable numbers for that era—in a loss to the Cardinals. The Eagles beat the Steelers the next week, but for some reason Steelers coach Buddy Parker took a potshot at McDonald, who caught four touchdowns against the Steelers in 1960 but had an off game that week. "How many touchdowns did McDonald score?" he asked rhetorically.

An angry McDonald pasted a copy of the article inside his helmet. He caught a game-winning touchdown the next week. "I didn't know anyone knew about that clipping," McDonald said after the game. "But it's going to stay in my helmet the rest of the season—just as a reminder." The Associated Press report of the game sums up the spirit of 1960s football in the final paragraph: "McDonald, incidentally, suffered two cracked teeth in the game."

A few weeks later, McDonald caught a 41-yard touchdown pass on a play called "Y-slot-cross" to beat the Redskins with just 16 seconds left in the game. "It was a wonderful feeling, just about the biggest thrill I had in football," he said after the game.

It was a thrilling season. The Eagles used a stack formation: three receivers to one side of the field, McDonald to the other, where he could operate in space. It was 21st-century football in 1961. The Eagles were 9–3 and in position to set up another battle with the Packers when they hosted the Giants on a rainy, foggy, December afternoon when snowdrifts lined the fringes of Franklin Field.

McDonald had as great a game as any receiver could ever have: seven catches, 237 yards, two touchdowns. But his unearthly numbers were hardly noticed in a game marked by phantom penalties and historic story lines. McDonald caught a 52-yard touchdown to give the Eagles a 10–7 lead, and the Giants recalled 40-year-old Charlie Conerly from the bench to replace fellow legend Y. A. Tittle. (In modern terms, they called in Kurt Warner to relieve Brett Favre.) Conerly threw two touchdowns to give the Giants a 21–10 halftime lead. McDonald caught a 66-yard pass to get the Eagles to the 12-yard line, but Sonny Jurgensen missed an open receiver in the back of the end zone. A Jurgensen touchdown to Timmy Brown was then waved off by offensive interference on McDonald, who allegedly set a pick on the play.

McDonald atoned for that real or imagined sin with a 30-yard touchdown. Then the referees got serious, calling a controversial roughing the punter penalty to set up another Giants touchdown. The Eagles answered, but time was on the Giants' side. With 18 seconds left and trailing by 4, Jurgensen threw to Pete Retzlaff, who lateraled to McDonald. But McDonald was knocked out of bounds and into a snowdrift.

What a way to end the season: McDonald, his teeth chipped, newspaper in his helmet, knocked out of the field of play, taking the Eagles championship hopes with him. Maybe it's best that 1961 is largely forgotten: we have enough stories with that kind of ending.

But there was once a risk we would forget everything except the encyclopedia line. Thanks to Didinger, that didn't happen.

. . .

RAY DIDINGER and Tommy McDonald were keynote speakers at the Katz Community Center in Cherry Hill in 2008. Aaron Schatz of Football Outsiders was the third speaker, and I was there as a one-man entourage. There was a meet-and-greet for the center's top donors, so I got to sit at the table with McDonald as he shook hands, told stories, and let donors' grandsons hold and wear his championship ring.

McDonald was bubbly and jovial. His tales of football in the 1950s and 1960s were long on emotion and short on detail. He had truly forgotten more about football than any of us would ever know. He was approachable, downright cuddly: a man as happy to be signing autographs in 2008 as he was to sprint onto the field in 1961. There was no anger, no pessimism, no resentment of the fact that times have changed and football players are millionaires.

In other words, there was no Bednarik. Our 1960 memory had faded down to that encyclopedia line and Concrete Charlie, who for all his greatness couldn't stop telling us that sports had changed for the worse. Our only well-known local football legend had a nasty habit of making us feel bad about our own fandom, which was the last thing we needed during a quarter-century wait for a championship.

McDonald gave us something we needed: an old timer who made us feel good, who allowed us to celebrate the past without denigrating the present. He gave us a relatable champion: not a granite-carved superhuman grouch, but a tiny, peppery, gracious, colorful fellow who loved us back for our rediscovered adulation.

That's what Didinger rescued for us: a bit of our self-esteem, a fond memory, a nice guy to round out a tiny pantheon overcrowded with tough guys. He gave us a football Richie Ashburn. We needed it. We've had too few champions in this city to let the best ones fade away into obscurity.

29

ANDRE WATERS

He Gave His Life for Philly Toughness

Greatness: ★ ½
Toughness: ★ ★ ★ ★
Eccentricity: ★ ★ ★ ½
Legacy: ★ ★ ★

WE LOVE GUYS who play with no regard for their own safety. We worship players who hit like disaster-movie comets, who use flesh and bone, spikes and sticks and helmets as battering rams, who get stitches between periods, take cortisone shots at halftime, leave the game bruised and bloody and in only slightly better condition than the other guy. We applaud this behavior, lionize and encourage it, sometimes forgetting that we are cheering for players to risk their lives.

Andre Waters treated every game like a blood feud. He attacked opponents viciously, subsidizing his meager talent with utter recklessness. He played through pain, played through concussions and cranial trauma that would eventually damage his brain, shatter his personality, and make him take his own life. As inspiring as Waters's game-changing tackles were, as exciting as he made Sunday afternoons, no one should have to pay the price he paid for just a few seasons of athletic glory.

· · ·

ANY HONEST LISTING of the Eagles greatest safeties would rank Waters sixth all time, at the highest, behind Brian Dawkins, Randy Logan, Bill Bradley, Don Burroughs, and Wes Hopkins. Guys like Joe Scarpati, Quintin Mikell, and Brenard Wilson could also make the case that they were better than Waters. Rank the Buddy Ryan–Bud

Carson defenders, and Waters would also find himself near the back of the line, behind not just Reggie White and Hopkins but Jerome Brown, Eric Allen, Clyde Simmons, and Seth Joyner.

But Waters is in this book because of what he embodied. Those Ryan-Carson defenses, with their Body Bags and Houses of Pain, were all about raw intimidation. White and Hopkins were intimidating, but they were also talented, capable of dominating opponents on skill alone if they had to. Waters was a clenched fist, a guy who had no business on the field except to throw his body at ball carriers and inflict as much damage as possible. He was the meanest cuss from the 700 Level, offered a helmet and cleats and told to work out his frustrations on the field, 15-yard penalties be damned.

Oh, Waters had a little talent. He was overlooked in the NFL draft because Cheyney State University didn't have a sports information director in the mid-1980s, so scouting film was hard to come by. But his workout times were fast by 1984 standards—he ran the 40-yard dash in 4.57 seconds—and he impressed secondary coach Fred Bruney in training camp. "He's got a feel for man-to-man coverage," Bruney said when Waters made the team. "He's tough; he'll challenge a receiver." Waters played special teams and returned a few kicks, taking one back 89 yards for a touchdown to help an awful Eagles team beat an excellent Redskins team in 1984.

When Buddy Ryan arrived, Waters came into his own. Ryan promoted Waters on the depth chart over the more reliable, less vicious Ray Ellis. Ryan encouraged Waters's line-blurring savagery, saying he liked the way Waters "turns people upside down and laughs at them." He reprimanded Waters, but only slightly, when Waters knocked Steve Bartkowski and David Archer out of back-to-back games with shots to their knees. "I don't want to be known around the league as a cheap-shot artist," Waters said after earning an ejection for the Archer blow, which occurred after the quarterback was out of bounds.

Waters acquired a dirty reputation, somewhat justly. He was a launch-with-the-shoulder, lead-with-the-head, lunge-for-the-knee tackler, the kind that was common in the 1970s but out of favor by the mid-1990s. Dan Dierdorf excoriated Waters on *Monday Night Football*, calling him "the cheap-shot artist of the NFL . . . a guy who goes after people with the intention of hurting them." We loved Waters even more for that, because Dierdorf was just another national-media blowhard picking on the scrappy Philadelphian, just like all those national columnists who wrote the fans off as drunken hooligans. The Dierdorfs of the world were supposed to misunderstand and disrespect a guy like Waters.

The casualty list was long: Bartkowski, Archer. Jim Everett, Rich Gannon, then Waters himself. After a 14–13 loss to the Buccaneers, Waters suffered a seizure as the team boarded a flight out of Tampa. Waters spent the night in the hospital with a concussion and "body cramps." A day later, coach Rich Kotite said Waters was fine, and Waters not only played the next week but elbowed a Saints receiver in the helmet after the game.

It's about the only Waters concussion we have a record of. In 1994, he admitted that he lost count at 15. "In most cases, nobody knew it but me. I just wouldn't say anything. I'd sniff some smelling salts, then go back in there." He described a feeling like "looking through a telescope" after the concussions. So he played football with telescopic vision, an undersized safety from a poor Florida family with 11 siblings, a guy from a tiny college with no game film, a guy less than a breath better than the next safety off the bench, a guy who couldn't afford to miss time or be anything less than a guided missile when he took the field.

When Waters shot himself in 2006 at age 44, neurologists discovered his brain had damage comparable to the brain of an 85-year-old Alzheimer's patient. For all those years, he was more a danger to himself than to others.

. . .

WE ALL LOVED Andre Waters, even if we winced at some of his knuckleheaded tackles. We can show that love, and show respect for his legacy, by remembering that toughness has its limits. Grabbing some smelling salts and running back onto the field (court, ice) can have tragic consequences. When a player is slow to come back from an injury, if he exercises a little more caution, it doesn't automatically mean he's soft or lazy. He may just want to reach his 45th birthday with a fully functional mind. The NFL is learning not to shrug off head injuries, thanks in part to Waters's tragic death and the study of his brain. Fans and teams are also learning, too late for Eric Lindros but just in time for Brian Westbrook and Kevin Kolb.

Let's honor Waters's memory by applauding toughness, celebrating aggressiveness, but recognizing that even Philly-style brutality, for everyone's sake, must be tempered with a little common sense.

30

ANDREW TONEY

The Agony of the Feet

Greatness: ★★★
Toughness: ★★★
Eccentricity: ★★★
Legacy: ★★

THE BOSTON STRANGLER sat fidgeting at the end of the bench as the Sixers beat the Bucks on a December night in 1986, wearing what he called one of his "stone looks." Team owner Harold Katz ordered him to be there, but Toney was too injured to play, and coach Matt Goukas was reluctant to call for him even if he could limp onto the court. "I hope this makes somebody happy," Toney said after the game. "Every time the horn blew, all it meant was, I had to go back to my seat."

Weeks later, the two-time All Star, one of the NBA's best pure scorers, watched the Sixers beat the Clippers from Section H of the Spectrum stands. Goukas had banished his shooting guard, once one of the brightest young stars in the city, for being a "negative influence."

Andrew Toney was unstoppable against the Sixers' greatest foes. He helped defeat the Celtics in the 1982 Eastern Conference Finals and the Lakers in the 1983 NBA Finals. But he couldn't win the Battle of Broken Feet, a one-man war against a debilitating injury, an intractable owner, and a sports culture that expects players to gut it out through even the most extreme situations.

· · ·

ANDREW TONEY had no conscience as a shooter. As a rookie, Toney had no qualms about waving Julius Erving out of the low post so he could penetrate on his defender. With less than two minutes left in a tie game against the Lakers in 1983, Toney ignored a Billy Cunningham play call, demanded the ball from Mo Cheeks, penetrated against virtually the entire Lakers defense, and sank a 10-foot bank shot to decide the game. Only Toney could ignore Dr. J on a fast break or Cunningham on a rant and get away with it. On a team full of All Stars and Hall of Famers, he was the best pure offensive player. "I've always said that Magic, Michael, and Isiah were the greatest players I went up against," Celtics guard Danny Ainge once said, "but Andrew was not far off."

Toney became the Boston Strangler in the 1982 Eastern Conference Finals. He scored 30 points in one game, 39 in another. The streaky shooter then shook off a 1-for-11 performance in Game 6 to dominate the final game of the series. He scored 14 first-quarter points. When the Celtics cut the lead to 64–62, Toney went on a one-man run, beating three defenders to sink a 12-footer, coming off screens by Erving and Mo Cheeks for two more buckets, losing Larry Bird for two scores, and faking Ainge out of his sneakers for another. The Sixers soon led by 17. The admiring Boston crowd exhorted the Sixers to go to the next round and "Beat LA."

On the court, he was a unique mixture of strength, speed, precision shooting, and, yes, occasional passing. "He sees things out on the court that other players just don't see," Erving said in 1983. Off the court, he was an easygoing young man who loved the game. He and teammate Franklin Edwards would cruise into rough neighborhoods to play pickup games with local kids. When Toney appeared at youth basketball camps, he would make star-struck kids laugh with the old "Pull my finger" gag. Julius Erving was all dignity, Moses Malone all intimidation, Mo Cheeks all professionalism. Toney was all fun.

That was before the Battle of Broken Feet.

•   •   •

THE STRANGLER was struggling, and the Boston press loved it. "The Boston Strangler performed as if he had a basketball lodged in his throat last night," the *Boston Globe* reported after a 3-for-17 night in Game 2 of the Eastern Conference Finals in 1985. Toney came back to score 26 points in each of the next two games, but the Sixers lost the series. Toney signed a seven-year, $4.72-million contract after the Celtics series, but he expressed his unhappiness with his role in the offense: the Sixers expected him to turn on his shooting like a spigot when they needed him, then to retreat behind Erving and Malone whenever he went cold.

But there was more. Toney was hurting. His feet and ankles bothered him all through the 1984–1985 season. Team doctors could find nothing wrong. They wrapped one right leg in a cast as a precaution during the summer, then sent him to conditioning guru Pat Croce. Toney worked diligently with Croce. The pain persisted. Toney played poorly and complained of pain in practices and preseason games. The team said it was all in his head. He sought a second opinion, then a third. Finally, a University of Pennsylvania doctor found a stress fracture in Toney's right foot, then another (plus bone spurs) in his left.

The battle was on.

Toney expected an apology from the Sixers, but the team shrugged its shoulders at the medical error. "You can't look back at what you did or didn't do yesterday," Goukas said. By March, the casts were off Toney's legs, and he was cleared to play, but he was still in pain. Katz saw Toney shooting around in practice and in pickup games and determined he was healthy, so he ordered Toney onto the court. Toney sat on the end of the bench, then came off the bench for a few games, then suffered another injury and was lost for the season.

The Battle of Broken Feet dragged on for two years. Toney was rarely healthy for any extended time. Whenever he missed a game or practice, Katz or another team official questioned his motives or his toughness. Toney landed on the injured list in January 2007, and two weeks later Goukas suddenly banished him from the locker room and the bench, calling him a "negative influence." Toney watched a game from the stands before burying the hatchet with his coach. "It is the soap opera that makes 'General Hospital' look like the prologue to 'Sesame Street,'" Phil Jasner wrote in the *Daily News*.

Players around the league sided with Toney. Celtics legend Bill Walton once suffered a similar injury and faced similar criticism. "I think the big problem with sports medicine in general is that not enough credence is given to an athlete's complaint of pain," he told the *Boston Globe*. "Why anybody would want to rush a player back is beyond me," said Larry Fleischer, general counsel for the Players Union, adding that "it's bad, it's sad. It takes a tough man to go through what he's going through."

The Sixers' arrogance in the face of their medical error is shocking in retrospect. By contrast, Toney comes across as mature and reasonable in the old clippings. He kept rehabbing, kept trying to play. He considered retirement but never asked for a trade, never blasted Katz the way Katz often blasted him. He even had his moments—in April 1987, he doled out 13 assists as Erving scored his 30,000th point—and finished every game by wrapping both feet in ice packs.

But the situation looked different to the everyday fan. Toney signed a huge contract, then refused to play through pain. He was benched, fined, banished. The Erving-Malone Sixers were falling apart, and Toney was their highest-profile problem. He was easy to write off as a me-first player, another faded prospect who let money go to his head. So the player Pat Riley once called "the best clutch player I have ever seen" faded out of Philadelphia, then retired during the 1989 preseason with no fanfare, just a series of squabbles with the team about his injury settlement.

. . .

YEARS LATER, Mo Cheeks tried to bring Toney back as an assistant coach. What sounded like a simple arrangement became suddenly complicated: the two sides couldn't agree on details, communications became muddled. It was a small aftershock of the battle, a reminder of how nothing was quite what it seemed with Toney.

The Battle of Broken Feet was as much about hurt feelings as bone spurs. Toney wanted an apology, recognition that he was right about his injury and was really trying to return to the form. Katz wasn't an apology kind of guy, and sports culture—particularly in Philly—isn't about apologies. Players know that criticism, much of it unfounded, some of it cruel, comes with the $4.72-million contract. Players cannot afford to be sensitive, but everyone else gets to be as insensitive as they want to be.

We fume when a team "coddles" an athlete, but a little coddling could have given us five or six more good years of Toney and an Erving-Toney-Cheeks-Malone-Barkley line up that actually played together and survived past 1985. An apology and some TLC would have yielded a few more wins, maybe another shot at the title. Given the choice of coddling Toney or telling him to shape up, many of us would have chosen the latter. But what if the choice had been coddling Toney or watching Sedale Threatt go 1-for-24 from the three-point arc for a season?

I know which one I would have chosen. Thankfully, the Sixers won a championship before they made their choice.

31

LENNY DYKSTRA

He Nailed the Good Ol' Boy Act

Greatness: ★★★
Toughness: ★★★½
Eccentricity: ★★★½
Legacy: ★

O UR PROBLEM AS FANS is that we want so badly to believe the image. If the take-out slide is hard, if the uniform is dirty, if the eyes glint with competitive fire, we assign virtues to a player that he may not really have. Combine the image with a little success, even if it's fleeting, and we might mistake the player for a leader, or a hero, or a role model.

Philadelphia has been cruel to many respectable athletes who committed very minor infractions like being "aloof." Yet we were inordinately kind to Lenny Dykstra, drinker, gambler, drug abuser, and thief. We loved the hard-nosed country-boy persona and ignored the fact that Lenny Dykstra was a true scoundrel, a man good enough to trust with the leadoff spot but nothing else.

· · ·

AGAINST THE 1993 Phillies, opponents started every game in trouble. Braves great John Smoltz faced Phillies nobody Ben Rivera on June 23, but Smoltz, winner of 213 major league games, didn't really have a chance.

Dykstra started the game with a walk. One batter later, John Kruk walked. Darren Daulton worked a 3–1 count before singling to center, bringing Dykstra home. In the fifth inning, Rivera walked, then Dykstra walked again. Kruk ripped a fly down the right field line that Dave

Justice mishandled, and Rivera scored. Smoltz needed 100 pitches to get through six innings. Greg McMichael relieved him.

Dykstra walked to start the seventh inning. He raced to third when McMichael overthrew the first baseman on a sacrifice bunt. Kruk walked. Daulton singled home Dykstra. The Braves brought in a new pitcher. Pete Incaviglia walked. Jim Eisenreich singled. And on it went, the Phillies batting around, scoring five runs on three hits, five walks, an error, and a wild pitch, burying one of the best pitching staffs in history beneath a pile of full counts and scratch hits.

It happened over and over again in 1993: the Dykstra leadoff walk that started the big inning. Dykstra walked 129 times that season, leading a team that featured disciplined hitters like Daulton (117 walks) and Kruk (111). He mixed in the occasional leadoff home run, but the walk was almost as deadly a weapon. Beneath the gritty exterior, beyond the rhetoric about hard-nosed play, the Phillies were a sabermetrician's dream, championing the kind of baseball endorsed by statisticians who argue that getting on base is the most important skill in baseball.

Dykstra's on-base percentage was .420, but Philly fans don't fall in love with percentages or with walks. So we attributed Dykstra's success to his image: the fiery, tobacco-spitting good ol' boy flying around the base paths and center field. If the walks were acknowledged at all, they became an extension of his orneriness: Dykstra fouled off pitches to tire or rattle the pitcher, which was true, but the end result (a fast runner on first) was far more valuable than any psychological advantage.

The persona was, admittedly, alluring. Dykstra was a joy to watch, and the tobacco spit and cocky smile gave the appearance of a troublesome rogue with a heart of gold. The rogue part was dead on; the heart of gold was debatable.

* * *

DYKSTRA DID EVERYTHING that baseball fans are supposed to hate.

He gambled so heavily that he received a year's probation from the league in 1991 after admitting that he had lost $78,000 playing high-stakes poker. Teammates wrote it off as part of his nature. "He just wanted to compete," said Howard Johnson, who played with Dykstra for the Mets. "If we were out in the field and all there was were horseshoes, he'd want to play you in horseshoes. He's just so confident and cocky and always wants to back his own play."

He drank so heavily that he almost preempted the magic of 1993. Driving home from Kruk's bachelor party in 1991 with Daulton in the passenger seat, he crashed his car into some trees. Dykstra's blood alcohol level was .179. Patrons at Smokey Joe's, where the party took place, said Dykstra was a regular customer. Dykstra and Daulton missed two months as they recuperated from their injuries. Dykstra apologized, and when his game matured (more walks, less salvos into the fence after fly balls) we assumed, or hoped, that the man had matured.

He took steroids, unapologetically. "You know, I was the pioneer of that stuff," he said in *The Zeroes: My Misadventures in the Decade Wall Street Went Insane* by Randall Lane. "I was like the very first to do that." Steroid use is baseball's mortal sin, inspiring Inquisitions and witch-hunts that tainted a generation of players and their achievements, fairly or otherwise. Dykstra hinted about steroids throughout his career, talking about his "special vitamins," and many of us chuckled.

It's hard to compartmentalize his success on the field when there was so much happening off it. "Everyone has always known Lenny to be a free spirit," said teammate Tom Herr. "Everyone who recognized those qualities also realized that he was doing some things that could possibly be dangerous. I'm talking about reckless behavior. He didn't pay attention to man's law or God's law."

After retirement, Dykstra dabbled in a vice worse than liquor, steroids, and gambling combined. He became an inside trader, a stock market snake-oil salesman who cultivated a trumped-up reputation as a financial savant (his hot tips came from legitimate financial advisor Richard Suttmeier, his record exaggerated and tirelessly promoted by television loudmouth Jim Cramer), then accepted money from a company to recommend its stock. Dykstra played the "investing is like baseball" angle, and investors loved the idea of an everyman who spewed common sense like tobacco juice and could outperform Ivy Leaguer economists.

Our problem as investors, and as citizens, is that want so badly to believe the image. Combine the right persona with a little success, even if it's fleeting, and we might mistake the wrong people as heroes. The 2007 crash was fueled by backroom tactics like Dykstra's and by the histrionic ignorance of friends like Cramer. Dykstra went bankrupt, claimed to be homeless for a while, then reappeared in 2010 as a financial advisor. Apparently, he still hasn't used up the last of his thrillbilly charm, and there are plenty of people ready for one more reckless ride.

. . .

DYKSTRA'S CAREER PEAK was brief: great seasons in 1990 and 1993, injury-shortened teases in 1991 and 1992, a few reputation-based All-Star appearances. Our rational minds tell us that his accomplishments are tainted by steroids, that his other infractions cannot be swept away, that he's more of an embarrassment who had a few good years than a true sports legend.

But our hearts dwell forever on the image forged in 1993, on tobacco spit, stolen bases, leadoff homers, and a dozen pitches fouled off to stay alive. Perhaps Dykstra deserves a little nostalgic appreciation; we may all be a little better off if we learn to separate beauty from virtue in sports.

Fair enough. Just do yourself a favor and don't invest with him.

32

CURT SCHILLING

He No Longer Takes That Fifth Day Off

Greatness: ★★★★
Toughness: ★★★
Eccentricity: ★★★
Legacy: ★

I N A FEW YEARS, Curt Schilling will give a Hall of Fame speech. When he does, make sure you are settled in and comfortable.

You'll have a few hours to kill while he philosophizes. To pass the time, play this bingo game: every time he mentions courage (in reference to himself), God, America, steroids, taxes, "values," and his own role in getting America past the tragedy of September 11, 2001, give yourself one point. Chances are, you'll reach 50 points before your first bathroom break.

Just don't hold your breath waiting for Schilling to mention Philadelphia or the Phillies. We're beneath his dignity.

. . .

CURT SCHILLING is a blogger now. Oh, he'll tell you he's a pundit, or a political analyst, or an entrepreneur who designs video games while offering incisive critiques of American cultural mores. He's always had that gift for self-aggrandizement. He's just a blogger. He updates his 38 Pitches blog semi-regularly to tell us how well his company is doing and how badly America is doing. Not surprisingly, a man who made $115 million playing baseball (according to Baseball Reference) doesn't like taxes. Ironically, a man who benefited from organized labor and collective bargaining to earn his riches is a proponent of the unfettered free market. As you might expect, a man who threw really hard for a living doesn't have the deepest insights into world issues that extend outside the strike zone.

Ed Wade once called Schilling "a horse every fifth day and a horse's ass the other four." Schilling doesn't take that fifth day off anymore. Giants broadcaster Mike Krukow also called Schilling a "horse's ass" after Schilling managed to take Barry Bonds criticism too far (a feat in itself) by saying, "It's just unfortunate that there's good people and bad people." Charles P. Pierce called Schilling "America's most beloved stigmatic" after Schilling pitched on a bloody ankle—my God, the blood was so magical that no bandage, brace, or towel could conceal it from the faithful!—then said afterward, "I just wish everybody on this planet could experience the day that I just experienced. I will never use the words 'unbelievable' and 'the Lord' again in the same sentence."

It takes unique gifts to be called a horse's ass by both your employer and your competitor. Schilling was gifted with a 6-foot-5 frame, a fastball in the 90s, a good slider, a deadly splitter (late in his career), and an almost delusional overestimation of his own intelligence and importance. His open letter to America after September 11 was one of the most unnecessary documents ever written, a sad attempt to grab attention when everyone else was busy trying to either help or cope. Even if you agree with Schilling's general political ideals, a few dips into 38 Pitches will convince you that his "principles" amount to little more than watered-down regurgitation. Schilling says what everyone else says, though not quite as well, and wants to make sure you know he's the one who said it.

He may think he was Don Drysdale on the mound and is Matt Drudge on the political scene. Really, he's just a pale imitation of Jim Bunning in both arenas.

* * *

LUCKY FOR US, we didn't have to deal with bloody socks or philosophical treatises in Philadelphia. Schilling wasn't just a Phillies pitcher, he was a 1993 Phillies pitcher, and while that team was guilty of its own kind of self-promotion, Schilling's bigger-than-the-game routine wouldn't have sat well in the locker room. John Kruk would have made him eat that bloody sock.

Schilling was a good pitcher in 1993, not a great one, and he missed most of the next two seasons with shoulder injuries. He returned to form in 1996 with a surgically rebuilt shoulder, better control, and a newly perfected split-fingered fastball. In 1997, he set strikeout records. In 1998, he started calling out teammates—most notably young pitchers Matt Beech and Garrett Stephenson—for not sharing his commitment to winning. By spring training of 1999, he was "holding out hope" for a trade to a contender while criticizing Phillies management for not surrounding him with the talent he so richly deserved. "I haven't seen any signs the last few years from ownership that they're committed to helping us win a ballgame," he said. Ed Wade, who admittedly pinched a few pennies in the 1990s, was still able to call out Schilling on his disingenuous reasoning. "Earlier this month, Curt was quoted as saying, 'It's up to ownership to get good players.' What message does that send to his teammates, the guys he shares the clubhouse with and the guys who play behind him?"

This being Philadelphia, we had to wait through another year of trade requests and self-serving interviews by the man Jim Fregosi once called "Red Light Curt" (television cameras use red lights to signify they are rolling, and Schilling loved those cameras) before anything happened. Schilling grew into the Great Thinker. He liked to lecture reporters about how much he knew about business, in contrast to Phillies management, whom he then ironically accused of hiding their huge profits. (If they have huge profits, then they must be doing well, right?) He wanted to be traded, but he didn't want to have to move his family (which hampered talks with the Indians), and he didn't want to have to pitch for a bad team (limiting interest from the Orioles). He wanted what he wanted, which is okay, but he couched all of his selfishness as some principled worldview: it's better for the Phillies, for the fans, for our way of life, if Curt Schilling gets what he wants.

You can read the same visionary rhetoric on his blog today, but now he's talking about the nation, not the Phillies. At least when he was here, he stayed on topic.

* * *

BOSTON, OF COURSE, lapped Schilling's shtick up. Boston columnists have always mixed their completely undeserved "underdog spirit" rhetoric with an insufferable dose of self-righteousness. Schilling fit right in. Bill Simmons bought Schilling's made-for-television World Series heroics sock, line, and sinker. "Sitting in the dugout between innings, he threw a towel over his head and stared at the ground, hands pressed against his ears, looking like someone who just finished a harrowing plane flight," Simmons wrote glowingly of Game 7, not quite realizing that someone who wanted to bear pain heroically wouldn't have made such a show of bearing pain heroically. "This was about heart. This was about coming through when it mattered most." In fact, it wasn't even the first appearance of the towel routine: Schilling used it when Mitch Williams pitched, and other Phillies copied it because they knew Red Light Curt was just trying to get a few close-ups.

It was always all about image for Schilling, which is the main difference between Boston and Philadelphia. Philadelphia fandom is about suffering. Boston fandom is about the appearance of suffering: complaining about the Red Sox while the Patriots win multiple Super Bowls and the Celtics pursue their millionth title. Schilling found a receptive audience, and he played to it ceaselessly, making sure to mix some calculated "Yankees suck" remarks with his political endorsements.

Even New England is starting to sour on Schilling now that he's a blogger, and not as good a blogger as Simmons. When Schilling demands that Roger Clemens return his Cy Young awards because of his steroid scandals, he's just another loudmouth at his keyboard. He tried to start a flame war with *Boston Globe* writer Peter Abraham—one of the city's most level-headed columnists—because Abraham poked fun at Schilling's eight-paragraph rant about Josh Beckett. The tirade was amateurish, even by blogger standards, but it was vintage Schilling: short-tempered, short-sighted, self-serving, and dumb, yet imbued with an air of superiority.

None of this would have played in Philly. We lost a great pitcher when we traded Curt Schilling, but good riddance. We prefer sports legends who don't spend all of their time telling us that they are sports legends.

33

JIM BUNNING
The Spirit of '64, the Year That Wasn't

Greatness: ★★★½
Toughness: ★★★
Eccentricity: ★★★
Legacy: ★

THE 1964 PHILLIES are our loose-tooth memory, our regional epic tragedy, our lost-innocence moment. They are also our civic hogwash.

When you read the memoirs or listen to stories of the Great Phold, you can drown in the blarney. Everyone in the city was a teenager in 1964, wide eyed and baseball obsessed, huddled under their blankets with transistor radios or sitting on South Philly stoops on hot afternoons, listening with awe as Jim Bunning won game after game. Then, September came and the Phillies choked—choked!—and the sun no longer rose for those disillusioned teenagers, who also lost their first girlfriends that summer and saw their emotionally distant fathers weep for the first time, probably when Bunning, pitching on two days' rest, got knocked out in the fifth inning by the Colt-45s on September 16.

If the memoirist really opens his malarkey throttle, he'll connect the dots between the Kennedy assassination, the arrival of the Beatles, and the 1964 Phillies. Essayist Joe Queenan can usually be counted on to cut through such balderdash, but even he succumbed to the nostalgic poetry when he called 1964 "*annus horribilis*." "The brief emotional uplift provided by the Fab Four quickly gave way to the catastrophe of late September," he wrote in *True Believers*. Bruce Buschel took the same regrettable path in an otherwise funny *Philadelphia Magazine* article. "Everything was beautiful and then it was all over. *Bang!* Lee

Harvey Oswald. *Woosh!* Chico Ruiz." The execrable Mark Harmon movie *Stealing Home* uses the 1964 Phillies as one of the framing devices for its drippy coming-of-age fluff. (If Jodie Foster were my babysitter and she spent the summer prancing around in bathing suits and miniskirts, I wouldn't have given a damn about the stupid Phillies, but never mind.) The 1964 Phillies have become our excuse for sackcloth-and-ashes whining after every short losing streak, our trump card in the game of long-suffering one-upmanship in our arguments with fans in other cities.

Let's reconstruct the facts for a moment. The Phillies were terrible from the late 1950s through 1962, and most fans had abandoned them. Attendance in Connie Mack Stadium averaged 7,565 fans per game in 1961 and 9,525 in 1962. The team got better in the second half on 1963, and by 1964 fans started to slowly return. The team averaged about 12,000 to 14,000 fans through early June, then began to consistently draw over 20,000 fans when the team was in the pennant chase in the summer. In other words, at least some of these memoirists were front-runners who discovered their lifetime love of baseball the moment the Phillies became good.

The fans who did fill Connie Mack Stadium to near capacity that summer weren't a knot-hole gang of hero-worshiping kids. They were the usual bellicose mob. A *Sports Illustrated* story of the time had one fan booing Tony Taylor after Taylor hurt his shoulder diving after a hard grounder. Dick Allen, of course, was already getting booed for every strikeout and error. Fans may have loved the 1964 Phillies, but it was our typical tough love. "The fans could cost the Phillies the pennant," Houston pitcher Hal Woodeshick warned before the Phold, having seen the crowd turn suddenly on Allen after a few miscues.

That insurmountable lead the Phillies coughed up had sprouted as quickly as it later withered. The Phillies were only a game and a half up when July ended, then enjoyed a 17-game stretch against the awful Cubs and two relatively new franchises: the Mets and Colt-45s. They held that mighty six- to seven-game lead for about a month. They weren't a great team that choked. They were a decent team that won because of a little luck and a soft schedule. A Houston sportswriter called them "Gene Mauch and the Philadelphia Department of Recreation Team." The stories of the era praised their pluck, teamwork, and moxie, just as stories always do when a surprise team goes on a

Jim Bunning
(Courtesy of Temple University Libraries, Urban Archives, Philadelphia, PA)

run against bottom feeders. But the Phillies didn't have the talent to compete with Bob Gibson's Cardinals or Willie Mays's Giants for any extended period of time. To believe that they could was the soul of fandom. To expect that they could—to accuse them of choking when they failed—was the soul of delusion.

Bunning encapsulates the 1964 Phillies in a way that Allen or the bland Johnny Callison does not. A 32-year-old fastballer with a jerky delivery and a moody, arrogant reputation, Bunning arrived in a trade from the Tigers, who were tired of his gopherballs and his frequent losses to the Yankees. He pitched exceptionally well for six months, throwing a perfect game against the Mets on Father's Day, but the Phillies rapidly became over-reliant on Bunning and second starter Chris Short. Bunning began to fade in September, but the desperate Mauch began starting him on two days' rest down the stretch. Bunning lost three games during the 10-game Phold, leaving before the fourth inning was over in two of them.

Bunning hung around as the star pitcher for the 1965–1967 Phillies, but no one cares about the 1965–1967 Phillies. He was traded to

Pittsburgh in December 1967. That's what all the fuss is about: a four-season rental. Bunning was a poor man's Roy Halladay. We remember him because he became a senator, his opinions drifting from fiscal conservatism in the 1990s to knee-jerk obstructionism in 2010 (Bunning no longer goes to baseball card shows in Detroit because his votes against the auto industry bailouts made him persona non grata). We remember him because he slid into the Hall of Fame, his political career making him more appealing than the Mickey Lolich–Luis Tiant candidates to whom he's most similar.

And of course, we remember him for 1964, the great watershed moment in Philadelphia history that is just a footnote everywhere else. Bunning was never blamed for the Great Phold, and rightly so, because he pitched himself to exhaustion for a team that would have been in fifth place without him. And while the Phillies did lose 10 straight games, and they did blow a six-and-a-half game lead with 12 games to play, we've heard quite enough already about how it scarred a generation of fans. Many of those fans jumped on the roller coaster when it was on top. They rooted for a team that didn't have the horses to finish, lost their hearts to a bunch of guys who were anything but lovable when they weren't scratching out wins against the Colt-45s. I've interviewed enough old-timers who claim to have "died in 1964," and while I can sympathize, I realize those deaths were greatly exaggerated. I died in 1981, and again in 1993, and again in 2005, plus a few other demises. They were tough losses, not the end of the damn innocence. The Phold of 1964 was a losing streak, not an assassination, for Christ's sake.

As for the boos, we booed before, during, and after 1964. We booed when the team was in first place for the first time in a decade. So it's time to stop using 1964 as a post-traumatic stress disorder excuse for all sports-related anxiety attacks, especially if you are 27 years old and know about 1964 only from half-read Bill Conlin columns. It wasn't a halcyon era. Those 10 losses didn't make anyone a world-weary adult.

And you weren't sitting in the stands next to dear old dad when Bunning threw that perfect game. It was in New York. And you weren't born yet.

34

RON JAWORSKI

The Quarterback We Grew Up With

Greatness: ★★½
Toughness: ★★★★
Eccentricity: ★★
Legacy: ★½

I CAME OF AGE the day I booed Ron Jaworski.

It's a rite of adolescence for every Eagles fan. You put aside the childish hero worship, see the game through adult eyes, and discover that the quarterback is not only mortal, but hopelessly and irreparably flawed. It happens about the same time that you discover your father is human, but your father can belt or ground you when you boo him, so you save the worst elements of pubescent rebellion for the quarterback.

When I was a child, Jaworski meant a lot, not just to me but to my family. My grandfather was a first-generation Polish immigrant. Thanks to Archie Bunker, Dumb Polack jokes were still common on television, and while we could laugh at the stereotype, men like my grandfather wished it would go away. By 1978, we had a Polish quarterback (not to mention a Polish pope), and my grandfather started watching football again, often with me on the floor next to him. Greg Luzinski was a great hitter, but Jaworski was a leader, a field commander, someone to truly idolize.

The Eagles rose to the Super Bowl, three exciting years of buildup that culminated with an NFC title victory over the Cowboys that remains one of my greatest childhood memories. But then they fell. In 1983, the Eagles got off to a 4–2 start but finished the year in a 1–10 slump. I had just discovered sports-talk radio (WCAU at the time, in two-hour blocks) and started absorbing the wisdom of the masses. They said Jaworski couldn't read defenses. I believed it, and I repeated it. They said he locked onto the first receiver. They said he was immobile, which was a shorthand way to lay the faults of the team's rotted picket-fence of an offensive line at his feet. I believed it, and I repeated it.

Randall Cunningham replaced Jaworski after the first game of the 1985 season. He ran around like a puppy in a playground, but for a week or two I joined the throng in convincing myself that he was better. I was ready to say good riddance to Jaworski, tear down the posters of him on my bedroom wall, put away my childish ways. It was, I thought, a very grown-up attitude.

. . .

THERE'S A PHOTO GALLERY in the Pro Football Hall of Fame, and one of the pictures perfectly captures the Jaworski experience. It shows Jaworski lying motionless, facedown on the Astroturf after a sack. A yellow penalty flag lies beside Jaworski as a referee whistles and motions nearby. Cowboys defender John Dutton is frozen in the moment between celebrating the sack and protesting the penalty.

There's so much drama in the photograph. Jaworski looks as rumpled and lifeless as the flag. He's the gazelle carcass, Dutton the triumphant cheetah. The referee stands as a testament to the inadequacy of justice: 15 yards wouldn't restore Jaworski's health or help the Eagles recapture the fleeting magic of 1978–1980.

Jaworski was sacked 363 times in his career, 174 times in his final five years, when the Eagles were bad and the NFC East was filled with marauders like Lawrence Taylor, Dexter Manley, Randy White, Ed Jones, and Dutton. Only 15 quarterbacks have endured more sacks (including Jaworski's two successors, Randall Cunningham and Donovan McNabb), but Jaworski kept staggering back to the huddle, starting every single game from 1977 through the last weeks of 1984, setting a record for consecutive starts that only Brett Favre could break.

His durability was a mixed blessing. As the Eagles rose from the depths of the league to the Super Bowl in the late 1970s, Jaworski, with his immigrant, factory-town background, represented the perceived virtues of Philadelphia: resilience, hard work, and defiance. The Polish Rifle was a gritty die-hard, and nothing the overpaid, glittery marauders on the Cowboys defense did could stop him.

But the '80s came, and when the Eagles quickly collapsed, we wished Jaworski would go away. Yes, there were doubters before that.

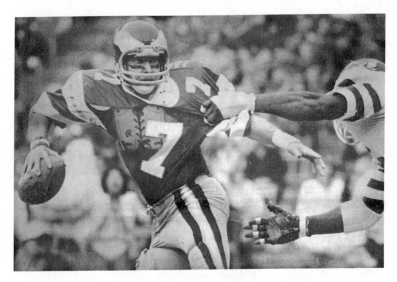

Ron Jaworski
(Courtesy of Temple University Libraries, Urban Archives, Philadelphia, PA)

Some chanted "We want Joe" for backup Joe Walton when Jaworski had a slow start in a 1979 playoff game. But there are always doubters, especially in Philly, where skepticism is a birthright. But by the mid-1980s, Jaworski was an anachronism: blood, guts, and bellbottoms in the world of personal computers and break-dance.

Cunningham, of course, was all break-dance. He received a standing ovation in the fourth quarter of a 1985 preseason game, a sign that we masses had made up our minds. Jaworski had played the 1984 season hurt. He faced Taylor and the Giants wearing a flak jacket to protect broken ribs. His ironman streak and his leg snapped against the Cardinals in late November; the Eagles were somehow 5–6–1 and still in the playoff chase when it happened, but they quickly faded under backup Joe Pisarcik. Jaworski rehabbed hard, fought his way back onto the field, and was pummeled by the Giants in the season opener: eight sacks in a 21–0 loss. Cunningham replaced him, and we cheered. It was time for a change.

Three weeks later, Jaworski came off the bench to relieve Cunningham in a tie game against the Giants at the Vet. Jaworski went 3-for-7 before delivering the game-ending interception. "There's no question

I hit rock bottom after being benched," Jaworski said. After that interception, he had no supporters. We all booed. We'd rather see Cunningham do doughnuts in the pocket than witness another sack, another crawl from the carpet, another loss.

*   *   *

THE JAWORSKI I see at NFL Films bears little resemblance to my boyhood hero, or to the battered quarterback I joined the city in rejecting as a teenager.

Jaworski is now the voice of technical football wisdom, a thinking man's expert on X's and O's, a guru of an inner game that most fans can't come close to comprehending. He's the most respected analyst in football, a *Monday Night Football* commentator who chooses knowledge over hype, a talk-show host who explains complex tactics in easy-to-understand terms. Once in a while, I get to ride shotgun as he prepares his weekly show. He leans back in a chair with a remote control, watching plays 25 times, pausing and freezing frames over and over to gain a complete understanding of what each player did, and why.

And I can only think, this is the guy we said couldn't read a defense? This is the guy we said telegraphed his passes?

Jaworski is also a respected businessman now, a local entrepreneur and the co-owner of the Philadelphia Soul. He is the voice and face of integrity in Philadelphia, always surrounded by well-wishers and autograph seekers when he makes a public appearance. After 33 years in the region, everyone knows him, or knows someone who knows him, or at least met him once at a fund-raiser or a golf tournament. Everyone respects him.

This is the guy about whom the *Daily News* once wrote: "With the possible exception of Mike Schmidt, no professional athlete has been booed more."

It didn't take long for us to realize that we were wrong about Jaworski. Cunningham was hopelessly unprepared as a rookie. Jaws returned to the lineup after that rock-bottom interception and threw six touchdown passes in his first two games. The Eagles went 6–5 after his return, though it was not enough to get the team to .500.

Buddy Ryan arrived in 1986 and tried to play to the boo birds. He traded for Matt Cavanaugh and gave him the starting job. Jaworski won it back and started five games before injuring his throwing hand. Ryan said Jaws was benched, hand or no hand. The Eagles released Jaworski in March 1987, no doubt believing that fans would welcome the change.

Instead, fans mourned the departure of a hero. "I never expected the kind of response that I've gotten, and I hear that the Eagles are flabbergasted by the way people have reacted," Jaworski told the *Inquirer* soon after his release. "I've never been the most loved guy here. I've been booed a lot. But I've always been respected, and the fans just feel that, after what I've done over the years, I deserved a thank you rather than a kick in the butt."

He did deserve better. Even a cocky teenager like me knew that.

. . .

AFTER JAWORSKI, I became more measured in my criticism, more wary of how fickle and uninformed the wisdom of the masses can be. I can be quick to criticize, but I'm slow to anger and more generous with my benefit of the doubt. In other words, I grew through adolescence into adulthood. Jaworski was a part of that growth, an in-my-face example of teenage snap judgment proven totally wrong.

As fans, we can still be adolescent at times. We're often moody and irrational, petty and judgmental. Maybe that's the nature of fandom: when you get right down to it, root-root-rooting for the home team is a juvenile impulse. But there's no reason the worst excesses cannot be tempered. Jaworski taught us to appreciate the sports heroes we have, to not rush too soon to the next distraction, but it was a lesson we learned only briefly. We embraced Jaworski just as he left us, but many others in this book weren't so lucky.

After his release, Jaworski told the *Inquirer* how he wanted to be remembered: "Maybe I wasn't the most talented guy, maybe I wasn't blessed with the ability of a Bobby Clarke, a Julius Erving or a Mike Schmidt. So I want to be remembered as a guy who just kept getting up, a guy who never said die."

That's how we remember him: the guy who never said die, even when we thought we wanted him to. Thanks, Jaws.

35

MO CHEEKS

Point Guard for a Nation

Greatness: ★★★
Toughness: ★★★
Eccentricity: ★★
Legacy: ★★

M O CHEEKS'S OFF-KEY baritone was hardly the Sound of Philadelphia, but his 2003 version of the national anthem was more moving than any sung by Teddy Pendergrass, or even Whitney Houston.

Everyone has seen the video: 13-year-old contest winner Natalie Gilbert forgets the words to the "Star-Spangled Banner" before a Portland Trail Blazers playoff game. She stands terrified on the court for a few seconds, blushing and giggling. Then Cheeks appears. "It's okay, c'mon, c'mon," he says, before cueing her with the next line, putting his arm around Gilbert and singing along, waving his right hand to exhort the crowd to help.

Cheeks cannot carry a tune. His knowledge of the words was about as cloudy as Gilbert's. (He feeds her the line "at the starlight's last dreaming." Close enough.) Still, the duet is beautiful, and the thousands of fans and players in the field house joined voices as we seldom do before a game.

No sportswriter could resist the obvious hook: it was the greatest assist ever by a player legendary for assists. The man known as one of the league's greatest team players coaxed the ultimate team performance from the Portland fans.

That was our Little Mo singing out there. Philly may have taken him for granted at times, and the Sixers may have left him out to dry in his final days, but Cheeks always came back, and he brought a little bit of us everywhere he went, even to Portland.

. . .

FOR THE RECORD, Cheeks did more in his 11 years in Philly than play tight defense and selflessly dish the ball to Julius Erving and Moses Malone. Cheeks averaged 14.5 points per game to go with 7.89 assists during the 1982–1983 championship season. He wasn't always a role player. Later in his Sixers career, with Charles Barkley in the fold and Erving and Malone aging, Cheeks was often the third option in the offense, scoring 15.4 points per game in 1985–1986 and 15.6 points per game in 1986–1987. In 1988, with Erving retired and Malone in Washington, Cheeks was still an All Star, representing the Sixers alongside Barkley.

Cheeks even dunked occasionally: nine times during the 1982–1983 regular season, four more times in the playoffs. Most famously he dunked in the final seconds of Game 4 of the 1983 finals, punctuating a sweep of the Lakers by going coast-to-coast after a Magic Johnson miss, high-stepping all the way and ignoring the wide-open Erving on his wing. "He dribbled the ball with his right hand and slapped his side with his left hand. It was like he was riding a hobby horse," the *Inquirer*'s Bill Livingston wrote of his journey to the rim.

In true Cheeks fashion, he later denied any desire to showboat, or even to dunk. "I should have passed the ball," he said years later. "It was just the euphoria of it all."

. . .

BY 1989, SIXERS OWNER Harold Katz had accused Andrew Toney of goldbricking, publicly insulted Malone, alienated Erving, and threatened to move the team to Camden as part of his stadium negotiations. It was inevitable that his ax would fall on Cheeks, by then a productive but aging remnant of a long-ago title team.

The Sixers wanted young point guard Johnny Dawkins. The Spurs wanted Cheeks as a mentor and leader for their young team. The two teams engineered a five-player trade, quickly but silently, worried that the deal might fall through. Sixers assistant coach Fred Carter shot hoops with Cheeks in the Saint Joseph's University Fieldhouse on an

August afternoon, obeying strict orders not to mention the nearly finalized trade. By the time Carter worked up the nerve to talk, Cheeks had already left the court.

Sixers coach Jim Lynam waited in Cheeks's driveway for 45 minutes to break the news, but when Cheeks was late, Lynam returned to the team's office. Cheeks learned about the trade, the first of his career, from Michael Barkann, then a young reporter for KYW Channel 3, who waited for Cheeks at his home. Shocked by the news, Cheeks rolled up his windows and drove away. "I'm at a loss for words," he said later. "To hear it the way I did, with a camera in my face, that's not the way I envisioned (being treated) after 11 years."

A few days later, the consummate professional collected himself and spoke hopefully of a return to Philly. "I really liked it here," he said, noting that he planned to stay in Philadelphia in the offseason. "I've talked a little about becoming an assistant coach here, and I still think I'd like to do that."

Cheeks returned as an assistant to John Lucas in 1994. Lucas noted that Cheeks brought more to the table than his knowledge of backcourt play. "Mo adds something else this team needs, which is a little tradition. There's a great response and love for him in this town." So much love that many thought the 37-year-old bench coach would take the court again as the awful 1994–1995 season unfolded. "We're going for youth," Katz said, nixing the idea. "I'm not interested in selling a few more tickets," he added. Of course not.

The Sixers retired Cheeks's jersey in February 1995. The Spectrum crowd gave him a standing ovation. Erving and others spoke. For a few halftime minutes, the Sixers were champions again, not an awful team en route to a 24-win season. "They say actions speak louder than words and that's the way it was with Maurice," former coach Billy Cunningham said that night. "Maurice led us with his defensive ability, his personality, the way he sacrificed himself for others."

*   *   *

CHEEKS STAYED on the Sixers bench when Larry Brown replaced Lucas and the team climbed out of the cellar and back to the NBA Finals. Later, when the Sixers again needed a dose of tradition, he rejoined the team as head coach. Cheeks suffered through three-and-a-half nondescript seasons, dealing with a talent-poor roster and a battle with gout, an illness so painful that Cheeks sometimes coached with one shoe on and one off.

In between Philly stints, Cheeks coached the Trail Blazers to the playoffs and helped a young girl remember the "Star-Spangled Banner."

If only that moment had occurred in Philadelphia, where Cheeks spent most of his playing and coaching career, instead of the Pacific hinterlands. Perhaps the national reputation of Philly fans would have changed forever. We might have become the city that rescued young girls, not the city that spits and throws up on them.

Cheeks may have been in Portland that night, but his Philly sensibility was with him. He wasn't swayed by pomp and circumstance, by camera crews and pyrotechnics. He didn't worry about how he looked or how he sounded. He performed a small, human gesture that was more moving than any charitable contribution or public service appearance.

He did the little thing. He tried. He helped. His actions were louder than words. And his words—sung with a wobbly determination—echoed through the sports world.

36

RON HEXTALL

Ameba, Enigma, Goaltender

Greatness: ★ ★ ★
Toughness: ★ ★ ★
Eccentricity: ★ ★ ½
Legacy: ★ ½

T HE 1986–1987 STANLEY CUP Finals were a shooting clinic for
Hall of Famers. The series was an exhibition of precision puck-
handling and passing by the Edmonton Oilers, one of the greatest
hockey teams ever assembled.

The series highlights are available on YouTube; watching them
brings back scary memories: Wayne Gretzky feeding Paul Coffey, Coffey feeding Jari Kurri, Gretzky and Mark Messier leading five-on-three
charges. The Oilers opened that series with two wins, and they took
2–0 leads out of the first period in three straight games. They swarmed
"like white-sweatered hornets," Adam Kimelman wrote.

The only thing standing between the Flyers and a sweep at the
hands of living legends was rookie goalie Ron Hextall.

Hextall was outstanding throughout the 1987 playoffs, saving 90.8
percent of shots, but he was extraordinary against the Oilers. He was
at his best in Game 6, as the Flyers clawed back from yet another 2–0
deficit to keep the series alive. In the second period, he stopped an
undefended two-man break, sprawling across the crease to stone Jaro-
slav Pouzar after a steal near the blue line. In the final seconds, with
the Flyers leading and the Oilers' goalie pulled, Hextall withstood a
furious onslaught by Messier and others. "Hextall had to make like an
amoeba over the last half minute of the game to cover the net," Gary
Blockus wrote in the *Allentown Morning Call* the next day.

The Flyers lost Game 7 and the series, but Hextall won the Conn Smythe Trophy and some noteworthy admirers. "Hextall is probably the best goaltender I've ever seen in the National Hockey League, that I've ever played against," Gretzky said after Game 6. Backup Flyers goalie Glenn Resch, a 38-year-old NHL lifer, offered praise as exuberant as it was ominous. "He is today, and he will be five years from now, and probably 10 years from now, the best goalie in the league."

Philly fans know better than to project 10 years into the future, or even 2 years. By 1989, Hextall was in a tailspin. By 1992, he was out of town, his Philadelphia story seemingly over, another star who burned out too quickly.

. . .

WHEN PELLE LINDBERGH died in November 1985, the Flyers promoted Darren Jensen, not the 21-year-old Hextall, to back up Bob Froese. Jensen was more NHL ready. Hextall was too raw. Froese made the All-Star team and helped the Flyers win 53 games. Hextall went to camp in the summer of 1986 just hoping to compete for a roster spot.

When Hextall went undefeated in the preseason, coach Mike Keenan took a gamble, naming him the opening-day starter against the Oilers, who were coming off a 56-win season. The move surprised everyone, even Hextall. Hextall gave up a goal to Kurri on the very first shot of the season. He stopped everything else: two Gretsky breakaways, an undefended charge by sharpshooter Esa Tikkanen. Hextall didn't wait for the Oilers to come to him: he attacked them, venturing beyond the crease to cut off angles and disrupt their shots.

Hextall won that game, then 8 of his first 10 starts, then Rookie Player of the Month honors for October 1986. Fans were skeptical at first, remembering Robbie Moore, who went undefeated in four games at the end of the 1978–1979 season only to wilt in the playoffs and disappear forever. But Hextall won fans and teammates over. He was a different kind of goalie, one who protected the crease with the ferocity of a checking-line goon and who stickhandled like an extra defenseman. He earned 104 penalty minutes in his rookie season, but he also recorded six assists and talked openly of becoming the first NHL goalie to score on a shot on goal. "Ron Hextall is a nuisance, an agitator, a whirlwind of constant motion and emotion," Bill LeConey later wrote of him. "Whether he's pounding his sticks against the goal posts or swiping at an opponent who crosses his path, Hextall always seems to be stirring things up."

After winning the Conn Smythe Trophy and battling the Oilers to the bitter end, Hextall was one of the brightest stars in the city. His reign was short. Hextall was the team's MVP in each of the next two seasons, scoring that elusive goal on December 8, 1987. But the penalties mounted (he set a record for goalies with 113 penalty minutes in 1988–1989), and Hextall's adventures far beyond the crease led to easy goals. The Flyers began to slip from contention. Hextall drew much of the criticism for the decline, and he deserved a lot of it.

Late in a Conference Final game against the Canadiens in 1989, with all hope lost and Hextall angry over a cheap shot against Brian Propp early in the series, Hextall charged Montreal defenseman Chris Chelios as he crossed the blue line, body-slamming him near the boards. The attack merited a 12-game suspension. That offseason, Hextall held out for six weeks. When he returned, he rushed to the ice before he was in playing shape. He pulled a groin on his first game back. After missing 10 games, he played again, beating the Islanders. But he pulled a hamstring in the next morning's practice and missed a month. The team sent him to Hershey to rehabilitate, but he tore a groin muscle in his lone start there. "It was like a nightmare," Hextall said after the injury. "But usually you're asleep when you have a nightmare, aren't you?"

Hextall recovered, and for a few seasons he split the goaltending chores with Dave Wregget and Dominic Roussel, prospects who were obviously being groomed as replacements. He was effective, but far from the player Gretsky and Resch thought he would be in 1987. He had mellowed: fewer fights, fewer journeys out of net, less talk about scoring. But he had lost some of his elite quickness. He became just another guy who wasn't as good as we thought he could be, another disappointment.

At a golf tournament in the spring of 1992, Mark Howe told Hextall to keep his bags packed. "Roussel's going to be taking your job within the next year, and that makes you expendable," Howe said later, recounting the story in the *Daily News*. "I hated to tell him, but I thought then he wouldn't be too surprised when the news comes." Two months later, Hextall became a key component in the Eric Lindros deal. "When the ax was dropped, he was pretty upset that it's come to be," Hextall's agent said, hinting that Hextall might not report to the Quebec Nordiques.

. . .

HEXTALL DID PLAY for the Nordiques, then the Islanders a year later. But his Philadelphia story wasn't over. Roussel didn't develop. Tommy Soderstrom, another goaltending prospect, was worse. The Flyers traded Soderstrom to the Islanders to get Hextall back in September 1994.

Hextall was thrilled to return. "My dad kept telling me, 'You don't look good in that blue,'" he told the *Daily News*. He put the booing and disappointment behind him. "I don't think they would have gotten me back if there were any hard feelings," Hextall said after the trade. "I'm not one to look back. I'd rather look forward." He even moved back into his old South Jersey home, which Lindros had been renting.

All of the "face of the franchise" pressure now belonged to Lindros. Speaking of Hextall, coach Terry Murray said, "We're not trying to make him the savior or the leader of the organization, or anything other than just be a player, a goaltender." The lowered expectations may have had an effect on Hextall's performance: he led the league with 2.17 goals against average in 1995–1996, then won 31 regular season games in the Flyers' return to the Stanley Cup Finals in 1996–1997. More likely, the team improved around Hextall, and we stopped obsessing about every minor injury or soft goal.

What's certain is that Hextall's second stint with the Flyers rehabilitated his image. It brought back memories of the tough guy who fought and puck-handled better than any goalie in history, erasing memories of holdouts, injuries, and costly acts of over-aggression. Hextall stayed around long enough to earn a reputation with a younger generation of fans, who gave him his own Facebook group ("Ron Hextall Is Tougher Than Chuck Norris") and Urban Dictionary listing ("The greatest goalie ever").

"Philadelphia will always be my home," Hextall said at his induction into the Flyers Hall of Fame in 2008. A goalie who fights, an ameba who battles hornets, belongs nowhere else.

37

JOHN KRUK

The Thinking Man's Slob

Greatness: ★★★
Toughness: ★★½
Eccentricity: ★★★
Legacy: ★½

I F THE 1993 Phillies played in any other city, we would have hated them.

Remember the overheated stories about their toughness, their sloppiness, their barbaric personalities? "If innocent Mariners could fly the Maple Leaf upside down during the 1992 World Series in Atlanta, imagine what the raffish Phillies could perpetrate in the next few days," George Vecsey wrote in the *New York Times*, perpetuating the team's Cro-Magnon stereotype. The media spun sloppy uniforms and tobacco spit into a marketable image: Philadelphia brand baseball, like the cream cheese, was high in fat and low in sophistication.

It was mostly snake oil, mostly image. The Phillies were no louder, ruder, or tougher than any other bunch of baseball players; they just had a few long-haired guys and a sudden knack for winning, so sportswriters found a hook and swam with it. Imagine the Mets or Braves trying to pull off that "hairy tough guy" routine. You'd only stop booing to laugh. You'd want to punch Len Dykstra in the face. You'd call Darren Daulton a pretty boy. You'd cheer for Mitch Williams to enter the game rather than reaching for the glycerin.

And John Kruk. . . . You would probably like him, even if he was on the other team, even if he was dwarfed by some silly Hagar the Horrible persona. Kruk was just that type of player.

. . .

WHILE RESEARCHING this book, I checked the statistics of the 1990 Phillies, and wept. The best thing about the 1990 Phillies season is that it was almost immediately forgotten. Von Hayes led the team with 17 homers that year. Pat Combs led the team with 10 wins. Bruce Ruffin. Sil Campusano. It was that kind of year.

It was also Kruk's first full season with the Phillies. The team acquired Kruk and Randy Ready from the Padres for Chris James in a deal that must still have Padres fans seething, assuming that there are Padres fans. Kruk was batting .184 when we dealt for him midway through 1989, but he batted .331 for the Phillies. Spring training of the 1990 season was our chance to get to know him, the time when sportswriters had the opportunity to write the profile pieces that shape fans' opinions.

We learned that Kruk was willing to take a low-ball salary rather than risk arbitration. "I didn't think arbitration was the right thing," he said. "The Phillies gave me a chance to play. So I wanted to be fair to them." We learned that he took dieting about as seriously as we did. "I cut all the junk food out," Kruk said of the regimen that helped him shed 20 pounds. "All the McDonald's, the Wendy's, the potato chips. And I cut down on the beer." We learned that his mental approach was nothing like Mike Schmidt's. "I don't sit down and analyze my swing. I've watched video tapes a few times, but it didn't help because I don't know what I'm looking for. I just swing." We learned he was funny: when a reporter criticized his grooming, he shot back: "I'm no Mr. GQ myself, but what you're wearing doesn't match."

All of this would become caricature in time, all of the burgers and beer drinking and one-liners and the aw-shucks approach to the game. But in 1990 it was real personality, and the team needed it. Watching Von Hayes and Charlie Hayes was difficult: they were as bland as they were bad. Kruk was fun, and before the slob-gawking story lines of 1993, he was a well-rounded individual, a beer-and-burger guy who really worked hard at his game, a prankster who got serious when calling out a player who wasn't giving his all. Kruk, Dykstra, and Daulton were all there in 1990, but the supporting cast wasn't, so the Phillies had a handful of colorful personalities, not a barbarian horde ready to storm the gates of Rome.

Kruk's bat also endeared him to us. Philly fans love contact hitters, love seeing the ball put in play, even if it doesn't go 400 feet. Yet we've had so few contact hitters. Pete Rose. Greg Gross. Placido Polanco. Heck, people loved Dave Cash, even if he was the weakest .305 hitter you'd ever see. Kruk was a brilliant contact hitter. He worked counts and sprayed the ball, flashed power when he needed to, and charged to first base with speed that shocked shortstops who thought they had time to throw. Baseball hasn't produced many big guys who slap out a .300 average while drawing walks in recent times. You have to go back to the 1940s to find guys like Kruk, players like Hoot Evers and Ernie Lombardi with quick wrists, great eyes, and tubby waists.

In other words, Kruk was a throwback.

. . .

THROWBACK. What a cliché. What a loaded term.

"These days, most ballplayers are businessmen. They are as much at home carrying a briefcase as a bat," wrote Paul Hagan in the *Daily News* in 1990. Kruk, to Hagan, was "slightly out of place, a player with a 1950s work ethic playing in the thoroughly modern 1990s."

Ah, the good old days. Kruk and the 1993 Phillies were often called throwbacks, and Bruce Buschel was suspicious of the term when he wrote for *Philadelphia Magazine*. "Maybe it's me, but there always seemed something racial, something coded, in the terms 'hard working' and 'blue-collar' and 'throwback,'" he wrote. He noted that the stars of the 1993 Phillies—and most of the supporting cast—were white, and suggested that the city's attitude toward color was "exclusionary." And Kruk? "John Kruk, bless his soul, may be the whitest man on earth. Overweight, overachieving and over-tussed."

Race had an impact on the way the 1993 Phillies were perceived. Country boys with untucked shirts and long hair were considered charming at a time when black guys with baggy pants and do-rags looked like criminals. Still, the "throwback" label had more to do with the fogy-driven tradition of sports journalism than with anything racial. The last century of sportswriting has been a ceaseless yearning for the good old days, just beyond memory, when players cared not a whit about their salaries, mastered all the fundamentals like bunting and backing up throws, and signed autographs for disabled children until sunset. In the 1990s sportswriters pined for the 1950s, in the 1950s for the 1930s, and at the turn of the century they yearned for players who were more like Harry Wright's Cincinnati Red Stockings. That myopic nostalgia allowed 1990s writers to gawk at the long-haired Phillies while half of major league baseball was on a steroid binge. Writers were too busy waxing rhapsodic about Mickey Mantle to notice a problem that nearly swallowed the sport, and they couldn't bring themselves to remember that in the "throwback" days, players cared just as much about money as now, and black players were accused of being stupid and lazy, assuming they were allowed on the field at all.

But none of this should be laid at Kruk's feet. He really was a man out of time. A wide-bodied singles hitter. A quipster who was never guarded, never surly. A man who played the final game of the League Championship Series with his pants ripped above the thigh, as if it were 1914 and the spare uniforms were a trolley-ride away. He knew about his persona, and he didn't care. He just wanted to play and win games.

. . .

FANS OF MY GENERATION tried to make the 1993 Phillies into our own Broad Street Bullies, because they were all we had. We still love them, but we need a little of that myopic nostalgia to think of most of those players as heroes today. They were steroid users and space cadets, pitchers who couldn't throw straight and blowhards who thought themselves more important than the game, bit players and hangers-on whom we remember only because they were part of a few months of magic, a time when the Phillies were in first place and we thought the world rooted against us because we didn't shave.

Much of 1993 was manufactured, but Kruk was real. Writers took his likeable personality and smeared it over the whole team, and they became likeable too. We could use a few more players like Kruk in all sports, in all of our eras. But if guys like Kruk came around all the time, we wouldn't keep calling them throwbacks.

38-39

Tie: **JEROME BROWN**
and
PELLE LINDBERGH

The Lost Brothers

Greatness: ★ ★ ★
Toughness: ★ ★ ★
Eccentricity: ★ ★ ★ Four from Jerome, minus one from Pelle
Legacy: ★

DEATH HAUNTS our sports memories.

In the lost quarter century from 1983 to 1998, watching great teams fall short and terrible teams linger wasn't bad enough. We also had to see heroes fall: brash young stars, full of promise, taken away just when we realized how special they were.

Pelle Lindbergh. Jerome Brown. You remember where you were when you heard about each of their deaths, don't you? Lindbergh and Brown: fallen sons, and true Philly players who endured boos and criticism, then earned our respect, all in the short time we had with them.

.   .   .

IT IS SUNDAY morning, November 10, 1985. The Flyers are on a 10-game winning streak. Pelle Lindbergh is brain dead at Kennedy Hospital in Voorhees, New Jersey.

The Flyers story in the Sunday *Inquirer* is about the Flyers victory over the Bruins. Tim Kerr had a hat trick. "It's just fun right now," Kerr said. "You know how it is—you get in a groove, the team's winning and

Pelle Lindbergh
(Courtesy of Temple University
Libraries, Urban Archives,
Philadelphia, PA)

everything is fun." Lindbergh had the night off, but the *Inquirer* article speculates at the end that "Pelle Lindbergh will start against the Oilers" on Thursday.

Lindbergh left the Coliseum sports bar after 5:00 A.M., long after the *Inquirer* went to press. He slammed his car into the wall sometime after 5:40 A.M. News seeped slowly back then: no blogs, no under-the-broadcast crawl. You went to church or breakfast beaming about a 10-game winning streak, and you heard rumors. Bad accident. Paralyzed. Brain dead. You rushed home and flicked through the stations, hoping it wasn't as bad as you'd heard. It was worse.

•   •   •

IT IS THURSDAY afternoon, June 25, 1992. It's a typically hot, dull Philadelphia summer. The Phillies are in last place. They lost 8–1 on Wednesday night because someone named Mickey Weston (making his first and last appearance with the Phillies) couldn't get out of the fourth inning. Charles Barkley was agitating for a trade. Randall Cunningham was rehabbing his knee. If you were thinking about sports at all, you were looking forward to training camp: there were plenty of questions about the Eagles offense, but you knew all you had to know about the defense.

News traveled faster in 1992 than in 1985: more cable television, more satellites, more sports-talk radio. By late afternoon, you knew. Jerome Brown was in an auto accident. Flipped Corvette. Nephew in the car. By evening, you saw videotape of the wrecked car, reaction shots of grieving family and teammates. We love to cheer. We like to boo. Once again, sports forced us to grieve.

.   .   .

WHEN WE LOSE loved ones, we remember the good things about them and omit the bad. Often, that does a disservice to them, and to us. Remembering the faults and flaws, the fights and disagreements, keeps the memory alive and real, makes the bonds stronger, preserves the moments that made the relationship special.

So let's remember how badly we booed Pelle Lindbergh, how harshly we criticized Jerome Brown.

Lindbergh was named to the NHL's All-Rookie team in 1982–1983, but he followed a fine regular season with three awful playoff performances. By the start of the 1983 season, he was rotating with Bob Froese and trying to shake off a slump. By February 1984, the slump became a crisis. He endured a stretch where he allowed 6.20 goals per game, with the Flyers going 1–4–1 in six games. At the Spectrum against the Canucks, he coughed up a 5–2 lead almost single-handedly, allowing a weak 70-foot slap shot to bounce off his leg for the game-tying goal. "Lindbergh covered his eyes for a full second, hoping the ice would open up and swallow him," Jay Greenberg wrote. "When it didn't, he got up. . . . And Lindbergh, naked now before fate and 17,001 taunts, faced the music." The Flyers shipped him to the AHL for a few games, as much for his own protection as for theirs.

Reading newspaper accounts of Lindbergh can be spooky. His Porsche—a different Porsche than the one he wrecked, because he purchased the one he wrecked after winning the Vezina Trophy in 1985—keeps popping up in stories. "The Flyers are slumping, and everybody knows that it's 100 percent Lindbergh's fault and now he can't find 75 cents in his $40,000 Porsche," wrote Greenberg in 1983, recounting an incident where Lindbergh left his wallet with his fiancée and had to borrow the bridge toll. (The "100 percent" remark was sarcastic, as the whole team was slumping at that point.) When Lindbergh stayed prone on the ice for 10 seconds in that Canucks loss, Greenberg wrote about him "not getting up" and the "Angel of Death" stalking him.

It's macabre, a reminder of how quickly we invoke death when a team loses a game—like the old-timers who claim to have "died in

1964." By the start of the 1985–1986 season we were done worrying about death every time Lindbergh took the ice. We were just starting to really enjoy living with him.

As for Brown, there were fights, weight issues, contract disputes, and camouflage pants. He was a Buddy Ryan favorite, and he had all the Buddy flaws: too blustery, too profane, too likely to follow a dominating performance with a disappearing act. When Ryan was fired after the 1990 season, Brown became the poster child for passé Buddy Ball. Brown held out in the summer of 1991. Holdouts were typical when Norman Braman ran the team like a water-ice stand, but Brown remained behind when fellow holdouts Seth Joyner and Clyde Simmons signed, and if there was one player Braman and Rich Kotite seemed comfortable living without, it was their overweight, outspoken nose tackle.

We can pretend now that we always loved Jerome, that we respected Ryan and knew from the beginning that Kotite was a ninny. But that's not how it was at the time. Most of us had soured on Ryan, and Brown had exactly one sack in 1990: one less than Mike Golic, his backup. It was time to buy into Kotite's system, to professionalize the team, to stop winning grudge matches and start winning playoff games.

Brown, it turned out, really was with the program. He arrived at camp weighing 297 pounds, a perfect playing weight for him. He toned down his public persona. He delivered a monster performance in 1991, that comically disheartening season when every quarterback within 10 miles of the Vet got injured but the defense still led the Eagles to a 10–6 record.

So by June 1992, we believed in Brown and looked forward to what a team that won 10 games with Brad Goebel and Jeff Kemp at quarterback could do with Cunningham back under center. Then we lost Brown, long before camp opened and we even had the chance to start really dreaming.

*   *   *

IT'S TIME TO GO BACK to the alternate universe, the world of "what ifs." In some alternative universe, Lindbergh and Brown are still alive. They had long, successful careers. They don't share this low berth on our pantheon of legends. They are elsewhere. Higher? Lower? At the very top?

They certainly aren't linked in our minds. Brown was boisterous and brash, Lindbergh quiet and a little sensitive. Brown was a huge man with a weight problem, Lindbergh a tiny athlete with dehydration issues. Brown was more like Charles Barkley, Lindbergh more like Mike Schmidt. The only thing that links them in our universe is their absence.

But in the other universe, this whole book is different.

Even in the other universe, the Eagles don't win a Super Bowl with Brown; we'd have to travel to the realm of No Kotite for that. The 1992 Eagles win an extra game or two with Brown, but one defensive tackle doesn't make a difference in a 34–10 playoff loss to the Cowboys. In the years that follow, Randall Cunningham grows nutty, Ricky Watters brings chaos to the locker room, and another big talker on defense does more harm than good. Brown joins Reggie White, Seth Joyner, and others in the Great Free Agent Diaspora and resurfaces on Buddy Ryan's Cardinals late in his career. Brown used to joke that after retirement, he would "get up to about 450 pounds." "I'm going to get myself a Kentucky Fried Chicken franchise, a big stogie and a white Caddy." In the alternate universe, he's smoking that stogie, driving that Cadillac, maybe telling jokes on a pregame show.

What about Lindbergh? In our universe, the Flyers lost the Stanley Cup Finals to the Edmonton Oilers in seven games in 1987. It's hard to imagine anyone playing better than Ron Hextall in that series. Anyone but Lindbergh, that is. All it would take was one game, one little edge, a veteran over a rookie. In that alternate universe, Lindbergh makes a few more saves, and the Flyers win Game 2 against the Oilers in overtime instead of losing in overtime. The Flyers win the Stanley Cup, and suddenly Brian Propp, Tim Kerr, and others skate into this book. Lindbergh has his career and Hextall's combined, plus a ring, and he's on the front cover next to Julius Erving.

Maybe. Or maybe both players fall short of expectations, get weighed down by controversy (or, in Brown's case, simply weighed down), get traded or play out the string. Maybe they were at their peak when they left us, each destined only for long, disappointing denouement. Maybe we remember them only because we lost them.

If so, let's remember more than the shocking headline or the idealized image. Let's remember how Lindbergh and Brown won and lost, amazed and frustrated. Let's remember how we felt when they played, the good and the bad, without forgetting how we felt when we lost them. And let's remember again that sport is just sport, not life and death, and that a lost playoff game feels like death only until you deal with the real thing.

HAL GREER

The Forgotten Hall of Famer

Greatness: ★★★★
Toughness: ★★★
Eccentricity: ★
Legacy: ★★

HAL GREER PLAYED 754 regular season and 66 postseason games for the 76ers, helped the team to a World Championship, represented the team in eight All-Star games (earning the MVP award in one), played 80 games per year and scored 20 points per night like clockwork, and found a way not just to peacefully coexist with Wilt Chamberlain but to thrive in his shadow. He played on arguably the greatest team ever, and inarguably the worst team ever, without ever having to leave the city. He embodied our greatest sporting ideals for an entire decade, a workaday everyman with a picture-perfect jump shot, always ready to battle the Celtics to the buzzer.

For these accomplishments, he earned our eternal amnesia. You can read a dozen books about Philly sports and barely notice Hal Greer. Unless you listen to Sonny Hill, you can go a full year without hearing his name mentioned on the radio. Look for him in Bill Simmons's *Book of Basketball*, and you'll find dirty jokes instead of a profile. Greer is our forgotten Hall of Famer, our lost champion.

. . .

THE 76ERS PERPETRATED a cruel joke on the city of Philadelphia. They arrived from Syracuse in 1963 to no fanfare, quickly acquired hometown hero Wilt Chamberlain, leapt into contention, and won a championship after just four seasons. They then embarked on a long, slow-motion swan dive, spending a few seconds as the Celtics' playoff

Hal Greer
(Courtesy of Temple
University Libraries, Urban
Archives, Philadelphia, PA)

playthings, then slip-
ping below .500, then
plummeting so low that
by 1972–1973 they were
the worst team in mod-
ern sports history with a
9–73 record.

In other words, they
became champions be-
fore anyone had a chance
to turn and notice them.
Then, once fans climbed
on the bandwagon, they took them on an express train straight to hell.

The only player who stayed along for the whole ride was Greer.
During the championship season, he was a 22-point-per-game scorer,
a smooth-shooting complement to Chamberlain. During the nine-win
season, he was a battered 36-year-old averaging 5.6 points per game.

Between the glory of 1967 and the futility of 1973, there were hundreds of games and thousands of points. Greer was one of the most
durable players in Philadelphia sports history, playing 80 or more
games per year nine times with the Sixers. He averaged over 20 points
per game from the time the team arrived from Syracuse until 1972.
Greer was a sniper at guard and small forward, and while it's told that
he resented Chamberlain's arrival at first, their games meshed perfectly. Greer roamed the perimeter, looking for 15- to 18-footers, making the most of the space Chamberlain created wherever Chamberlain
wasn't. He defended Sam Jones and other Celtics snipers. He kept battling, long after Chamberlain left and the Sixers went on a bad-draft
binge and tried to win games with Bob Rule at center.

Greer was everything we claim to like in a player. "Hal Greer was such a smart player," teammate Billy Cunningham said of him. "Hal Greer never forced things or did things that would not be beneficial to the team." The NBA Hall of Fame Web site quotes Sixers coach Dolph Schayes: "Hal Greer always came to play. He came to practice the same way, to every team function the same way. Every bus and plane and train, he was on time. Hal Greer punched the clock. Hal Greer brought the lunch pail."

A smart player. A lunch-pail type. A tough guy—Greer committed 3,855 fouls, among the most in NBA history, and played through numerous injuries. A guy who scored 32 points to beat the Celtics—finally—in a championship game the Sixers tried to lose.

Where is his statue?

.   .   .

WHEN POLLING FANS for the Greatest Athlete in Philadelphia Sports History in 2010, the *Daily News* included Eric Lindros, Donovan McNabb, and Ron Jaworski, but not Greer. *The Great Philadelphia Fan Book* devotes pages to Mike Mamula and Derrick Coleman but mentions Greer just twice, both times as part of novelty lists. (Greer gets to be the best Sixers player whose name begins with "G" and one of the best players ever to wear #15. What a fitting reward for a guy who outscored Chamberlain in the playoffs in 1967.) Press coverage of Greer's Hall-of-Fame selection was shrugged off in "oh-by-the-way" articles. Talk-radio debates about the all-time greatest Sixers focus on-list Allen Iverson and Andrew Toney at two-guard, as if there were no Hall of Famers around to push them. Chamberlain biographers mention Greer only when he's passing or being passed the ball.

It's not just Philly fans. Simmons wrote a 60,000-page basketball book (give or take), but when it came time to profile Greer, he cited the "lunch-pail" quote and likened Greer's press notices to oral sex. Simmons's point appears to be that even Greer's former coaches and teammates have cloudy memories of him, so they fall back on sticky clichés—a valid point, perhaps, but one that could be made without compounding the problem with crude jokes.

It's not like we have champions and Hall of Famers by the bushel in Philly. New Yorkers can overlook a superstar or two because their trophy case is so crowded. Boston sports history is so crowded with old basketball and hockey legends—and new football ones—that it's understandable if some 1960s Celtics star is forgotten (though Simmons won't let that happen). We don't have that excuse.

Sure, the Sixers weren't as popular then as they would be in the 1970s and 1980s. And 1960s legends fade from memory over time. Greer played not just in Chamberlain's shadow, but in the shadows of NBA greats Jerry West and Oscar Robertson, who garnered more national attention. Billy Cunningham also played on those great Sixers teams, and he later got more attention because he had a cool nickname and coached the team to another championship.

There's more to it than that. Greer gave us nothing to kvetch about. Celtics losses were usually laid at Chamberlain's feet. Greer provided no controversies, no unfulfilled expectations, no reasons to boo. Even the 1972–1973 season was far out of his control: he was over the hill, riding the bench, suffering along with the fans. It's the peculiar fate of the Philadelphia legend: if we don't have to rehash your failures, or devote book chapters to justifying why you were ridiculed/traded/accused of faking injuries, you leave us with nothing to talk about. So we forget you.

It doesn't help that the Sixers tried to erase Greer from memory as soon as the Julius Erving era arrived. Greer felt he was forced into retirement in 1973, then ignored when he looked for a coaching job. Greer wound up coaching minor league teams in Cherry Hill and Philadelphia, and coaching at high schools. The team tried to honor him when he reached the Hall of Fame, but Greer wasn't interested. "There's nothing there," Greer said of his relationship with the team in 1982. There's even less now.

Greer is ultimately a victim of Philly sports pathology, of the masochistic, codependent need to dwell forever upon toothache memories of 1964, to identify ourselves with the tragically flawed, to take reassuring delight in misery. He doesn't quite fit the story line, so he gets forgotten. That's a shame, because Greer provided basketball fans with a decade of excellence, of victories, of *memories*. This book's list of greats is about to tumble into some not-so-greats. Let's celebrate a guy who punched the clock—and once punched out the Celtics—before we take that tumble.

41

RICKY WATTERS

All He Had Was Four Little Words

Greatness: ★ ★ ½
Toughness: ★ ½
Eccentricity: ★ ★ ★ ½
Legacy: ★ ½

REVISIONIST HISTORY has grown around Ricky Watters in recent years. According to the new chronology, the "For Who, For What" incident was blown out of proportion. Watters may have been brash and cocky on the field, but that was just a manifestation of his competitive fire, not a sign of selfishness. Watters was not only a very good running back, but an all-time great, and the only thing standing between Watters and the Hall of Fame was a regrettable postgame quote, one that didn't really reflect his toughness or his passion for the game.

A segment on the NFL Network's *Top 10* television show reflected the new perspective on Watters. Watters ranked seventh on the top-10 list of players who weren't enshrined in the Hall. The show highlighted Watters's impressive career numbers—including 10,643 rushing yards—and his Super Bowl exploits (three touchdowns in the Niners rout of the Chargers in Super Bowl XXIX), and experts suggested that Watters's "personality shouldn't be a strike against him."

It's a fascinating whitewash, one that plays upon the permanence of statistics and the impermanence of everything else. Watters has been out of Philadelphia for 13 years and out of football for 9, so all that remains for most fans is "For Who, For What" and the 10,643 yards. It's easy, under the circumstances, to say the former unfairly overshadowed the latter, to write the controversy off as media gone wild, and to rehabilitate Watters as something more than what he really was.

Unfortunately, the Watters rebranding overlooks a few key facts.

. . .

THE EAGLES LOST 21–6 to the Buccaneers on September 4, 1995. Watters, the high-priced free-agent running back acquired from San Francisco to help bring the West Coast offense to Philly, rushed 17 times for 37 yards and caught five passes for 34 yards. Worst of all, he short-armed two passes over the middle. One of the passes can be seen on the *Top 10* program (easy to find on YouTube): Watters pulls up to avoid contact on a pass that looks catchable.

After the game, Watters ripped Randall Cunningham for delivering the ball too late. The next day, he changed the course of his career. "I'm not gonna jump up there and get knocked out. For who? For what?"

The press attacked. "They are words that today might as well be stamped on the enlarged forehead of Ricky Watters," Kevin Mulligan wrote in the *Daily News*, "or, better yet, dipped in 14-karat gold and dangled from Watters's ear lobes." Watters tried to un-pop the balloon the next day with an apology, but no one remembers the apology. Television analyst Ron Jaworski noted that the pass indeed arrived too late, but no one was concerned about the semantics. Watters rushed for 94 yards in a win against the Cardinals the next week. He gained 229 yards from scrimmage in a win over the Redskins, then rushed for 122 yards and a touchdown against the Giants. He helped the Eagles go 10–6 with few other offensive weapons, and he made the West Coast offense viable when Rodney Peete replaced Cunningham, but his words chased him through the entire season.

If that's how the story had ended, the revisionists would be right. Watters played poorly in one game, heard the Vet Stadium boos, reacted badly one time, and could do no right after that, earning nothing but scorn while he carried the Eagles on his back to the playoffs twice. Unfortunately, that's not what happened.

After a loss to the Bills in November 1996, Watters criticized the game plan, saying that he would call more running plays if he were the coordinator. Watters carried 19 times but gained just 51 yards in that game; he carried the ball 20 or more times in each of the previous seven games, a high total for a runner in any scheme, let alone the pass-oriented West Coast offense. Watters wasn't being ultra-competitive, he was just grandstanding. The team held a closed-door meeting to warn Watters about negative remarks.

In December 1996, in a playoff-relevant game against the Jets, offensive coordinator Jon Gruden replaced Watters with smaller, quicker Charlie Garner for a third-quarter series of plays. Watters fussed on the sidelines, then donned a green parka and sat down. (Players who expect a quick return to the game are supposed to stand near the coaches.) Garner's brief drive ended when the Jets returned an interception for a touchdown, but after the next kickoff, the coaches couldn't find Watters. He was on the bench, blending in with the defensive players and backups. "Some of the guys started freaking out, telling me to go get in the game. I'm like, 'Hey, I'm not supposed to be in there,'" Watters said during his television show during the week. The incident led to another set of meetings and warnings.

In 1997, the Eagles beat the Cowboys in a sloppy 13–12 game at the Vet. After the game, Watters's girlfriend, Catherina Chang, approached Gruden in the tunnel. In front of reporters and other witnesses, Chang berated Gruden for not getting Watters the ball enough. Watters had 20 carries in the game.

Watters arrived at training camp in 1997 with a full entourage, three 4×4 vehicles carrying nine supporters and well-wishers. He was in the final year of his Eagles contract, but with free agency looming he kept sabotaging attempts at image repair. *The Sporting News* published a lengthy feature on Watters, the kind a savvy athlete can use to make himself more marketable. All Watters did was ladle on more egotism: "My teammates are positive and in good spirits. And you know why? Because I am positive and in good spirits, that's why."

. . .

THAT'S THE WATTERS the revisionists forgot. It's true that he played hard, kept himself in great condition, and was sometimes the only fully functioning component in the Eagles offense. But it was all about Ricky. That's why he complained about his carries, even after victories. His on-field histrionics, the "competitive fire" his supporters talk about, were all about his individual accomplishments, not about the team. The Eagles were supporting characters in his show. Teammates supported him publicly, talking about his competitive spirit and separating the "real Ricky" from the "TV Ricky." But the most honest statements came with a weary sigh. "Ricky is Ricky, and each week, each year, a new chapter unfolds and you never know what's going to happen," said teammate Guy McIntyre, who played with Watters in San Francisco and Philly.

Ultimately, Watters became detrimental to the team, despite all those yards. Garner, a multitalented runner who would go on to two 1,000-yard seasons with the 49ers, stayed nailed to the bench. Gruden wasted time on spin control that could have been better spent on quarterback development. Ray Rhodes's disciplinarian credibility evaporated. The Eagles stagnated, then eroded, and all the while Watters kept demanding his touches and wondering why no one gave him the respect he "deserved."

. . .

ALL THAT'S LEFT of Watters's arguments to greatness, then, are his yards, many of them compiled in nondescript seasons for the Seahawks at the end of his career. That's what Watters did best: he compiled statistics, protecting his workload while his teams finished with six wins. The numbers may still allow Watters to sneak into the Hall of Fame, but it's more likely that they'll be buried. A new generation of players are compiling even more impressive statistics, sliding Watters down the all-time leader boards, and many of them have behavioral problems that would shame even Watters. When we think about a 49ers star who came to the Eagles, mixed highlights with extreme selfishness, and left destruction and ill feelings in his wake, we now think of Terrell Owens, not Watters.

Watters has been forced to the sidelines of even the "Philly infuriation" debate. It's a fitting punishment for a man who could never answer his own infamous questions, because he couldn't look beyond himself.

HAROLD CARMICHAEL

He Was Too Tall to Disappear

Greatness: ★★★
Toughness: ★★★
Eccentricity: ★★
Legacy: ★

IMAGINE IF HAROLD Carmichael played today.

Imagine a 6-foot-8 wide receiver lining up against 5-foot-10 cornerbacks who aren't allowed to bump after 5 yards. Imagine him running quick slants, shielding defenders from the ball with his body. Imagine him breaking tackles on receiver screens.

Imagine him in a league where teams throw 40 passes a game, not 25. Imagine him catching passes from Michael Vick or Donovan McNabb, not Mike Boryla.

In today's NFL, Carmichael would be a hybrid of Randy Moss and Antonio Gates. He would line up all over the field, sometimes at tight end, sometimes in the slot. He would catch 100 passes per year, easily. Imagine the announcers gushing over him. Imagine drafting him in the first round of your fantasy football league, knowing the king-sized receiver could be counted on for a few extra touchdowns on fade routes and jump balls.

In the modern NFL, Carmichael would be a superstar wide receiver, with all the responsibilities and privileges, his end-zone celebrations considered distractions, his dropped passes inviting ESPN scrutiny. His relationship with the media and fans would short-circuit the talk-radio phone lines. He would be, in all senses of the word, larger than life.

Instead, he has become the most inconspicuous 6-foot-8 Pro Bowler in history.

. . .

CARMICHAEL LED THE NFL with 67 receptions and 1,167 yards in 1973. He was the only receiver to top 60 catches or 1,000 yards that year, when defense reigned in the NFL. He led the Fire High Gang, a trio of tall targets (with Charle Young and Don Zimmerman) who helped broken-down quarterback Roman Gabriel win a Comeback Player of the Year award.

Two seasons later, Carmichael was benched.

"Hal" Carmichael was considered a showboat in those days. His Fire High Gang celebrated touchdowns with a "Roll-six" routine, shooting imaginary craps in the end zone. Carmichael later said that he rolled six only because fans loved it: Eagles fans had little to cheer about, so a little end-zone tomfoolery lightened the mood.

But Carmichael also dropped a lot of passes, often because he didn't want to expose his ribs to marauding 1970s safeties by reaching for high passes in traffic. That was a problem: reaching for high passes was one of his primary jobs.

Carmichael dropped three passes in a blunder-filled October game against the Cardinals in 1975. Then, with the Eagles trailing 24–13 late in the game, he caught his first pass, a 15-yard touchdown. Carmichael didn't roll six, but he spiked the ball, hard, and watched it as it floated high in the air off the bounce. As end-zone celebrations go, it seems tame today, but it was a big mistake in 1975, especially for a player and team having an awful game. When coach Mike McCormack benched Carmichael midweek, he made it clear that the spike was as big a problem as the drops. "After he drops one, I wish he would quit the theatrics and get back in the huddle."

When Carmichael came off the bench the next week against the Cowboys, the Veterans Stadium crowd booed him hard. He responded with a touchdown catch. Then another. Each time, he rolled the ball onto the field and ran to the sidelines—no spikes, no dice. "Even at 6-foot-8, he grew," Paul Giordano wrote.

There were other dropped passes, other boos, other losses. He voiced his frustration to the press. "I dropped some passes I should've caught, and we were losing too many games, but maybe some people thought I was losing those games all by myself," Carmichael later said. Carmichael was on the road to becoming a classic Philly disappoint-

Harold Carmichael
(Courtesy of Temple
University Libraries,
Urban Archives,
Philadelphia, PA)

ment, starting his career hot, buckling under expectations, even daring to admit sensitivity to the withering criticism of the Boo Birds.

Only one force on earth could save him: Dick Vermeil.

• • •

DICK VERMEIL SAW THROUGH the dropped passes, saw through the hot-dog reputation. "When I got the job, Harold was beaten down emotionally," Vermeil later said. "He was booed; he was maligned unfairly." Vermeil rebuilt Carmichael's confidence, got him to tone down his celebrations. He made the Eagles better, too, and it's no surprise that Carmichael's numbers improved when Ron Jaworski replaced Mike Boryla at quarterback.

In 1979, Carmichael caught two touchdown passes in a November win against the Cowboys. The win ended a three-game losing streak, touched off a four-game winning streak, and vaulted the Eagles into a wild-card game against the Bears. Carmichael caught an early touchdown pass in that game, but the Bears rallied and took a 17–10 halftime lead. With the Vet Stadium crowd booing (Jaworski, not Carmichael, was now their target), Carmichael delivered again, catching a 29-yard touchdown pass up the seam to tie the game. Carmichael finished the game with six catches for 111 yards, plus a collision/block/illegal pick that turned a Billy Campfield swing pass into a game-winning 63-yard touchdown. The Eagles won their first playoff game in 19 years.

One season later, they were in the Super Bowl, and Carmichael was the NFL's Man of the Year, recognized for his on-field excellence and off-field charity. Roll-six, the dropped passes, and the boos were long forgotten. He was soft-spoken, humble, a philanthropist and a leader.

• • •

CARMICHAEL WAS NEVER a finalist for the Pro Football Hall of Fame. There are two reasons why: Hall of Fame voters are distracted by shiny objects, like Super Bowl rings, and Carmichael played under the worst circumstances of any wide receiver in modern history.

Soon after Carmichael retired, Hall of Fame voters went into an all-Steelers, all-the-time mode. Faced with a backlog of overqualified candidates in the 1990s, voters went on a Steel Curtain binge, stopping occasionally to grab some Raiders, Cowboys, or 49ers. If you weren't a member of a dynasty, you practically didn't exist. When it came time to nominate wide receivers, the voters selected Steelers greats Lynn Swann (a debatable choice) and John Stallworth (a laughable one), ignoring Carmichael and many other qualified options.

Carmichael had the misfortune of playing his best years in the mid-1970s, football's Dead Ball Era. Teams began to pass more often in 1978, and 70-catch, 1,000-yard seasons were common by 1984. Hall voters were fooled by the early accomplishments of Stallworth and Charlie Joiner, good but not great players whose careers bled well into the passing revolution. Carmichael had a few great seasons under the relaxed post-1978 passing rules, but by the 1980s he was worn down by a decade of pounding.

Carmichael was better than Joiner, better than Stallworth, better (in a different way) than Swann. In 2008, he became eligible for selection by the Hall of Fame veterans committee, but there was no drumbeat to elect him, and Carmichael is too low key to start one.

Maybe we should.

* * *

PHILLY FANS GREW to love Carmichael, but time has eroded his legacy. The 1980 Eagles didn't win. The Fire High Gang is forgotten. Carmichael's club records were eclipsed by other receivers who benefited from a more pass-heavy NFL. After watching a shirtless Terrell Owens exercise in a driveway, a hard spike in the end zone sounds like a silly reason for controversy, so we don't even remember the flamboyance. Carmichael still works for the Eagles, and fans cheer when they see him hovering around training camp—it's hard not to notice and recognize a 6-foot-8 man. We admire him, but we may not realize just how exceptional he was.

"Horizontal Harold presented the most unusual offensive threat in the history of Pro Football," John Facenda once intoned in an NFL Films feature. He's also one of the most unusual Philly legends, one who overcame his cocky-kid reputation and became both a great player and a class act. His reward is underappreciation, nationally and locally, an ironically low profile for such a huge man.

If he played today, things would be very different.

43

MITCH WILLIAMS

The Wildest Thing We'd Ever Seen

Greatness: ★★
Toughness: ★★
Eccentricity: ★★★½
Legacy: ★½

THE PHILLIES KNEW what they were getting when they traded for Mitch Williams, and so did we. Williams was already the Wild Thing, a Charlie Sheen character from a silly baseball movie, when Lee Thomas coveted him in the spring of 1991. Williams had saved 36 games for the Cubs two seasons earlier, but his record in 1990 was 1-8, and after he blew three saves in one week Cubs coach Don Zimmer no longer had the physical and mental health to pitch Williams in save situations. Thomas was willing to move heaven and earth to acquire the closer, but the Cubs settled for Chuck McElroy and Bob Scanlon, toying with the Phillies until opening day before making the trade.

The Phillies knew what they were getting. "There will be days he can't find the plate," manager Nick Leyva said. "He doesn't know where it's going and he throws hard," said John Kruk, who saw Williams throw pitches over the screen when both were Padres farmhands.

Was this a practical joke? Were the Phillies trying to make fans crazy? The Phillies had two acceptable closer candidates in Roger McDowell and Joe "the Saver" Boever, two ground-ball pitchers who might lose a few games but never looked ugly doing it. But they traded two prospects to acquire a baseball cliché, a Nuke LaLoosh, a million-dollar arm with 10-cent control.

One week later, we learned what a Williams "save" looked like. He entered a 2–0 game with two on and two out in the eighth inning against the Cardinals. He walked his first batter on four pitches. He walked in a run on his next batter. A strikeout ended that inning, and the ninth was uneventful, but we knew we had a fireman who arrived at the scene with both lighter fluid and water.

But for some reason, we loved it.

Maybe it was Williams's simple-minded approach to his craft. "My approach to the game is to go after people hard. I want to throw something that is hard," he said after that high-wire save against the Cardinals, the first of what would be many tightrope walks across the mound. Maybe it was the roller coaster experience itself. He left the bullpen, and the previous eight innings were suddenly irrelevant, your stomach was churning, and if he struck out the side after hitting the first two batters, the final out felt that much sweeter.

That was it: the dirty pleasure. Rooting for the Wild Thing was like dating the wrong girl, the one with the miniskirts and mood swings, the sexy strut and wandering affections. You knew how it was going to end, with your heart broken and your mind shattered. You knew it the moment your eyes met hers. But hot summer nights are about thrills, not good judgment, and the thrills made you just crazy enough to come back for more.

*   *   *

WE SPENT A LOT of hot summer nights with Williams, some that dragged on far too long. On July 2, 1993, the Phillies hosted a doubleheader against the Padres. Game 1 lasted until 1:00 A.M. because of five hours of rain delays. As players headed to the locker room to dry off after a loss, assistant coach John Vukovich announced "25 minutes." Game 2 was not postponed; it would just be played in the wee hours of July 3.

And it would last into extra innings.

Williams took the mound in the ninth inning of a tie game sometime around 4 A.M. He walked the second batter, then threw a wild pitch that moved him to second. Go figure: the guy who's wild at 10:00 P.M. only gets wilder after closing time.

But Williams pitched out of that jam, then pitched a 1-2-3 10th. The Phillies were out of pitchers—Danny Jackson, the next night's starter, was home in bed—so after a Pete Incaviglia walk, a Jim Eisenreich single, and a Darren Daulton single, Mitch Williams had to bat.

He ripped a game-winning single.

And the fans, the few thousand crazies who sat through five hours of rain delays, a Phillies loss, and 10 more innings, plus a few night owls who heard about the marathon and came back to the Vet, demanded a curtain call. "We want Mitch!" they chanted.

Williams tipped his cap. Then he went out to his truck to wake his father, who had driven from California to see the doubleheader and needed to rest during the rain delays. "He was kind of ticked off that he missed it, but I think his sleep was more important."

Only the Wild Thing's dad could fall asleep when he was on the mound.

. . .

THIS IS THE PART of the story when Joe Carter steps to the plate, and our knees buckle, our hearts shatter, the skies darken, and hope dies. It's the part where Williams blows Game 4 of the World Series, receives death threats, and stays up at night with a 9-mm handgun at the ready, policemen patrolling his Moorestown home. It's the part where Williams pitches his way out of the league in 1994 and ends up running a Pennsauken bowling alley.

It's the part where we're reminded how terrible we are as fans, except that we weren't that terrible. Death threats are a sad part of sports these days: every kicker who misses a field goal can count on a phone call from a drunken prankster. Williams heard some boos, but he chose to stay in the Philly area, even though he was born in California and owned a Texas ranch. Other players in his situation had it worse—heck, Donnie Moore killed himself after allowing a home run in the 1985 ALCS. We didn't hold Joe Carter against Mitch Williams for very long.

How could we? We knew from the beginning what we were getting. You don't blame the wrong girl for slipping back to the roadhouse, the scorpion for biting, or the out-of-control closer from finally finding the heart of the plate at the worst possible time. Lee Thomas acquired more than a closer in 1993. He acquired a blinking neon arrow. This is where everything goes wrong. This is the guy who will dash your dreams. It's inevitable, and it's obvious, so all you can do is enjoy the ride and brace yourself for the crash.

Even though we were braced, that crash hurt. But the ride really was worth it.

44

BRAD LIDGE

The (Briefly) Perfect Reliever

Greatness: ★★½
Toughness: ★★
Eccentricity: ★★
Legacy: ★★

BRAD LIDGE HAD something to get out of his system: earned runs. It was Christmas in July at Citizens Bank Park in 2008, and Lidge was a Santa who served grand slams.

What an odd promotion: Christmas in July. Here, in the city where the burgermeister banned Christmas for a quarter century, where (by law, it must be mentioned once per book) we booed Santa. It was a manufactured holiday for a team with squatter's rights to second place. The Phillies spent most of the previous month (Advent in July?) in a slump, so Charlie Manuel held a 20-minute closed-door meeting to wake the team up in his sleepy way. The Phillies responded by getting shut out through eight innings by Jair Jurrjens. Lidge entered the ninth inning with the Phillies trailing 1–0. The Phillies needed to keep it close, and Lidge, having pitched just twice in two weeks, needed the work.

Oh, how he needed the work. The first batter doubled. The next singled. The third walked. The fourth singled. Four batters, a total of two strikes. Then Brian McCann came to the plate with the bases loaded. Pow. The Braves led 6–0. At that point in 2008, the Phillies couldn't score seven runs in a three-game weekend series, let alone the ninth inning. Exit Lidge, his ERA nearly doubled from 1.29 to 2.36.

Lidge gave Philly a gift that night. He got all the failure out of his system at once. As we all know, Lidge didn't blow a single save in 2008.

That's because he saved all his mistakes for times when they caused the least harm. When Lidge allowed a run, it was with a three-run lead. When he allowed a grand slam, it came when the bats had already settled in for a long summer's nap.

If only all of us could compartmentalize failure like Lidge did for that magical season: run amok for one debauched weekend, then be perfect for 363 days, all our indecencies and indiscretions left behind in Vegas or Cabo, no nasty consequences. Life doesn't work like that. Baseball doesn't either. And Philly sports history is just a series of consequences. But for Lidge, for one year, everything worked perfectly.

. . .

ONE OF THE THEMES of this book is that the difference between hero and goat is almost always something small: a bad pitch or a dumb remark, a dropped pass or a missed shot, bad karma or bad timing. Tug McGraw is a hero forever because Garry Maddox and Dick Ruthven bailed him out in Game 5 of the 1980 League Championship Series: McGraw blew a save in the eighth, but Maddox doubled home in the tenth and Ruthven pitched two scoreless innings of relief. Had Roger Mason relieved Mitch Williams and pitched to Joe Carter, Williams might be remembered as something more than a hangover with a fastball. Every hero is a flawed hero, even Julius Erving and Bobby Clarke. We have no perfect players or perfect seasons.

But Lidge, for one year, was as close to perfection as we'll ever see.

Once the grand slam was out of his system, Lidge went on a tear. A save the next night, Boxing Day in July or whatever. Another save the next night to win the series against the Braves. A travel day, then two more saves. Manuel is a slow talker, so his speech must have taken a day to sink in. The Phillies started winning 12–10 and 8–5. The bats were awake, and Lidge had the ninth inning locked down.

He kept getting better and better. He gave up one run in 12 September games. You're not a Philly fan if you didn't spend the month waiting for the shoe to fall. It never fell. He saved seven postseason games, but these weren't white-knuckle McGraw saves or Williams horror shows. The Phillies gave Lidge two-run leads, and he gave us peace of mind.

It was perfection, save for that one midsummer night's comedy that ultimately meant nothing. Perfection is fleeting under any circumstances. In Philly, it disappears between heartbeats.

. . .

LIDGE RUINED 2009 as perfectly as he saved 2008. The stat wizards at Baseball Prospectus even crunched the calculations: no reliever in history has ever followed such a great season with such a 162-game catastrophe, in part because no pitcher was allowed to grope around the mound as long as Lidge without losing his closer's role.

The first blown save was a doozy: Lidge faced the Padres with a 5–4 lead in mid-April but allowed a single, two walks, and a home run to Kevin Kouzmanoff. Soon there were others, home runs leaping off the bats of Albert Pujols and Andre Ethier like it was Christmas in May, June, whenever. Manuel kept throwing Lidge out there, because there were no other options. By the postseason, we had no hair left to tear out, but we were still there, and Lidge flew right and threw straight for a few weeks, saving playoff games against the Rockies and the Dodgers.

When Lidge entered Game 4 of the World Series in the ninth inning with the score tied, down came the dangling shoe. Johnny Damon singled and went on a base-stealing binge. Matt Teixeira singled. Alex Rodriguez doubled. Jorge Posada singled. Some cosmic scale balanced, but better for it to happen then, with a championship ring on one hand and a pennant in the other, than on some random September night in 2008 when the whole city was championship starved and doubt ridden.

. . .

IT WAS BETTER to have Lidge back in 2010 than to toss him away after that dreadful season. You've already read about 20 guys in this book who lingered far too long after their failures, marking time for season after unwanted season with no hope for redemption. Lidge started 2010 shaky, spent a few weeks on the disabled list, then returned looking a little like the perfect pitcher from 2008. He gave up just two runs in 26 games from August through October, keeping the Phillies in the pennant race through another summer of strange scoring droughts, saving 1–0 games for Roy Halladay and Roy Oswalt. Had the Phillies bats not fallen asleep again in the NLCS, Lidge might have gone from hero to goat to hero. No one in Philly sports history has ever taken that trip.

Lidge pitched poorly in Christmas in July in 2008, but he gave us Christmas on Halloween, parade and all. He may still keep on giving. We've never had a reliever—not even Tugger—who was quite so generous.

45

BRIAN WESTBROOK

The Man Who Got the Credit

Greatness: ★★½
Toughness: ★★★
Eccentricity: ★
Legacy: ★★

ASINGLE PUNT RETURN can change history.

The Eagles were about to go 2–4. The Giants held a 10–7 lead and the ball after the two-minute warning in the fourth quarter. The Eagles had started the 2003 season with two ugly losses, and Rush Limbaugh had enlightened us that Donovan McNabb's apparent success the previous season was just part of a liberal conspiracy. On that October afternoon, Limbaugh appeared to be correct. McNabb was flailing, completing just nine passes all game, most of them 3- or 4-yarders. He'd had three chances to bring the Eagles back in the fourth quarter, but it was all he could do to hold onto the football while getting sacked.

The Giants handed off, and we took time-outs. Hand-off. Time-out. It was the fourth quarter in the Meadowlands, so we watched each hand-off with crossed fingers. Maybe Joe Pisarcik would appear from the mists of time, Giants coach Tom Coughlin would call "65 Power-Up," and Herm Edwards would snatch a loose ball. No. Kerry Collins handed the ball cleanly to Dorsey Levens. All we could do was burn time-outs, force one more punt.

Brian Westbrook dropped deep to return it. The punt bounced at the 21-yard line. Westbrook snatched it on the bounce at the 16. A Giants defender missed him. Westbrook made one cut, then darted up the left sideline. Two defenders trailed him, one of them Brian Mitchell, who returned punts for the Eagles the previous year. Westbrook won the footrace up the sideline. "Here comes Westbrook! He's got a lane!" the television announcer shouted. "Here comes Westbrook! He can fly!" Merrill Reese's call is not on the Internet. It probably reached the soprano range when Westbrook crossed midfield.

The Giants cried for penalties, and the replay zombies reviewed the return for evidence of foul play, but there was none. "Eagles pull off another Miracle of the Meadowlands," read the headline at CBSSports. com. A miracle that made them 3–3 instead of 2–4. A miracle that touched off a nine-game winning streak and another trip deep into the playoffs. A miracle that saw Westbrook rescue McNabb for the first time, but not the last.

• • •

WESTBROOK WAS a breathtaking, dynamic, thrilling player. For a few seasons, he was a great player. But he was overrated.

Eagles fans faced a dilemma from Miracle of the Meadowlands Part Deux until 2009. During that time, the team regularly won 9–12 games and reached the playoffs. Their offense moved the ball pretty well for most of that era. But it was politically incorrect to give McNabb any credit whatsoever, at least publicly. The McNabb Deniers took over the taprooms and airwaves right around the loss to the Buccaneers in the 2001 playoffs and still haven't relinquished them. If you thought McNabb played pretty well, you bit your tongue.

So if the offense is playing well, McNabb doesn't deserve credit, and the receivers are a bunch of guys named James Thrash or Kevin Curtis, who gets all the props? Why, Westbrook, of course: the tough, scrappy, well-spoken Villanova kid with the soft hands and electrifying moves.

As integral as Westbrook really was to the Eagles' success, the Cult of Westbrook grew downright silly at times. We obsessed over his workload constantly: he needs more carries, he can't handle any more carries, we need him to return punts in the big game, we could not risk letting him return punts until the big game. When he was injured, we fretted about his return. When he was playing, we lived in fear of injuries. When Westbrook did do something bad, when he fumbled while trying to run out the clock against the Giants (Week 2, 2006) or muffed a punt in the Super Bowl, he had the good fortune to live in blame's blind spot.

Westbrook earned much of that adulation, not just with his talent, but with his grit and intelligence. He played through injuries. He caught hundreds of passes in traffic that Ricky Watters wouldn't have lifted his finger to point at. He made smart plays, like the decision to fall at the 1-yard line so the clock would run out against the Cowboys in 2007.

But he was a role player, a third-down back and a punt returner, during many of the Eagles' best seasons. He missed a game or two every year. His best season was in 2007, the year the Eagles went 8–8 and lost four different games by a field goal. His peak was brief. He was at his best when he was part of the three-headed monster with Duce Staley and Correll Buckhalter, or when McNabb was throwing 50 passes per game and he could catch screens and run draws.

McNabb and Westbrook complemented each other. Neither one "carried" the other. Westbrook bailed McNabb out with a few 50-yard touchdowns on the end of 6-foot screens, but that is how football works.

Westbrook and McNabb left the Eagles in the same year. They will probably enter the Eagles Hall of Fame together. Let's honor them together, and remember them together: two exciting players, each great for a time, at their best when we were cheering them both on.

.   .   .

IT WAS 2008, and hope was dying, again. The Eagles faced the Giants in the Meadowlands, again, this time on an icy day with 20 mile per hour wind gusts. McNabb was faltering (again) and in the middle of a controversy (again). The Eagles were 6–5–1, and McNabb was trying to bounce back from an ugly tie against the Bengals, followed by a benching against the Ravens. The Giants were the defending champions, and they had beaten the Eagles a month earlier.

The 2008 season was miserable for Westbrook. He missed some early season games with injuries. He was never 100 percent healthy, and his workload had diminished. He had a lot of 14-carry, 60-yard games, with only a handful of receptions. On the rare occasions that he burst into the open field, you prayed he would run out of bounds before getting hit, so he could live to see the next play.

On that windy December day, with McNabb bumbling and the Giants seething, Westbrook had one miracle left. He churned out a

33-carry, six-catch, 203-yard, two-touchdown performance. He ran up the middle for a 30-yard touchdown to give the Eagles a 10–0 lead. Then he caught a short pass over the middle and ran 40 more yards to keep the Eagles up by two scores. Most miraculous of all, when the Eagles got the ball back with over nine minutes left in the game, Westbrook ran for 13 yards, 6 yards, 5 yards. He rushed 11 times on one drive, gaining just 34 yards but eating up seven minutes and all of the Giants time-outs to put the game away.

It was Westbrook's last great performance, and it was unlike any of the others. We had seen the return man, the burner, the water bug, and the quick thinker, but never the battering ram. Westbrook beat the Giants, rescued McNabb, and set up yet another sprint to the NFC Championship game.

It happened all the time around here. Just not quite as often as we remember.

46

MARK HOWE

The Defenseman in the Shadows

Greatness: ★ ★ ★
Toughness: ★ ★ ★
Eccentricity: ★
Legacy: ★

THE GREATEST DEFENSEMAN in Flyers history wasn't a Broad Street Bully. He didn't ride shotgun with the Legion of Doom. He was Mark Howe: four-time NHL All Star, three-time Norris Trophy winner, and key player for the magnificent but overlooked Flyers of 1984 through 1987.

Howe is one of the best players never talked about, a player who accomplished more in his career than about half the guys in this book could ever hope for. Unfortunately, he was overshadowed by

1. His father
2. The Edmonton Oilers
3. The legacy of the Broad Street Bullies

In 1980s hockey, there were the Edmonton Oilers and everybody else. The Oilers were the 1927 Yankees or the 1960s Celtics. You didn't try to win a Stanley Cup from them. You hoped to steal it: to catch a break, to meet them in an off year. The Flyers were the second best team in the NHL, but there was a huge gap between first and second, between a Team of the Century and a team destined to be forgotten by its own city.

You'd forgotten them too, until you read Howe's name at the top of this chapter. Sure, now you remember Tim Kerr and Brian Propp, Dave Poulin and Brad McCrimmon and the rest. When's the last time you really thought about them? This was a team that went to the Stanley

Cup Finals twice and took the Oilers to Game 7 once. But if you are my age and you reminisce about Philly sports, you talk about Buddy Ryan and Mitch Williams. The 1980s Flyers come up only when Pelle Lindbergh is mentioned. When I asked hockey fans on my Facebook page whether any 1980s Flyers should be in this book, several people told me to dig deeper into the 1973–75 team instead. That team has a hundred books written about them. Memories of the 1980s team are kept alive only by the hockey purists.

That's a shame, because Howe was a great player on a great team. He was a converted winger playing defense, a smooth skater who could act as an extra forward on offense without sacrificing anything on the defensive end of the ice. He had that quick lefty wrist shot, which would either reach the net or reach the crease, where Kerr owned a cherry orchard. Howe scored 20 goals once and topped 40 assists almost every year. The Flyers won 53 games in two straight years, more than the Bullies ever won.

But the Bullies never had to face Wayne Gretzky. They also didn't have to overcome their own legacy. It had been only 10 years since the Flyers last won the Stanley Cup; many of the Bullies had only just retired, and their shadow still loomed. It was easy to make direct comparisons back then, to say Kerr was no Reggie Leach, Propp was no Bill Barber, Lindbergh and Ron Hextall weren't Bernie Parent, and nobody was Clarke. The Howe-Kerr-Propp Flyers even spent more time in the penalty box (thanks to Rick Tocchet and Dave Brown) than the Bullies did. It didn't help: fans my age loved Howe's Flyers, but our fathers, uncles, and big brothers kept comparing them to something they could never be.

It went beyond the still-fresh memories of Clarke and company. We took excellence for granted in 1985. The Phillies won the World Series in 1980 and visited in 1983. The Sixers had just won the title. Mike Schmidt, Julius Erving, and Moses Malone were still playing well. With those guys stomping around, with another parade seemingly just a year or two away in some sport, it was easy to overlook Howe. He was a good little player, Gordie Howe's kid, damaged goods the Hartford Whalers let go because he nearly killed himself running into a goal-post bar and was always playing through back pain. We were so laden with all-time greats for a few years that we forgot about the kind of player we are supposed to love: a tough, heady, selfless, no-

nonsense leader who won lots of games and fought as hard against a juggernaut as Allen Iverson ever did.

So let's give Howe his due. Let's remember that the Flyers lost three first-round playoff series in a row from 1982 through 1984—two to the Rangers—while Clarke and Barber shared the ice with Howe and Kerr. Then, the legends left. Howe scored an overtime goal in Game 1 of the 1985 quarterfinals against the Rangers, finally ushering in the new era of Flyers hockey and launching the team toward the Stanley Cup Finals.

Let's remember that Howe was injured for the first two games of the 1987 Finals, both Oilers wins, then limped back onto the ice to tangle with Gretzky and bring the Flyers within one goal of the impossible. Let's remember that the era between the glory days and the frustrations of the Legion of Doom was hardly a wasteland: it was filled with exciting hockey, brought to us by admirable stars.

The next time you're reminiscing about Philly teams of yesteryear over a few beers, and someone brings up Randall Cunningham or the 1993 Phillies for the umpteenth time, remind him of Howe, Kerr, Propp, Tocchet, Brown, Brad Marsh, and all the winter nights you spent watching the Flyers skate circles around the Rangers and Islanders. The memories will come flooding back, and most of them will be good ones.

47

SCOTT ROLEN

Backache, Headache, Heartache

Greatness: ★ ★ ★
Toughness: ★ ½
Eccentricity: ★ ★
Legacy: ★

FOR SEVEN YEARS, Scott Rolen was one of the most important people on the Philadelphia sports scene. It was, admittedly, a dark, dark era.

Rolen joined the Phillies in 1996, when the team was foisting a lineup full of Todd Zeile and Mark Whiten on the public. The Sixers were in their Derrick Coleman–Shawn Bradley 64-loss era; rookie Allen Iverson hadn't yet taken the court. The Eagles were in their Ty Detmer–Rodney Peete holding pattern. Rolen was a 21-year-old rocketing through the minors, batting .324 at Reading and Scranton–Wilkes Barre before finally getting an August call to the big leagues. A year later, he was the National League Rookie of the Year; a year after that, he hit 31 home runs. The future of Philadelphia sports belonged to Rolen, Eric Lindros, and Allen Iverson. You're forgiven if you think that feels like an eternity ago.

Rolen reminded everyone of Mike Schmidt. He had the effortless swing, the plate discipline, the reflexes and consistency at third base. But he wasn't Schmidt. He was an imposter, sent by some higher power to torment Phillies fans for their sins against Schmidt. We tormented Rolen back, because that's what we do. It was another ugly, dysfunctional little dance, another round of sniping and accusations, another completely unnecessary grudge between a player and the fans.

. . .

"SCOTT ROLEN DAY" wasn't a big deal when it happened. The Phillies gave away Rolen T-shirts on August 22, 1998, but after taking the lineup card to the umpires, Rolen disappeared. Terry Francona had decided Rolen needed rest, despite 12 RBIs in the previous four games. It might have been a defensible decision—the Phillies were playing a day game after a night game and they'd had a double-header earlier in the week—if not for the T-shirts. The Phillies lost to the Rockies 5–2 that day; kids who attended the game hoping to watch their favorite player left with a feeling of hollow disappointment. In that respect, it was a uniquely Philadelphia sports giveaway.

But Scott Rolen Day was soon forgotten, at least temporarily. Rolen was still the toast of the city. "This kid is special," Bill Lyon had written a few days before Rolen's day off. "And he couldn't have come along at a better time." He had two doubles and two RBIs in a 10-inning win against the Giants a few days later. He hustled on the base paths. One day off—his only one of the season—was forgivable.

Years later, Scott Rolen Day became a symbol of the rift that grew between Rolen and the fans, and of Rolen's knack for engendering ill-will. Like Donovan McNabb's phantom puking at the Super Bowl, the story has taken on tall-tale proportions: it's said that Rolen demanded regularly scheduled rest days, which came later (he played 161 games that season) and that Francona tried to talk him into playing (Francona benched Doug Glanville on the same day for the same reason).

The next season, Rolen took off on Scott Rolen Beamer Bear day to mourn his grandfather, who had passed away the previous evening. The Phillies lost, 1–0. Few could fault Rolen for the decision—"there's no close second to family," Francona said after the game—but Rolen was now 0-for-2 on fan appreciation opportunities, and he was suddenly slumping, his batting average at .258 on the day off and not destined to climb much higher. Schmidt was in the owner's box for Beamer Bear day. He said that he planned to have a talk with Rolen about baseball—and life—later in the season.

Getting "handle the media" advice from someone like Schmidt is like getting fielding tips from Greg Luzinski. But Rolen soon had other problems.

* * *

WHEN ASKED IN 1998 what the Phillies needed to turn the corner, Rolen answered "leadership." In 2000, after the Curt Schilling trade, Rolen tried to become a leader. He did so by criticizing the organization for the trade. "I think we might have taken an immediate step backward," he said. "It's almost a start-over, we're still rebuilding." Rolen added that he was "miserable" at the treatment of Rico Brogna, the pesky first baseman who lost his starting job to slugger Travis Lee in the deal.

Rolen began taking games off to rest his back, which he said was aggravated by playing on Vet Stadium turf. Francona was generous with rest days; once, Rolen told him that while he could play, he probably shouldn't. Francona gave him the day off. "I feel like a crybaby, a big wuss," he said after missing that August game. After the 2000 season, Francona was fired, and Rolen quickly defended the coach while criticizing management. "I'm certainly not downgrading the talent of the team, but I don't think we're as good as the Mets or the Braves or a lot of other teams in this league."

Rolen and the Phillies tried to agree on a contract extension in 2001. Negotiations went nowhere in February and March. The new Veterans Stadium turf passed Rolen's inspection, but the new Phillies, helmed by prickly Larry Bowa, clearly didn't. Rolen reportedly turned down a $120-million contract because he wanted a guarantee that the Phillies' overall payroll would remain high. The season began, and contract negotiations ceased. Rolen wanted days off to rest his back but refused to ask for them. Bowa refused to offer them unless he was asked. By May 3, Rolen was batting .202, and the boos rained down at the Vet. "I have no excuses for anything. I stink. I'm not hitting the ball," Rolen said.

Rolen raised his batting average to .270, only to read about Bowa ripping him in the *Daily News*. Bowa had told Bill Conlin that his cleanup hitter wasn't putting forth enough effort. Bowa later denied the quotes attributed to him, saying he wasn't singling any one player out, but the gist was clear: despite the fact that the Phillies were in first place, the manager was dissatisfied with Rolen's production. Rolen waited outside Bowa's office for half an hour before a road game, then argued at length with the manager. "I found out in that article what a bad player I was," Rolen said after the meeting.

The boos intensified when the Phillies returned home. Dallas Green piled onto Rolen, criticizing him on 610-WIP as "satisfied" with being a so-so player. At the time, Rolen was on a tear, erasing memories of his early-season slump while raising his batting average near the .300 mark. Still, it was clear that there would be no extension, no "Phillies for life" status for Rolen. The organization was tired of him. The fans had turned on him. "How did it come to this? And why?" pleaded Conlin in a *Daily News* column, forgetting that he was the one who published Bowa's inflammatory quotes a few weeks earlier.

• • •

ON SEPTEMBER 11, 2001, baseball took a backseat to real life. A week later, the second-place Phillies hosted the first-place Braves. Rolen hit two home runs off Braves ace Greg Maddux in a 5–2 victory. The crowd demanded a curtain call after the second homer. Rolen was reluctant, uncomfortable with the spotlight on a night when the World Trade Center bombings were still so fresh in everyone's mind. Bowa told him to take his bow, and Rolen sheepishly tipped his hat to the fans. "We finally agreed on something. I'm glad I did it. It was the right thing to do."

Somehow, that curtain call seems more important than a day off on T-shirt day.

Green later backed off his comments, and Bowa went out of his way to praise Rolen, but the damage was already done. "There were loyalty and respect issues that were tarnished a bit this year," Rolen said, telling the team that he refused to resume contract talks.

One day after the 2001 baseball season ended, Eric Lindros played his first game against the Flyers, scoring a goal for the Rangers. It was a time for eras to end. Rolen played through half of 2002, a miserable player waiting for a trade that finally came in July. He said good riddance to Philly, and we took it personally, though anyone in his right mind would be thrilled to get as far away from Bowa and Green as possible after a year like 2001.

It was a start-over. We were rebuilding again.

• • •

BY ROLEN'S ERA, the local media had perfected the art of extracting negativity from even the most benign player comments, in a manner much like extracting oil from sunflower seeds. Anytime a player expressed anything other than appreciation for the incessant criticism ladled upon him by the media and fans, his quotes were immediately dissected, and any elements of sensitivity, self-pity, or excuse-making were harvested, distilled, and enhanced for their full airwave controversy value. Rolen made matters worse because he actually was sensitive and sometimes petulant, plus he was suspicious of the notorious local media and unwilling to open up.

He was also, as Conlin once described him, "soft-spoken, intelligent, truthful, respectful of his elders," and, as Sam Donnellon called him, "a guy who dives for baseballs and runs out ground balls." There was a lot to like about him if we weren't so obsessed about what he couldn't do.

Rolen's payroll-related contract demands were silly, his complaints about the turf and the team's roster decisions grating. He ran afoul of the stubborn Bowa and buffoonish Green at a time when not everyone had caught on to their out-of-touch act, and he bore the brunt of fan frustration with the Phillies—heck, with all four teams—when he became "just" a .290-hitting Gold Glover with 25 home runs. His greatest crime? He was too much like Schmidt off the field and not enough like Schmidt at the plate. And he played in an era when players didn't have to hang around and take the abuse.

Rolen hit his 300th home run in July 2010, making the All-Star game as a member of the Reds. He still pulled himself from the lineup from time to time, and we all got a laugh at his expense when he kept striking out in the 2010 playoffs. But he's been to five All-Star games since leaving the Phillies. Green's appraisal of the "so-so" Rolen was as off the mark as nearly all of his post-1980 opinions.

The Phillies became great without Rolen, but they never really replaced him at third base. They made it to the World Series with Pedro Feliz, who wasn't half the player Rolen was, and they reached the playoffs with Placido Polanco, who fits better as a super-sub than a starter. If they had signed that lifetime contract in 2000—if both sides were a little more practical and a little less obstinate—Rolen could still be here, starting a hundred games a year, pinch hitting, batting around .300. And if we didn't harp on all the negatives, we might be happy to have him. We might even have won more than one World Series in the last three years. We'll never know.

48

SHAWN BRADLEY

The Greatest Mistake

Greatness: ★
Toughness: ★ ½
Eccentricity: ★★
Legacy: ★★★

WHEN NOTEWORTHY PLAYERS retire, ESPN often produces a Top-10 highlight reel for SportsCenter. In 2006, ESPN produced a montage of the top 10 dunks *against* Shawn Bradley. It may be the greatest lowlight film of all time.

The video is available on YouTube, and it is comedy gold. Penny Hardaway dunks, and the ball hits Bradley squarely on the cheek on its way down. Yao Ming brushes Bradley away from the basket with one quick nudge. Chris Webber hangs from the rim, his legs spread in the air, and Bradley briefly finds himself with a face full of Webber's jock. Bradley didn't just allow dunks: he stumbled away from each dunk, limbs flailing at odd angles, like the victim from a crime scene. Most of the ESPN lowlights came from Bradley's days with the Mavericks, but the joke was still on the Sixers, who had spent the second overall pick and $44 million on him.

This isn't a book about famous flops. Too much ink, airtime, and agita is wasted in Philly revisiting the failures of Mike Mamula and Jeff Ruland, Lance Parrish and Derrick Coleman, squandered draft picks and free-agent bumbles. But Bradley was too huge a mistake to exclude. Fans were suspicious from the start, then spent two seasons watching Bradley confirm those suspicions. Few players in sports history were so wrong for their city and team, on so many levels, as Bradley, a 7-foot-6 novelty act with indifferent athletic desire and an exorbitant price tag, was for the Sixers and Philadelphia.

* * *

LET'S FLASH BACK to January 1995. The Sixers are 10–23. They are at the tail end of what will become a nine-game losing streak, and they are facing Shaquille O'Neal and the Orlando Magic. The Sixers' starting lineup: Dana Barros, B. J. Tyler, Clarence Weatherspoon, Sharone Wright, and Scott Williams. Bradley, the second-year hope of the franchise, the $44-million center, can't crack the lineup of a terrible team.

Bradley plays just 13 minutes against the Magic, fouling out while allowing many of O'Neal's dunks during the game. He scores one point, has two rebounds, and needs five stitches in his lower lip. The Sixers lose 91–70.

It was one of Bradley's worst games, but it wasn't atypical. That was a night at the office for the Sixers in 1995. Bradley didn't just help the Sixers lose. He made you cringe, made you tuck your jersey under your jacket and hope no one saw you leaving the Spectrum in the third quarter.

Bradley's game was excruciating to watch. He was so angular and awkward that it was impossible for him to gain leverage, so centers and bigger forwards could push him all over the paint. At the same time, his body control was so bad that he would pick up sloppy fouls, meaning he was forever on the bench, which was a blessing in disguise. He sometimes showed a soft touch on hook shots and jumpers, teasing you into thinking he might develop a high-post game, and of course he blocked a few shots every game. But he lacked strength, aggression, and technique in the low post. He was always a step slow in support defense and was both unable and unwilling to box out.

Worst of all, he didn't care much about getting better. His game regressed after his rookie season. Bradley took a long honeymoon after his rookie season instead of refining his game or gaining strength, and it showed. He was content to be tall and block shots, then spend most of the second half on the bench with four fouls, none of them very hard. "This kid is more than an empty uniform," Bill Conlin wrote in 1995. "He is a thief who turned the bad judgment of everyone with a dream of what he could become into the biggest daylight heist since the Brinks Robbery."

He regressed further, somehow, in the 1995–1996 season, his third and last in Philly. Bradley played 20 minutes against the Pistons, scoring five points with zero rebounds. He followed that with 23 score-less minutes off the bench against the Warriors. After that, 24 minutes against the Hawks with four points, four rebounds, six turnovers. "Make a trade. Do what you're going to do," rookie Jerry Stackhouse said after the loss to Atlanta. "We've got to be able to compete in the middle."

A day later, the Sixers sent Bradley to the Nets for Derrick Coleman and others. It was a headache-for-headache deal, but at least the new headache knew how to play basketball. A little.

. . .

BRADLEY WENT ON to play nine years with the Mavericks. The Mavericks knew what Bradley was: a curiosity, a backup center who could come off the bench and disrupt the opposing offense for a few minutes at a time. Mark Cuban transformed the Mavericks into an exciting sideshow attraction, and Bradley was part of the carnival. Fans in Dallas embraced him, or at least got used to him.

Philly fans, well, we needed a few years to recover. His game, such as it was, was wrong for the team. His attitude was wrong. Naturally, he was booed viciously, vilified on the radio and in the papers. Give us a bad player with bad work habits, a huge salary, and the toughness of a Popsicle stick, and you'll get a few boos. Make him 7-foot-6, so he stands out on the court like an elongated scarecrow, tumbling to the floor after an O'Neal dunk or trudging to the bench with three first-quarter fouls, and you've created a lightning rod for scorn.

That's the one good thing about running so many guys out of town: at least, a few times, we pick the right guy. Bradley didn't linger very long, just long enough to make you shake your head the moment you read his name.

49

PAT BURRELL

The Bat Who Wouldn't Leave

Greatness: ★ ½
Toughness: ★ ★
Eccentricity: ★ ★
Legacy: ★ ★ ★ ★

SOME PHILLIES SLUGGERS, like Del Ennis and Mike Schmidt, inspired boos and derision. Others, like Greg Luzinski and Ryan Howard, inspired awe and admiration. Pat Burrell was the only one ever to inspire reverse psychology.

After hitting 37 home runs in 2002 and signing a lucrative contract extension, Burrell endured a season-long slump in 2003, ending the year with a .209 batting average and 21 home runs. Fans booed him early in the year, then suddenly switched tactics and began cheering, not derisively but hopefully. "The fans are no dummies," Mike Newall wrote in *Philadelphia Weekly*. "They realize that playoff success hinges greatly on Burrell getting it going in the late season." In the same article, Burrell expressed surprise at the kid-gloves treatment he was being given by the fans. "As bad as I've been these people have been behind me. It has been almost shocking at times."

The cheers didn't work, and soon the boos returned, joined by the usual harping and carping that filled every summer day in the middle of the decade. Burrell was the Phillies whipping boy for so long that it's hard to remember that he was once Pat the Bat, the face of the franchise and the team's top young prospect. It also became impossible to notice that, after the miserable 2003 and 2004 seasons, he turned out to be a pretty good player.

. . .

MANY READERS will object to Burrell's inclusion on this list, but his was a quintessentially Philly career. He was the first player taken in the 1998 draft, signing for a then-record $8 million. He flew through the minors, batting .320 with 29 homers in his lone full season in the bush. He hit 18 home runs as a 20-year-old outfielder, finishing fourth in the Rookie of the Year voting. As he improved, expectations rose, always a step ahead of him. Then he signed a $50-million contract extension. The only way he could justify that kind of money was by leading the team to the World Series. Instead he went into a two-year slump.

Burrell lived down to his billing for a few years. He really was the overpaid underachiever, particularly in 2003–2004. Then, Charlie Manuel replaced Larry Bowa. Cue Handel's *Messiah*. With no one screaming in his ear about not reaching his potential every day, Burrell was free to come closer to his potential.

He slowly rebuilt himself as a serviceable player: not a great one, but a useful one. He hit 92 home runs in 2005–2007. His defense was poor and his batting averages were low, but he averaged about 100 walks per year, meaning his on-base percentages were high. The Phillies were loaded with left-handed sluggers—first Jim Thome, then Ryan Howard and Chase Utley—and Burrell became the righty bat that kept the team from being lopsided. We always wanted someone better, but the major leagues weren't teeming with guys who could bat .260 with 30 home runs per year.

By 2008, Burrell was the left fielder and five-hole hitter for a playoff team. He was 0-for-8 in the first three games of the divisional series, and Brewers pitchers were pitching around Howard and Utley to get to Burrell. Burrell expected to be benched, but Manuel kept him in the fifth spot. "People come up to me and say, 'How can you play him today?'" Manuel told Bob Ford in the *Inquirer* after the fourth game of the series. "And I say, 'Yeah, well I've played him four years and I'm playing him today.' I stick with my players, the ones I think can put it on the board."

Burrell hit two home runs to help the Phillies to a 6–2 series-clinching win in Game 4. "It's very fulfilling," said Burrell. "What we've gone through to get here, this makes it worthwhile." A few weeks later, Burrell rode in the lead float of the World Series parade.

* * *

FOR SOME FANS, neither the two home runs nor his supporting role in the World Championship makes up for all the disappointment of the years that came before. When Burrell returned to Philadelphia in the summer of 2010 as a member of the San Francisco Giants, the WIP hosts asked callers if Burrell's 2008 heroics changed their minds about the slugger. Most callers still held familiar grudges: Burrell was a lackadaisical outfielder, he had a penchant for meaningless home runs in blowouts, and he dared to exercise his no-trade clause in 2006.

These are familiar charges. Disliked sluggers are always branded lazy fielders in Philly, where we expect outfielders to crash head-first into the wall for every play. Greg Luzinski used to do that: he would chug as hard as he could toward the wall, even when it was obvious that the ball was going to ricochet hard over his head. Burrell was a poor fielder, and he got worse as he got older, but it was a weakness, not a character flaw. The "meaningless homers" charge is another default accusation that was hung on Schmidt and others. The four home runs he hit in an August sweep of the Mets in 2007, the ones that turned the tide in the NL East race and got the Phillies into the playoff hunt, felt pretty meaningful, but maybe they were isolated incidents. The non-clutch hitter got a few last laughs in the National League Championship Series, and he now has two World Series rings. As for the trade veto, when the fans have turned on you, the only thing worse than wanting to leave Philly is wanting to stay.

Strip away the usual rancor, and Burrell's story is really the story of the 2000–2008 Phillies. He was the first of the champs' homegrown prospects. He was the veteran who welcomed Jimmy Rollins, Utley, and Howard. When the Phillies moved to Citizens Bank Park, he was one of the guys who sold tickets. At times, he was the criticism magnet that protected the younger players. The conventional wisdom states that the Phillies couldn't win until bad seeds like Scott Rolen, Burrell, and Bob Abreu were gone, but Burrell stuck around and won, suggesting that Bowa simply reaped the misery he sowed. Burrell hung around long enough to earn at least a taste of redemption. He proved that the classic Philly prospect story can have a happy ending. All he needed was the guts to overstay his welcome.

50

MICHAEL VICK

The Face of the Future

Greatness: ???
Toughness: ???
Eccentricity: ???
Legacy: ???

OUR JOURNEY ENDS with a risky selection, but an appropriate one. We've looked to the past for the last 49 players. Michael Vick forces us to project into the future.

There were a lot of guys named Johnny and Bobby vying for the final spot: Johnny Callison, Bobby Jones, John LeClair, Bobby Abreu. Their stories have all been told, their legacies assured. Three of them were admirable supporting actors; Abreu was an enigmatic criticism sponge. If you want to read about lovable shotgun riders, this book has them: Hal Greer, Mark Howe, Brian Westbrook. If you want another tale of a pretty good player blamed for all of our nation's woes, the previous chapters offer about 25 choices.

Vick is still telling his story, and it could be something new. His tale has evolved during the writing of this book. In the summer of 2010, he was a backup quarterback embroiled in another midnight scandal, a birthday-party shooting involving members of his peripheral posse. In mid-September, he replaced Kevin Kolb, looked great while beating some terrible opponents, and he became the flavor du jour. Beating the Detroit Lions doesn't get you onto a list like this. If it did, Bobby Hoying would have a chapter.

Vick then beat Peyton Manning's Colts, and what he did to Donovan McNabb's Redskins doesn't qualify as a beating: it was termite extermination, only more lethal and stylish. Vick threw for four touchdowns and ran for two more on *Monday Night Football*; Tom Brady and Steve Young lined up to shower Vick with accolades, and the Pro Football Hall of Fame took the jersey off Vick's back and shipped it straight to Canton. Vick escaped flash-in-the-pan territory like he was escaping the pocket. He has become part of Philly sports history, our next tale.

A tale of what? Redemption? Disappointment? Glory? Crime and punishment? The possibilities are endless.

. . .

TEN YEARS FROM now, we may fit Michael Vick into any of the following categories.

The Troubled Veteran Who Taught Us How to Win. Vick could be Pete Rose. We didn't know about Rose's gambling problem when we signed him—it may not have been that bad at the time—and Rose was a superstar when the Phillies acquired him, not a down-and-out ex-con. Still, you can force-fit him into the same story line: he arrived, and a great team that always fell short suddenly climbed over the hump.

The Criminal Who Redeemed Himself to Become a Champion. Vick could be Bernard Hopkins, but on a bigger stage.

The Cad Who Was So Much Fun to Watch. Vick could become Len Dykstra, a guy who provided some playoff wins, a lot of exciting highlights, and the creepy feeling that we didn't want to look too closely at his private life.

The Dangerous Troublemaker. If you don't see Allen Iverson potential in Vick, you aren't looking. Remember how certain we were that Iverson had changed his ways by the time the 2001 NBA Finals came around?

Just Another Eagles Quarterback. Randall Cunningham and Donovan McNabb enjoyed meteoric rises and fawning headlines for a few years. Ron Jaworski wasn't an instant success, but 2,183 yards and 18 touchdowns looked pretty exciting in 1977 after a few seasons of Mike Boryla. We've gotten hooked on Vick-like substances before, and we pay for the brief high with a five-year pessimism hangover.

That's the most depressing possibility. After reading the Ultimate Weapon article in *Sports Illustrated* in 1989, after reading some of McNabb's early notices, I find that déjà vu overpowers my optimism about Vick. Rich Hofmann wrote about the Vick-Cunningham comparison in November, noting that both grew into serious quarterbacks after years of silly scrambling. To extend the metaphor, Vick's time with the Falcons was like Cunningham's time with the Eagles, and Vick's forays into dogfighting coincide with Cunningham's descent into infantile behavior. Our Vick is like the Randall Cunningham who played for the Vikings late in his career, tossing touchdowns to Randy Moss and Cris Carter.

It's an appealing metaphor. Remind me again: how many Super Bowls did Cunningham win with the Vikings? Zero. What do we do to quarterbacks who don't win the Super Bowl in this city? Gotcha. Even the most optimistic comparison we can muster, the one that gives Vick all the credit in the world for changing his ways and realizing his potential, leaves us back at Square 1: a quarterback who doesn't win. We're victims of our own imagination.

Something New

Every new superstar inspires hope. That's why we clamor onto bandwagons again and again. We've covered a lot of stories from the last 50 years in the previous 49 chapters: stories of champions and losers, superlative athletes and self-made men. But we haven't seen it all. Maybe this is the new story.

This is the story of an athlete of almost indescribable gifts, one who started out as a city's hope but became its downfall. Only this time the city is Atlanta, not Philadelphia. It's the story of a man capable of incredible stupidity (smuggling marijuana onto a plane) and unspeakable brutality (executing animals), an athlete who caused unfathomable disappointment, shamed an entire sport, and wound up in jail.

It's the story of an Eagles coach taking a low-risk gamble, a literal leap of faith. Andy Reid hoped to rehabilitate Vick the man as much as he wanted to coach Vick the athlete into Vick the quarterback. So the Eagles signed a favorite villain, a fun player to laugh about, a guy we loved to beat up in the playoffs, and stowed him on the bench for a year. We rolled our eyes and shook our heads while the penitent ex-superstar learned, and worked, and grew.

It's the story of a charmed era. Let's speculate now: Vick signs a contract extension, leads the Eagles to a Super Bowl victory. No, two of them. Schools and businesses close for the parades, the largest Philadelphia has ever seen. Vick rides in the first float, then Andy Reid, DeSean Jackson, Trent Cole, Stewart Bradley, other stars who haven't risen yet. Then the legends of 1960: Chuck Bednarik, Tommy McDonald, and others, enjoying another ride. Jaworski, Cunningham, and McNabb share a float, and they are cheered for 30 years of effort. Ryan Howard and Chase Utley hug Vick at the podium of the Lincoln Financial Field 50-yard line. Bob Clarke holds up a vintage 1973 Flyers jersey with a black "C" on the front and "Vick" on the back. Vick holds up the Lombardi trophy.

Vick stays for five more years. There are playoff wins and losses, lots of cheers and some scattered boos. Vick ages into a distinguished veteran. Books are written about the player and team that transformed a city. Our sports culture changes, and we become more like homers than haters. Our critical edge never goes away, but we unsheathe it less swiftly, and we become protective of our stars instead of suspicious of them.

Eventually, Vick gets a retirement send-off that rivals that of Mike Schmidt or Julius Erving, only it's sweeter, because Vick climbed out of the deepest gutter to achieve what he did, making his a story like none other, none in Philly sports history, none in sports history.

We tell our grandchildren that their favorite players are nothing compared to the champions of yesteryear, champions like Michael Vick.

. . .

MORE LIKELY, VICK won't become that champion, the transcendent star who wipes the slate clean and resets our expectations. Maybe Chase Utley is that player, and the Phillies are just another World Series away from making faith in the home team our rule and not our exception. Maybe Jrue Holiday or Mike Richards is that player. Or it's someone who hasn't been drafted yet, hasn't been born yet, will never come.

But we still have the dream of our champion. He thrills us. He terrifies opponents. He teeters on the edge of madness at times. He crawled up from the depths of Hell to lead us. We fasten the dream to whomever offers the most hope. Right now it's Vick, who admittedly fits the mold well. The palm branches are scattered at his feet. The crucifixion is scheduled for next Friday. Maybe this time it won't come off as planned.

Acknowledgments

THIS BOOK BEGAN as several articles and essays that appeared in the *New York Times* and on FootballOutsiders.com. Aaron Schatz, editor-in-chief at Football Outsiders, created a forum for thoughtful sports analysis, then gave me the leeway to write about old Eagles players instead of the latest Brett Favre or Randy Moss sagas. Colleagues like Bill Barnwell, Doug Farrar, Russell Levine, Michael David Smith, and others helped shape many of the ideas in this book. At the *New York Times*, Bob Goetz, Toni Monkovic, Naila Jean-Myers, Patty LaDuca, Judy Battista, and others gave me opportunities to become a humorist and Philly sports psychoanalyst, two highly related occupations.

Others who provided opportunities, bylines, or guidance include Luc Rheaume and Mario Prata of *Sports Forecaster*, Gregg Rosenthal of Rotoworld, and Mike Miller of NBCSports.com. The administration at Audubon School District in New Jersey was supportive of this project and gave me the extra time I needed to complete it, so thanks to Superintendent Don Borden, Principal Jack Ross, and School Board President Ralph Gilmore.

Thanks to Micah Kleit at Temple University Press, production editor Peggy Gordon, agent John Wright, and Brenda Galloway at the Temple University Urban Archives. Thanks to Eileen and Houston

Stevenson for hours and hours of babysitting and to dozens of friends who provided input, pep talks, and insights.

My wife, Karen, offered nothing but encouragement in the days when I had no bylines or readers, then kept the household running during the writing of this book, putting up with mood swings, sudden schedule changes, and long conversations about Scott Rolen. This book would never have been written without her love and support.

Mike Tanier

Mike Tanier covers football, baseball, and the wacky side of sports for the *New York Times*. He is a senior writer at Football Outsiders, where he is the coauthor of the *Football Outsiders Almanac* and writer of a regular column on football strategy and history. His work has also appeared in *ESPN The Magazine* and on NBCSports.com, Deadspin, and many other Web sites and publications. He has also taught high school math in New Jersey for nearly 20 years. Tanier lives in Camden County with his wife and two sons.